IVAN THE TERRIBLE

Henri Troyat was born a Russian Jew (Lev Tarassov) in 1911, but was educated in France. He is a member of the Académie Française, and in 1938 he won the Prix Goncourt. He has written numerous biographies, novels, short stories, essays and travel books.

A Selection of works by Henri Troyat

Catherine the Great (Phoenix Press)
Alexander of Russia
Balzac
Baudelaire
Everyday Life in Russia in the time of the Last Tsar
Flaubert
Gogol
Gorki
Pushkin
Tolstoy
Turgenev

IVAN THE TERRIBLE

Henri Troyat

Translated by Joan Pinkham

PHOENIX
PRESS

PHOENIX PRESS
5 UPPER SAINT MARTIN'S LANE
LONDON WC2H 9EA

A PHOENIX PRESS PAPERBACK

This book was first published in France under the title
Ivan le Terrible by Librairie Flammarion
First published in Great Britain
by The New English Library in 1984
This paperback edition published in 2001
by Phoenix Press,
a division of The Orion Publishing Group Ltd,
Orion House, 5 Upper St Martin's Lane,
London WC2H 9EA

A CIP catalogue record for this book is available from the
British Library.

Printed and bound in Great Britain by
Butler & Tanner Ltd, Frome and London

ISBN 1 84212 419 6

Contents

Contents

Illustrations

vii

Translator's Note

Few readers of this book, I imagine, will be curious to know what sources were used by the translator. However, to those who may have a scholarly interest in such matters, I owe the following explanation with regard to the many quotations to be found in the text.

In M. Troyat's French book, all quotations from contemporary (sixteenth-century) writers are naturally given in French, no matter what the language of the original. Whenever the work quoted was written in English—the letters of Edward VI and Elizabeth I of England, for example—I have tried to find and reproduce the authentic original, instead of merely back-translating the passage from M. Troyat's French. Similarly, if the work quoted was written in German or Latin, I have used the published English version of it instead of retranslating from the French. In all these cases a source citation appears in the Notes section at the back of the book. (Where no note is provided for a direct quotation, the reader will know that I have simply rendered the given French into English.)

The quotations from Russian—notably, Ivan's remarks, speeches, and letters—presented a different problem. Most of these I was obliged to retranslate from the French, with the inevitable loss in authenticity that results from double translation. Prince Andrei Kurbsky's *History of Ivan IV* does exist in English. A bilingual (Russian/English) version—edited, translated, and annotated by J. L. I. Fennell—was published in 1965 by Cambridge University Press. Accordingly, the quotations from this work I took from Mr. Fennell's translation, as indicated in the notes. The famous correspondence between Ivan and Kurbsky is also available in a bilingual edition by the same translator, published by the same press in 1955; however, a number of passages quoted by M. Troyat either do not appear in Mr. Fennell's version, or appear there in quite different form; in the end, therefore, I made my own English translation of the extracts from these letters, based on the French.

I am pleased to take this opportunity to express my long-standing gratitude to Paula Mark and the other reference librarians at the University of Massachusetts at Amherst. In doing research required for the present translation, as well as for the two preceding ones (M. Troyat's *Catherine the Great* and *Alexander of Russia*), I have come to rely heavily on their professional competence and unfailing helpfulness. In this particular case, I also wish to thank the library's Slavic bibliographer, Stanley Radosh, for his kind assistance in checking certain passages in Russian authors and in advising on the translation and transliteration of many Russian words.

JP

Ivan the Terrible

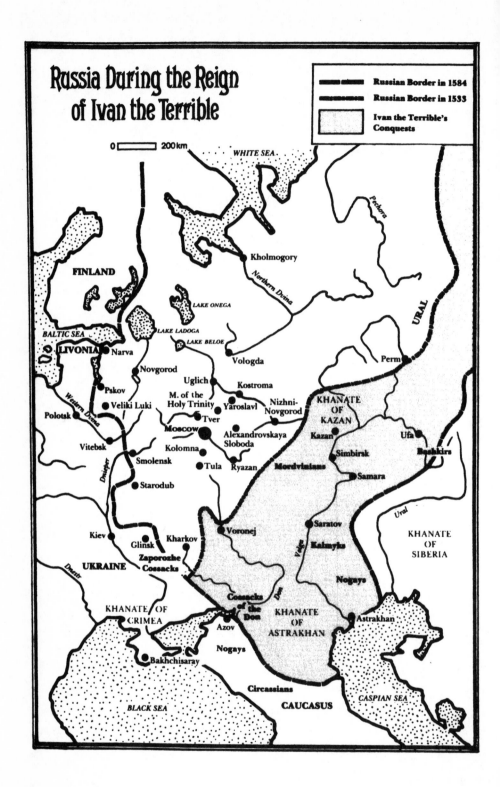

Russia During the Reign
of Ivan the Terrible

Russian Border in 1584
Russian Border in 1533
Ivan the Terrible's
Conquests

0 _____ 200km

WHITE SEA

Pechora

Kholmogory

FINLAND

Northern Dvina

LAKE ONEGA

URAL

LAKE LADOGA

BALTIC SEA

LAKE BELOE

LIVONIA Narva

Vologda

Perm

Novgorod

Pskov

Uglich

Kostroma

KHANATE
OF
KAZAN

Veliki Luki

M. of the
Holy Trinity

Yaroslavl

Nizhni-
Novgorod

Ufa

Polotsk

Tver

Kazan

Bashkirs

Moscow

Alexandrovskaya
Sloboda

Simbirsk

Vitebsk

Kolomna

Western Dvina

Smolensk

Tula

Ryazan

Mordvinians

Samara

Dnieper

Starodub

Ural

Voronej

Saratov

KHANATE
OF
SIBERIA

Kiev

Kharkov

Glinsk

Volga

Kalmyks

Zaporozhe
Cossacks

UKRAINE

Dniestr

Nogays

Don

Cossacks
of the
Don

KHANATE OF
CRIMEA

Azov

KHANATE
OF
ASTRAKHAN

Astrakhan

Nogays

Bakhchisaray

Circassians

CASPIAN SEA

BLACK SEA

CAUCASUS

I

The Parents

Twenty years of marriage and not the least sign of a child. It was a harder trial for a princely couple than for ordinary mortals. At least that was what Vasily III, Grand Duke of Moscow, thought in 1526. Worried about the continuation of his line, he wondered if notwithstanding the affectionate regard he had for his wife, the beautiful Salomonia Saburova, he ought not to replace her before he grew too old to have children—he was forty-seven. Salomonia, who shared her husband's disappointment, made pilgrimages, consulted sorcerors, and rubbed the most intimate parts of her body with a mixture of oil and honey —a sure way, it was said, of being impregnated. There was no result.

Vasily was in despair: He could no longer see a nest on the branch of a tree without tears coming to his eyes. Turning to his retinue of boyars, he sighed, "The birds are happier than I. At least they have children! . . . Who will become my heir and heir to the Russian empire? My brothers are unworthy of it, they can't even govern their own appanages!"* At these words, the boyars felt the time had come to put forward a daring suggestion. "Sire," said one of them, "the barren fig tree is cut down so that another may be planted in the orchard." That was exactly what Vasily wanted to hear. Salomonia's sterility was a welcome pretext for the sovereign to open his bed to a fresher partner. Without a shadow of compunction, he advised his wife to withdraw to a cloister. She protested that she did not deserve such penance after a lifetime of faithful love. Confronted with her refusal, Vasily employed force. She was carried off from the palace, shut up in the convent of Suzdal, and shorn as a nun. During the ceremony of taking the veil, she struggled so violently that one of the Grand Duke's officers struck her with his stick to recall her to order. "God sees me; he will avenge me on my persecutor," she cried through her sobs. Old Prince Simeon Kurbsky and the monks Maxim the Greek and Vassian Patrikeyev dared to intercede on the poor woman's behalf and were promptly banished. But most of the boyars and ecclesiastics, with the Metropolitan Daniel, at their head, approved the Grand Duke's decision.

Now that he was rid of his wife, Vasily could hardly wait to take another. To be sure, according to the rule of the Orthodox Church, a man who had repudiated his wife did not have the right to remarry, so long as she was alive. But the laws that govern the behavior of the humble fade away in the presence of crowned heads. At least that was what Metropolitan Daniel said. Nevertheless, Vasily decided to consult the Greek Patriarch of

---

*At this time Vasily III had two living brothers: Yuri (called George by certain authors, born in 1480) and Andrei (born in 1490).

Jerusalem, for greater security. That prelate was a strict and stubborn man, and far from applauding the Grand Duke's intention, he fulminated against it. "Vasily," he wrote, "if you contract a second marriage, you will have a wicked son; your states will be prey to terror and tears; rivers of blood will flow; the heads of the mighty will fall; your cities will be devoured by flames." Not in the least impressed by this prophecy, Metropolitan Daniel declared proudly, "Very well, we shall do without his blessing!" His assurance gave new energy to Vasily. Convinced that he no longer had anything to fear from the wrath of heaven, he began preparations for the wedding. In reality, he had already made his choice.

According to custom, the sovereign of Moscow was supposed to summon all the marriageable young ladies in the Grand Dukedom to the palace for the ceremony of the *smotriny* (from *smotrit,* to look), after which he would designate the one who would thenceforth share his bed. Vasily, however, decided to dispense with this beauty contest and announced out of the blue that he wished to take to wife Elena Glinskaya, the daughter of a Lithuanian refugee. The boyars were stunned: The fiancée came from a Catholic family. Would it not have been better to reserve so great an honor for a daughter of their own race and religion? Vasily remained deaf to their complaints. Elena was beautiful, intelligent, passionate. Brought up "in the German fashion," she had a cultivation and freedom of manners that set her apart from the Russian virgins of her age, who were locked in ignorance, prudery, superstition, and modest domestic virtues. The sovereign was so much in love with her that in order to look younger he did not hesitate to shave his beard—an act which to the pious men of his time bordered on sacrilege.

The marriage festivities lasted three days. Before the religious ceremony, the betrothed couple appeared sitting at a table draped with a cloth, on which lay a dish containing bread and salt. Their seats were covered with eighty black marten skins to keep away evil spirits. The wedding candles were likewise wrapped in marten skins. A dignitary fanned the fiancés with a bundle of marten skins tied together. The wife of another dignitary smoothed their hair with a fine comb dipped in mead. A cap and a white veil were placed on Elena's head. Hops, a symbol of fertility, were thrown over the couple. The whole company— with candles, lanterns, icons, and cakes—set out for the Cathedral of the Assumption. There the fiancés walked on a carpet of damask and sable. The Metropolitan presented them with a glass of Italian wine. Having drunk, the monarch broke the glass under his feet. After the blessing the newlyweds, seated on cushions of crimson velvet, received the congratulations of the clergy and the court while the choir sang, "Long life!" In the bedchamber to which they then retired there were icons everywhere, jars of mead, candles planted in kegs of grain, mountains of marten and sable skins. On the nuptial bed lay twenty-seven sheaves of wheat. The wife of the captain of the guard, who wore two fur pelisses, one of them inside out according to custom, once again sprinkled hops over the bride and groom, while courtiers brought them roast cock to eat. All night long, the Prince's equerry stood guard on horseback with his sword drawn under the bedroom windows. Next day, the couple went separately to the steam baths, then returned to their room and ate gruel in bed. The marriage being considered consummated—a bloodstained shift was the proof—the boyars congratulated their master and the feasting resumed.

In spite of all the hops that had been scattered during the various ceremonies, Elena proved no less barren than Salomonia. As in the case of the first wife, neither prayers nor relics, neither magic practices nor Italian and German ointments could overcome the curse that hung over her. The people whispered that God disapproved of Vasily's second union and had decided not to give him a child. The innocent Salomonia, on the other hand, was supposed to have secretly given birth to a son in the convent to which she had been relegated. But fortunately, thanks to the prayers of a monk named Paphnuty Borovsky, the anger of heaven was finally appeased: Elena was pregnant. Vasily was exultant. Behind his back, scandalmongers claimed that credit belonged not to the man who was officially rejoicing over it but to a member of the Princess's intimate circle, Prince Obolensky-Telepnev. No matter. Vasily thought he was a father, claimed to be a father; he loaded Paphnuty with gifts, declared him a miracle worker, and had him canonized. Another monk, by the name of Domitian, prophesied to Elena that she would be "mother of a Titus of great genius."

On August 25, 1530, Elena Glinskaya gave birth to a healthy son with strong lungs: Ivan. At the moment he was born, a roll of thunder shook the heavens and lightning struck the Kremlin. The court soothsayers concluded that a great reign was in prospect. Ten days later, Ivan was baptized at the Monastery of the Holy Trinity,* and his grateful father, with tears in his eyes, laid the little swaddled body on the tomb of St. Sergius so as to call down upon the infant the saint's protection. Intoxicated with happiness, Vasily lavished gold on the churches, opened the prisons, pardoned a few high noblemen who had formerly earned his disfavor, and tirelessly received delegations of his subjects, from the poorest to the most magnificent.

Far away among the Tatars, the Khan of Kazan, learning of the birth of Ivan, told the Russian boyars who had come to visit him, "A sovereign has been born to you and he already has two teeth. With one, he will devour us; but with the other, he will devour you!"

Two years later Elena, who was decidedly favored by the Almighty, gave birth to a second son, Yuri. The dynasty was assured. Vasily felt that he had fulfilled his role as sovereign both on the battlefield and in bed. On September 25, 1533, in a spirit of gratitude, he went with his wife and children to the Monastery of the Holy Trinity, received the blessing of the Ar-

---

*This, the great Troitsa-Sergeyevsky Monastery founded by St. Sergius of Radonezh in the fourteenth century, is located some forty miles north of Moscow.

chimandrite, and fasted and prayed among the pilgrims come from every corner of Muscovy. Then he went hunting, surrounded by his dogs, his foot archers, and his horsemen armed with hunting forks. As he was riding through the forest not far from Volokolamsk, he felt a pain in his left thigh, which showed as a purplish, running abcess. The next day, despite the sore, he decided to participate in a battue. Suddenly he felt dizzy. He was brought back to the village of Kolp on a litter. Elena was worried, and sent for her uncle, Mikhail Glinsky, and two German physicians, Theophile of Lübeck and Nicholas Luef. They started with "Russian remedies": poultices of wheat flour, honey, and boiled onions. In vain. Pus flowed out by the cupful. Transported to Volokolamsk by his boyars, Vasily felt certain he was done for. Every time poultices were applied, the foul discharge increased. The bewildered doctors ordered a laxative of seeds, only weakening the patient. He demanded to be brought back to Moscow, for he wanted to die in his capital.

The first stop on the journey was the St. Joseph Monastery, where the patient lay on his bed exposed to public view in the church. While the deacon recited prayers for his recovery, Elena and her children, the hunters, boyars, clergy, and the common people who had flocked to the monastery knelt sobbing around him. The procession resumed the road to Moscow. It was snowing. The sleigh bearing Vasily jolted over the track. Since he wanted to enter the city secretly and thus avoid the malicious curiosity of the foreign ambassadors, the boyars threw a bridge over the Moskva River, breaking still-thin ice. Hardly had the sleigh entered upon the flimsy structure when it gave way under the weight of the team. The horses slipped into the water; the boyars cut the traces, held back the sleigh, and drew it up on the bank. At last, at dawn on November 25, 1533, Vasily found himself back in his apartments in the Kremlin, so exhausted that he barely had strength to thank God for having brought him to safe haven.

It snowed unceasingly on churches, palaces, huts. The sentries, numb with cold and blinded by the whirling flakes, called out their challenges to phantoms hurrying toward the Staircase of Honor. All the court dignitaries knew that their sovereign was dying. At his orders, they hastened to his side: Princes Ivan and Vasily Shuisky, Mikhail Zakharin, Vorontzov, Kurbsky, Glinsky, the treasurer Golovin, the chamberlain Shigona, boyars of less importance. . . . Crowded into the vestibule, they waited in silence in the wan light falling from the mica windows. At last a servant opened the doors of the bedchamber. Tapers burned in front of the bed where the dying man lay. Around him monks were murmuring prayers.

Gathering his strength, Vasily dictated a last testament in the presence of the boyars. He designated as successor to the throne his son Ivan, who was still only three years old, placing him until the age of fifteen under the guardianship of his mother and the boyars. The courtiers were none too pleased with these dispositions. They rebelled at the notion of having a little child for sovereign and, for regent, a foreign woman with a large and rapacious family at her side. But they bowed respectfully to the will of the dying man. Sensing their displeasure, Vasily told Mikhail Glinsky, "Although you are a foreigner by birth, you have become Russian among us. I therefore entrust you with my wife and son."

As his sore was discharging increasing amounts of evil-smelling pus, the Grand Duke begged the doctors Luef and Theophile to wash him with vodka. While they were doing so, he said to them, "Tell me frankly if it is in your power to cure me." Luef admitted that he had lost all hope. "Well, my friends," sighed Vasily, "you have heard him, I must leave you." Metropolitan Daniel was there with the priest Alexeyev, bearing the holy bread and wine. With a superhuman effort, Vasily stood up to receive communion. Having lain down again, he summoned his wife and children and blessed them with the sign of the cross. Then, addressing the boyars, he said: "Serve my son as you have served myself. Do everything in your power to see

7

that he reigns over this country. . . . Do not abandon Mikhail Glinsky, for he is bound to my wife by ties of blood." At these words, Elena's sobs redoubled. On her knees she uttered piercing cries and struck her head on the floor. She was dragged away, her garments torn, her hair disheveled.

As soon as she was gone, Vasily asked Metropolitan Daniel to make him a monk. For the salvation of his soul, he said, he wanted to be buried not as an all-powerful monarch but as the humblest servant of the Lord. His brother Andrei and Vorontzov opposed this wish, which they deemed incompatible with the dignity of the Grand Duke of Moscow. With his tongue half paralyzed, Vasily insisted. He kissed the hem of his sheet, made a wavering sign of the cross, and cast an entreating look at the icon of the Madonna of Vladimir. Metropolitan Daniel had a black cowl brought and exclaimed, "No, no one shall rob me of his soul! A silver vessel is no doubt precious, but when it is gilded its worth increases!" The prayers resumed. Vasily was tonsured. He became a monk under the name of Varlaam. The Scriptures were placed on his chest. He was scarcely breathing. Suddenly Shigona cried, "It's over, the monarch is no more!" Not long after, he was to declare that the Prince's face had lit up at the moment he gave his last sigh, and that the foul exhalations of his wound had changed to a sweet perfume. Metropolitan Daniel washed the body of the deceased, wiped it with linen cloths, and dressed it in a monk's habit. On learning the news, Elena fainted and, we are told, did not regain consciousness for two hours.

It was midnight on December 4, 1533, and no one in Moscow was asleep. Despite the snow, the people stood waiting in the streets. When the great bell of the Kremlin tolled the knell, the crowd burst into sobs and fell to their knees. They wept for a great prince who in the course of a twenty-nine-year reign had subdued the boyars, fought the Crimean Tatars, and added to the provinces and towns he had inherited Pskov, Ryazan, and territories taken from Lithuania. The next day, at the Cathedral of St. Michael the Archangel, Metropolitan Daniel pronounced the eulogy of the deceased: ". . . a skillful administrator, a true pilot, the image of divine goodness, a pillar of patience and firmness, the father of the nobles and of the people."

Having wept floods of tears for her fifty-four-year-old husband, Elena turned bravely to her new duties as sovereign. She was surrounded by a Council of Regency composed of the brothers of the deceased, Yuri and Andrei, and of twenty distinguished boyars including Ivan Belsky, Ivan Shuisky, Obolensky, Vorontzov, Zakharin, Morozov, and others. This assembly was dominated by the Regent's uncle, old Mikhail Glinsky, an ambitious and enterprising man, and by the Grand Equerry Ivan Obolensky-Telepnev, a handsome young man of limited intelligence whom Elena had taken for her lover. On their advice Elena sent ambassadors extraordinary to Emperor Charles V and to his brother Ferdinand, King of Hungary and Bohemia; renewed friendly relations with Sweden, Moldavia, Livonia, the Khan of Astrakhan, and a few Nogay princes; continued the war against the Tatars of the Crimea; made an incursion into Lithuania; and fortified the walls of Moscow. In 1536, little Ivan, barely six years old, received the Lithuanian ambassadors. Rising from his throne, he asked in a piping voice, "Is our good brother, King Sigismund, in good health?" Then he held out his hand for them to kiss. Everyone praised the boy for his dignified bearing and clear enunciation. Without question the little fellow had the makings of a sovereign. But according to his father's testament, it would be a long wait before he took power. And between now and then, how many plots lay in store!

No sooner was Vasily dead than a struggle broke out between the boyars, who were anxious to take back their prerogatives, and the Regent, who meant to govern the country with a stronger hand than the deceased Prince's. Fearing that in spite of their oath her husband's two brothers, Yuri and Andrei, would try to seize the crown, she had them both arrested on the pretext of insubordination. The first was thrown into prison, where he starved to death. The second was captured while trying to foment a revolt, and was incarcerated and poisoned. His supporters were given the knout and then tortured; some thirty of them were hanged on gallows placed at intervals along the road from Moscow to Novgorod. Andrei's wife and son were locked up in an oubliette. Lastly, Mikhail Glinsky, Elena's own uncle, who had dared to remonstrate with her on the subject of her affair with Obolensky-Telepnev, was relieved of his responsibilities and taken to prison. Other princes were strangled or exiled on the most trivial grounds. The boyars were indignant over all this violence. "Obolensky-Telepnev is the only powerful man at court," said one of them. "The others, of an older nobility, are boyars in name only. And no service is recognized unless one makes oneself agreeable to the favorite!" The number of persons in the Kremlin who longed for a change increased with every day that passed. Suddenly, on April 3, 1538, Elena died, seized with horrible pains. There was no doubt in the minds of the ambassadors that she had been poisoned. In the palace, behind the masks of grief was unanimous relief. In the great political upheaval that was to follow, no one paid any attention to little Ivan, eight years old, who had just lost his mother.

II

Childhood

Ivan, a child without mother or father, did not even have his uncles to turn to in his confusion, since both Andrei and Yuri had died in prison. It was true that the proud Princess Elena, a "distant" mother absorbed in the preoccupations of power, had never paid much attention to her sons, and her disappearance made no great hole in their lives. Nevertheless, Ivan felt that a source of warmth was missing. Accordingly, he transferred all his affection to his dear nurse Agrafena, the sister of Obolensky-Telepnev.

When the Regent died, the favorite realized at once that his situation was gravely threatened. For the boyars the hour of revenge had struck. The first to raise his head was Prince Vasily Shuisky. Like the late Grand Duke and his successor, Ivan, Shuisky was descended from the illustrious Alexander Nevsky; in fact, he prided himself on belonging to the elder branch of a family of which the reigning house represented only the younger branch. What he coveted, therefore, was not a place near the throne but the throne itself. His first concern was to sweep from his path the former favorite: Obolensky-Telepnev was thrown into a dungeon, where he died tormented by hunger and crushed by the weight of his chains. Immediately afterward, Shuisky ordered that the condemned man's sister, the nurse Agrafena, be seized and sent to a distant convent. When they came to arrest the poor unfortunate, Ivan clung to her skirts, wept, stamped his feet, and begged the guards to take pity on this woman who was not guilty of anything. To no avail. They pushed him aside and carried off his only friend; he was never to see her again.

Left alone with his brother, Ivan wondered whether next day it would not be his turn to be arrested. But curiously enough the boyars, who were busy fighting among themselves, considered him a negligible quantity. No doubt they thought there would be time enough to get rid of him when they had settled their personal rivalries. The first decision of the Council of Boyars was to free the political prisoners who had been victims of the Regent's moods. Among those who returned were Ivan Shuisky, Prince Vasily's brother, and Ivan Belsky, a descendant of the Gedimin princes of Lithuania. Belsky, too, dreamed of seizing power and, instead of thanking Vasily Shuisky for having had him released, hastened to oppose him. Each of the two champions had resolute supporters. Sometimes one, sometimes the other tightened his authority over the orphans.

In this climate of spying, poisoning, and violence, Ivan came to have the conception of life of a predatory animal, eager to pursue his prey and to enjoy its suffering. Everything he saw and heard in the palace taught him cruelty and trickery. Woe to the weak! Success excused everything. God was on the side of poison, the garrote, and the sword. While still very young he took pleasure in bloody games. Observing the brutal treatment that grown men inflicted on their fellows, he made ready to imitate them by tormenting animals. It was more than an amusement: it was an apprenticeship. He would tear the feathers from birds he caught, put out their eyes, slit their stomachs with a knife, delight in watching the stages by which they died. Standing on the ramparts of the Kremlin fortress, he would whirl young dogs above his head and hurl them down to the courtyard to break their bones. Their plaintive yelps satisfied an obscure need for revenge, as if these were hateful boyars he was putting to death.

Ivan could not forgive the boyars for the disorders into which their quarrels had plunged the country, for the contempt they showed their young sovereign. To be sure, on days of official ceremonies they dressed him sumptuously, surrounded him with imperial pomp, and escorted him with feigned deference, but on other days these same men treated him with disdain, as if he were the son of some servant girl. Stripped of his cap and coat and of his caftan decorated with precious stones, he would be relegated to his room to suffer the snubs of the very men who a few minutes earlier had been bowing before him. Speaking of this period twenty-five years later, Ivan wrote to Prince Kurbsky as follows: "When our mother, the pious Czarina Elena, left the earthly kingdom for that of God, my brother, Yuri, and I remained orphans in the absolute sense of the word. . . . Our subjects saw their desires fulfilled: they received an empire without a master. Paying no attention to us— their sovereigns—they rushed to conquer wealth and glory, falling upon one another in the process. . . . As for my brother Yuri and me, they treated us like foreigners or beggars. How many privations did we not endure, lacking both food and clothing! We were allowed no freedom. We were not brought up as children should be. Here is a scene I remember: We were playing at some childish game and Prince Ivan Shuisky was sprawled on a bench, with one elbow leaning on our father's bed and his feet on a chair. He paid not the slightest attention to us, neither as parent, nor as potentate, nor as servant of his masters. Who could endure such arrogance? . . . Many were the times when I was not even served my meals at the appointed hour! And what of my father's treasure that was mine by right? It was all looted. . . . The sons of boyars carried off that treasure, they melted it down to make vessels of gold and silver; they engraved their parents' names on them as if they had been hereditary possessions!"[1]

But it was not only resentment and humiliation that fed Ivan's hatred of the boyars. There was also constant fear: The child lived in dread of being murdered. Everywhere he saw enemies lying in wait for him. That curtain—was there a mercenary behind it, dagger in hand? The water in that ewer—was it poisoned? Every day he was a witness to quarrels, brawls, murders. At times he felt as if he had a temporary reprieve from execution, as if he had been miraculously forgotten by the brutes who were fighting over his empire. One night, guards pursued the new Metropolitan, Joseph, into the child's very room, where the prelate had taken refuge. Stoned, spat upon, his gown torn, Joseph begged the protection of his young prince, who, sitting up in bed and trembling for his own life, said not a word. Metropolitan Joseph was taken away to be shut up in a monastery in Belozersk. His crime? To have been a supporter of Ivan Belsky.

For, of late, the Shuiskys had seized the initiative again. Three hundred of their henchmen invaded the Kremlin, dragged Ivan Belsky from his house, and threw him in prison. His trusted adviser, Mishurin, was turned over to the sons of boyars, who flayed him alive; the bloody body was then pushed to the block, where an executioner beheaded him. In the midst of these events, Vasily Shuisky died, abandoning power to his brother Ivan. Ivan, weaker than Vasily, permitted the return of

Ivan Belsky, who immediately fomented a revolt. Captured and again dragged off to prison, he was put to death in his cell. Ivan Shuisky's own death—but of an illness—soon followed. His cousin, Andrei Shuisky, took his place at the head of the boyars. Meantime, young Ivan had made friends with Feodor Vorontzov. This was enough to convince Andrei that the favorite must be destroyed. In the course of a stormy argument in the presence of Ivan and Metropolitan Macarius, Andrei Shuisky and his companions, drunk with rage, struck Feodor Vorontzov in the face, dragged him to the palace courtyard, beat him unmercifully, and ordered the guards to throw him in prison. Ivan and Macarius, appalled, tried to intercede on behalf of the wretched man. But the boyars would hear none of it, and one of them, Golovin, tore the prelate's gown as a gesture of contempt. Once again, with glittering eyes and pale forehead, Ivan swallowed his terror and disgust and fell silent. He was thirteen years old.

A short time later, after the Christmas holidays, Ivan invited the boyars to a banquet. His hatred for them, having slowly accumulated, gave him the courage to strike a great blow. After months of uncertainty, he felt at last that through his princely birth he had been placed directly under heaven's protection; though he was still young and weak, his arm was an extension of the arm of God. Standing before his bearded, tipsy guests, he addressed them in a firm voice. He accused them of having taken advantage of his extreme youth, of having abandoned themselves to looting, of having arbitrarily carried out death sentences. Many of them, he said, were guilty, but he would be satisfied if only one, the greatest criminal among them were put to death, as an example: Prince Andrei Shuisky. Having uttered these words, he felt a mortal terror at his own audacity. Would the guards obey him? Wouldn't the boyars take advantage of the opportunity to seize him and tear him to pieces? He had staked his all. He waited, his heart in a knot. And the miracle happened. The guests around the table, dumbfounded by this act of authority, made not a move. Suddenly they had a master, a master who was scarcely more than a child. The guards seized Andrei Shuisky and turned him over to huntsmen, who had him devoured alive by hunting dogs in the middle of the street.

Nevertheless, this sudden act of self-assertion on Ivan's part had no sequel. He was not old enough to govern by himself. Taking advantage of the downfall of the Shuiskys, the Glinskys —who had returned in force—killed or exiled various enemies and, accusing the boyar Buturlin of having made scurrilous remarks, cut out his tongue. The Glinskys were soon driven out by the Belskys, who in turn were forced to bow before the Shuiskys, who were finally defeated by a last, unexpected revival of the Glinskys. The same families, with the same ambitions, succeeded one another in an infernal round. When one of the leaders fell, his brother, uncle, son, nephew, or cousin took his place. It was impossible to cut off all heads at once. Ivan was to confess later, at the opening of the *Stoglav* Council of 1551: "Our boyars governed the country as they pleased, for no one opposed their power. . . . I grew up. . . . I adopted the devious ways of the people around me, I learned to be crafty like them."

At fourteen, Ivan's great passion was hunting: bears, wolves, white foxes. He would roam the forests surrounded by the sons of boyars, tracking wild beasts or following wild swans with a gyrfalcon on his wrist. Then, excited by the ride, the merry band would attack villages, beat the peasants, knock the girls down in the straw, drink and eat till they were ready to burst. Although Ivan participated in these wild expeditions, unlike his companions, he kept his head in the midst of debauchery. He would watch as the others manhandled muzhiks and merchants, enjoying the sight of the women with their skirts turned up, and reveling in the smell of the wine, sweat, and blood. But at the height of these orgies he never lost the notion of his exceptional dignity. When he became drunk, when he fornicated, it was God who was getting drunk and fornicating, through him.

Though his half-idiot brother Yuri took no interest in anything except games and food, Ivan, after a day of marauding, liked to plunge into a book. By candlelight he would read over the pages of the Bible, the lives of the saints, the commentaries and exhortations of Saint John Chrysostom, the chronicles of the Russian monk Nestor. The prophecies of the Apocalypse mingled in Ivan's mind with the old Slavic legends. Metropolitan Macarius introduced him to history and theology. Thanks to him, Ivan became familiar both with Muscovy's past and with the mysteries of religion—he felt a connection to his Russian roots, and at the same time was uplifted. With an insatiable appetite for information, Ivan questioned the secretaries of the chanceries, the foreign ambassadors, the craftsmen working in the palace. Foraging left and right, he acquired information haphazardly, depending on the persons he happened to meet. This miscellaneous knowledge was jumbled together in his head, and primarily self-taught, he was unable either to organize what he knew or to use it judiciously. Reading gave Ivan the desire to write. He had a veritable passion for handling the Russian language. Magnificent sentences danced in his brain, and he set them down on paper solely for his own pleasure; later, he would offer them to the whole world. He also loved the art of oratory. When he spoke, he felt as if he were singing. Rolling, biblical periods flowed from his mouth. Intoxicated by the sound of his own voice, he was long-winded, bombastic, and impassioned—after the fashion of the time.

To become more familiar with his country, which he could not yet govern, Ivan roamed over it in all directions. Now he was in Vladimir, now in Mozhaisk, now in Rzhev, Tver, Novgorod, Rostov, Yaroslavl. In the course of these travels he went hunting, of course, but he also devoted himself fervently to pious exercises: There was not a monastery that he failed to visit on his way, not an important priest whose blessing he failed to solicit. He would go carousing with his companions, then remain standing for five hours at a stretch during a religious service, his soul rapt in beatitude. He prostrated himself so often before icons that a callus formed on his forehead.

The Russian people, ground down by the boyars, tried in vain to attract the attention of their young sovereign. Ivan refused to see the abject poverty of the provinces he traveled through. It did not matter to him that his journeys were a heavy expense to the towns that sheltered him. At each stop, he demanded feasts and gifts. If a few of the more daring townsmen ventured to present him with a petition, it was intercepted by those around him—and lucky were its authors if they were not immediately punished! The only hope for the humble was the thought that as the years passed, the character of the inexperienced adolescent might mature, that he would learn the duties of a monarch toward his subjects.

Drunk with arrogance, violence, hypocrisy, and piety, Ivan could not be troubled even by external events. The boyars, busy with fratricidal struggles in the Kremlin, were unable to resist the incursions of the Tatars of Kazan and the Crimea. A contemporary chronicler described these raids on Russian territory as follows: "The wretched, defenseless inhabitants were reduced to hiding in the forests or in the depths of caves. The places formerly peopled with villages were covered with brush. The infidels lived amid the ruins of burned monasteries, sleeping in the churches, drinking from the sacred vessels, plucking the ornaments from the holy images to make them into earrings and necklaces with which to adorn their women. They would slip hot ashes mixed with burning coals into the boots of the monks and force them, despite the pain, to dance for them. They raped the young nuns; they put out the eyes, cut off the nose, ears, hands and feet of those whom they did not take away in captivity. But the most horrible thing of all was that many Christians adopted their belief. . . . What I write is not what I have heard tell, but what I have seen with my own eyes and will never forget."[2]

With great difficulty the Russians, answering the call of their sovereign, finally repulsed the Tatars on the Oka, then on the Volga. The danger seemed to have been temporarily averted. Ivan, who was then sixteen years old, joined the army quartered in Kolomna. But the enemy had not shown himself for a long time. The military camp, transformed into a court, became the scene of countless intrigues.

One day when Ivan was out hunting in the environs, he saw approaching some fifty harquebusiers from Novgorod, bearing a petition. They were coming to complain of oppressive measures that afflicted them. Ivan refused to listen, and had his mounted boyars charge them. The harquebusiers defended themselves and, pierced by the boyars' arrows, collapsed on top of one another. In vain was Ivan assured that it was a misunderstanding; he believed himself to be the victim of an attempt on his life. Immediately he named the perpetrators: Ivan Kubensky, Feodor Vorontzov (the former favorite lately freed from prison), and the latter's brother Vasily. Without allowing them time to vindicate themselves, he had them decapitated in front of their peers. Three times the ax fell and the blood spurted forth. Not a muscle quivered in Ivan's face. No one in his entourage dared protest. This horrified acceptance of the sentence strengthened him in the belief that his justice was infallible and his power sacred.

III

Czar Ivan IV

From year to year, Ivan became increasingly aware of the borders of his empire. Freed from the yoke of the Tatars, the principality of which he was Grand Duke extended from the northern Volga to the Dnieper and from the Arctic Ocean to the Don. Beyond this Russia, which was still relatively small, stretched the mysterious steppes of Siberia; the unconquered regions of the Volga; Astrakhan and the Crimea; the western Ukraine; the Grand Duchy of Lithuania; and the countries on the shores of the Baltic. So many territories—Ivan looked upon all of them with covetous eyes. His ancestors had made Russia into a powerful state by enrolling under their banners all the petty princes whose domains surrounded Moscow. It was up to him to complete the work of his fathers by pushing back the frontiers and by subduing the boyars once and for all.

The city of Moscow itself had recently expanded considerably. It already included 40,500 houses. In the heart of the capital rose the sacred fortress of the Kremlin. Its crenelated battlements sheltered princely residences, palaces ornately decorated by Italian architects, and cathedrals with gilded, onion-shaped cupolas glittering in the sun. Around the Kremlin stood a city of wooden buildings, flourishing gardens, and broad streets that the least shower turned into rivers of mud. Craftsmen's hovels stood next to the mansions of important personages, "miraculous" chapels next to bathhouses. Every Russian, of whatever condition, went to these baths once a week to perspire in the steam. Among the booths on the great square of the Kremlin a noisy, colorful fair was always in progress. Tumblers, bear trainers, and blind minstrels attracted idlers, and the idlers attracted cutpurses. People crowded around the vendors of bliny and kvas. Amid the songs and laughter, quarrels would break out; sometimes these turned into fistfights, and guards would roughly intervene. On the Lobnoe Mesto,* near the Gate of the Savior, clerks shouted out government ordinances. No one listened to them. A little farther on, the executioner would be administering the knout to some petty criminal. Heedless of the victim's cries, sleeping drunkards would be sprawled on the ground among the throng. Passersby would step over them and go on their way, avoiding the piles of horse manure.

At night, all roads leading into the Kremlin were barred with chevaux-de-frise. The walls of the citadel bristled with cannon. A large company of guards watched over the security of the

---

*The Lobnoe Mesto (Place of Execution) is a round stone dais still standing in Red Square, Moscow, on the site where it was originally constructed in the 1530s as a rostrum for the announcement of government decrees, solemn ceremonies, church services, and executions.

Grand Duke, who resided there. It was in the Kremlin too that meetings of the Duma, the council of boyars, were held. The colors red and gold dominated in the council's low-ceilinged, vaulted rooms with squat pillars. There was more gold in the profusion of icons decorating the Kremlin's churches, audience chambers, and bedrooms; gold again in the garments of the nobles; and in the dishes used during their interminable banquets.

The nobles, who made up the Grand Duke's entourage, were all descended from appanaged princes and represented families as illustrious as their master's; hence, their reluctance to let themselves be governed by him. The rest of the population included functionaries, merchants, workers—and above all, peasants, whose chief role was to feed the army when it was on the march. There was, in principle, no serfdom: Whether the land they worked belonged to them or to another, the peasants were masters of their persons and of their labor. But in either case they were overwhelmed with taxes. True slaves—captives of war, men who had been deprived of their liberty by a judicial decision or by contract with a landowner—were then relatively rare. A privileged place in this Russian social hierarchy belonged to the merchants, some of whom amassed enormous capital through the boldness of their undertakings. Ignorant of western Europe, they preferred to trade with central Asia and the Far East. The Nizhni-Novgorod Fair welcomed foreign buyers. Russian caravans ventured as far as Peking. The greatest fortunes in Russia were, nevertheless, in the hands of the Church. The vast domains of the clergy were exempt from taxes. More than 100,000 peasants worked the lands belonging to the monasteries. Other sources of wealth for the monks included the industries they managed, the taxes they levied, and the pious gifts that rained down upon the brotherhood from all sides.

The Russian people as a whole, ground down by the Church on the one hand and the state on the other, were poor, in debt, subjugated. They were extremely religious, but their faith was identified with ritual; for them, strict observance of ceremonies took the place of profound conviction. To a simple man, it was a more serious crime not to cross oneself before an icon than to rob one's neighbor. Eating meat was permitted only three times a week, and sexual relations were prohibited on holidays and during Lent.

In general, the Church considered woman the chief emissary of the demon. The more beautiful she was, the more pernicious. To mitigate the evil, she was shut up in a gynaeceum, the *terem*. Made of ox bladders, the windows of the *terem* of a rich house opened on an interior courtyard. No man except the husband had access to the recluse. The wife lacked nothing, except the essential thing: to see the world and be seen by it. Surrounded by a swarm of serving women, she appeared before her husband's guests only at the most solemn banquets. Her existence was devoted to the care of her master, prayer, and the interpretation of dreams. In more modest circles, of course, this cloistering was less strictly observed. But what the poorer woman gained in freedom she lost in consideration. The first one to rise in the house, she toiled at household tasks until she was exhausted. "The condition of the women is most miserable," wrote von Herberstein, a contemporary ambassador of the Holy Roman Empire, "for [the Russians] consider no woman virtuous unless she live shut up at home, and be so closely guarded that she go out nowhere."[1] She was even forbidden to chat with a neighbor woman. But female fortune-tellers gained entry everywhere.

The whole country was steeped in superstition. In all classes of society, Christianity and paganism mingled together. The smallest events of life took on prophetic meaning. A buzzing in the ears indicated that someone was speaking ill of you; an itching of the fingers promised a journey; the quacking of ducks foretold a fire. Pregnant women gave bread to the bears of itinerant jugglers and listened to their growls to learn the sex of the child they awaited. If you wanted a man to die, you picked up a handful of earth he had walked on and threw it symbolically into the fire. On the Saturday before Pentecost, people danced in the cemeteries. On Maundy Thursday, they burned straw to call up spirits. None of this, however, kept the churches from being crowded with people making deep genuflexions and broad signs of the cross.

The magnificence of the Russian Orthodox liturgy was matched, among the nobility, by the magnificence of the garments of the faithful: when they came onto the parvis, they were as sumptuously dressed as the priests. A high-ranking worshiper wore a conical cap in the Persian style, trimmed with black fox. Several richly embroidered colored shirts, one on top of another, fell to his knees; covering these was a narrow tunic made of cloth of gold, reaching to the ankles. A belt tied very low, below the waist, accentuated the proud protuberance of the stomach and served to carry a dagger and a spoon. On top of all this, lastly, was an even longer silk garment edged with fur, from which emerged at every step morocco boots embroidered with pearls. A woman of the aristocracy was muffled up even more completely in an extraordinary layering of gowns—some loose, some tight, some of silk or cloth of gold or studded with precious stones and lined with fur. Her hair would be covered with a bonnet of fine cambric tied under the chin; her neck, ears, and wrists would be loaded with gems, her feet encased in ankle boots of bright-colored leather sewn with pearls. She was a veritable jewel box, stiff and heavy, hardly able to move under the abundance of ornaments. Whereas Russian men wore beards—as a symbol of their power and their privileged position in the eyes of God, who Himself had a beard—women covered their faces with thick red and white paint, not to make themselves more attractive, we are told, but to hide for shame their bare skin, which was a constant temptation to sin.

The ample garments of both sexes only emphasized the opulent proportions of the Russian figure. According to Western travelers, the men were potbellied and the women fat, thanks to the overrich diet and lack of exercise. Russian cooking was varied and heavy,* seasoned with garlic, onion, and hemp-seed oil. On the tables of the nobility were served roasts, chickens with lemon, *shchi* (the national cabbage soup), meat pies (*pirogi* with rice or fish, *pirozhki* with eggs), *bliny* with cream, *kasha* (a gruel of buckwheat and millet), *kissel* (cranberry juice thickened with potato starch and sugar), sweets made with ginger and honey. . . . On days of abstinence the sturgeon, pike, and salmon appeared in triumph, along with fish fritters and caviar. For drink there was *kvas*, Hungarian wine, mead, and vodka. Drunkenness was rampant at every level of society. A male worthy of the name should be able to drink like a fish; then he took a nap. Even the merchants closed their shops after the midday meal.

While still very young, Ivan had been attracted to women. But after having turned up the skirts of laughing servants and straddled terrified village girls, he began to think of more refined amusement. He was aroused by the idea of marriage. . . . He was soon going to be seventeen. Tall and thin, hawk-nosed, his face lengthened by a reddish-brown beard, he fascinated his interlocutors with his small eyes—blue and piercing, set deep in their sockets. His long brown hair fell on either side of his face and was cut short on the back of his neck. A shudder sometimes ran over his hard-featured countenance. It was whispered that he drank too much and that alcohol was shattering his nerves, already weakened by an unhappy childhood of constant fear.

In December 1546, Ivan summoned his theology instructor, Metropolitan Macarius, and announced that he meant to take a wife. The prelate rejoiced at this virtuous intention after so much debauchery, but he doubted that a foreign princess would

---

*Most of the dishes that were prepared in Russia in the sixteenth century are still popular there. Russian cuisine is the most conservative in Europe.

agree to settle in a country that for ten years had known nothing but violence. Wisely, he advised Ivan to give up his plan for an alliance with a European court, which might end in rebuffs, and to look for a Russian bride in the traditional way, gathering all the young maidens of great or petty nobility so as to choose the worthiest among them. Ivan, who for the moment had no preference, was delighted with the proposal and decided to put it into action at once. At his order, the Metropolitan called all the boyars, including those who had recently fallen from favor, to a religious service in the Cathedral of the Assumption.

The boyars hurried to the cathedral, sensing that some important revelation was to be made. After having celebrated a Te Deum even more solemn than usual, Macarius assembled all the nobles in the reception room of the palace, facing Ivan, who was seated on his throne. When all had taken their places before him, the Grand Duke rose and addressed the Metropolitan in these terms: "Placing all my trust in the mercy of God and the intercession of the patron saints of Russia, and with your blessing, Father, I have resolved to choose a wife. At first I thought to seek a bride in foreign lands. But after mature reflection, I have put that idea from me. Since I was deprived of my parents from earliest childhood and raised as an orphan, it is possible that my temperament might not agree with that of a foreigner. Could such a union be happy? I therefore wish to find a wife in Russia, by the will of God and with your blessing, Father!" The Metropolitan, who probably knew what Ivan was going to say beforehand, answered with gentle serenity, "Prince, it is God Himself Who has inspired in you an intention so favorable to your people. I give it my blessing in the name of the Heavenly Father."

The boyars, "moved to tears," according to the chronicler, cheered their sovereign and embraced each other. They were delighted that Ivan had decided to marry a Russian. Their national pride was flattered; besides, most of them had a daughter, a cousin, or a niece who, with a little luck, they said to themselves, might capture the Prince's attention. If so, the whole family would profit from it. Already each in his own head was spinning the golden threads of his particular dream of matrimony. The nobles were preparing to disperse, to run home and announce the great news, when Ivan stopped them with a gesture. He hadn't finished. There was something else he had his heart set on: Before marrying, he wanted to be crowned Czar. He proclaimed this in a loud, clear voice. The boyars exchanged glances of surprise: "Grand duke" or "Czar," what was the difference?

For Ivan there *was* a difference, and he had been thinking about it for a long time. This title "Czar" was one the holy books in the Slavonic language gave to the kings of Judea, Babylon, and Assyria, and even to the Roman emperors. They spoke of "Czar David," "Czar Ahasuerus," "Czar Julius Caesar," "Czar Augustus." Thus, for Ivan, the word "czar" carried all the prestige of the Bible, the Roman Empire, and Byzantium. The man who bore that title was the heir of ancient Rome and new Byzantine Rome. He was the head of the Third Rome, whose power was to surpass that of the two others. Thanks to him and his successors, Moscow would supplant Constantinople, Muscovy would be the "Sixth Empire" announced by the Apocalypse. Moreover, according to a genealogy hastily constructed for the occasion, Ivan was the direct descendant of the Roman emperor Augustus. As the legend went, Augustus had divided the world among his closest relatives and allotted to his brother Prus (or Prussus) the basins of the Vistula and the Niemen. Rurik, the ancestor of the Muscovite dynasty, was alleged to have been a legitimate successor of Prus, and thus the Russian sovereigns could claim an unbroken tradition reaching back to the beginning of the Christian era. This ancient lineage should guarantee the new czar indisputable primacy over the other kings and princes of Europe: by virtue of his birth, he was already the greatest of the great. One day, in the world of the future, in accordance with the will of God, everything would be subject to the law of Moscow. And it would be he, Czar Ivan IV, who had launched this vast movement of Slavic hegemony. This last was something he did not talk about to the boyars. His audience would have been incapable of understanding it. But Macarius was privy to this secret imperialist dream, and he approved of it. After a moment's hesitation, the boyars applauded their young master's second proposal. The important thing was not that he wanted to be czar but that he should choose a wife from among their daughters.

The coronation took place on January 16, 1547, in Moscow. Preceded by his confessor, who held a crucifix in one hand and with the other sprinkled holy water on those present, Ivan left the palace to the sound of bells and made his way to the Cathedral of the Assumption. He was followed by his brother Yuri and the members of the court, who vied with one another in the richness of their dress. It was a river of brocade, gold, and precious stones that flowed into the sanctuary and advanced slowly toward Metropolitan Macarius and the assembled archbishops, bishops, and priors. An invisible choir feelingly thundered forth, "May he live for long years, long years!" The Metropolitan blessed the sovereign and led him to a dais with twelve steps, at the top of which stood two seats covered with cloth of gold. Ivan and the prelate sat down side by side. The regalia were laid out on a stand in front of the dais. The Metropolitan gave his blessing to the monarch a second time, placed upon his head the crown—or rather, the Cap of Monomakh*—and offered him the scepter and the globe, praying aloud to the Almighty to confer on "this new David" the strength of the Holy Spirit. "Grant him long days," he continued. "Place him upon the seat of justice, strengthen his arm, and make all the barbarous peoples subject to him." And then, before his subjects,

---

*"Monomakh" means "one who likes to fight in single combat." It was the name of the oriental Emperor Constantine IX and the surname of the Grand Prince of Moscow Vladimir II (1053–1125). The Cap of Monomakh was the symbol of power in old Russia.

Ivan was named "holy Czar, crowned by God, Autocrat of all the Russias." At the end of the ceremony, the priests sang again, "Long years to noble Ivan, the good, the honorable, the favorite of God, Grand Prince of Vladimir and Moscow, Czar and Monarch of all the Russias!"

After having received the congratulations of the clergy and the dignitaries, Ivan attended the liturgy. The service lasted four hours, but the young Czar felt no fatigue. On the contrary, the magnificence of the coronation ceremony filled him with exaltation and confirmed the correctness of his decision. Now he felt safe from attack both from below (the boyars, the people) and from above (God had consecrated him). Only one coronation had taken place in Russia before his, and that had been the coronation of Dimitri, grandson of Ivan III, who had never reigned. To organize the exceptional solemnities of 1547, the priests had searched the archives and reproduced every detail of the ancient rites of Byzantium.

At last, Ivan set out for the palace again, walking on a carpet of velvet and damask. Behind him came his brother, Yuri, who from time to time scattered over the head of the newly crowned potentate gold coins which he took from a vessel carried by Mikhail Glinsky. As they passed, the people threw themselves to the ground in silence and crossed themselves. When the procession had disappeared, they rushed into the cathedral and ripped the cloth of gold from the Czar's throne—for everyone wanted to take home a souvenir of this day of pomp and ceremony.

Ivan was scarcely back in the palace when he sent a letter to the Greek Patriarch, Ioasaf of Constantinople, asking to be formally installed as czar. The investiture, although paid for handsomely, was long in coming. It was only in 1561 that the Patriarch granted it, and only after he had received three times the sum agreed upon. The charter confirming Ivan in the title of czar bore the signature of thirty-six Greek metropolitans and bishops, but only two of them were authentic: those of Ioasaf and his vicar. The others had been forged by a clerk, Phanar, who had been assigned to draw up the document. In any case, Patriarch Ioasaf's reply was only a formality so far as Ivan was concerned. The blessing of Metropolitan Macarius was all he needed to consider himself henceforth the repository of the divine will. At the coronation ceremony the high clergy had recognized him as both the master of all that breathed on Russian soil and the champion of the true religion. Indeed, faced with the German Holy Roman Empire of Charles V, the France of François I, and the England of Henry VIII—all of them divided countries opening to Protestant influence—he stood as the principal defender of the Orthodox faith. Moscow became the spiritual capital of the Greek Church, whose liberty was threatened by the Turks in Constantinople.

Now Ivan had to turn his thoughts to marriage and assemble the largest possible number of candidates. Emissaries left Moscow for all the provinces, bearing the following circular: "From Ivan Vasilyevich, Grand Prince of all the Russias. I have ordered my envoys to examine all the maidens, your daughters, who are [potential] fiancées for us. . . . Any among you who might hide their daughters and not bring them to our boyars would bring down upon themselves great disgrace and terrible punishment. Circulate my letter among you, without keeping it so much as an hour in your hands."

In the chief town of each province the Czar's agents made a first selection, after which the young ladies judged most appetizing were sent to Moscow. A thousand of them came. Too many! Further eliminations were undertaken. Finally, the chosen virgins, after a thorough examination by duennas, were lodged a dozen to a room in a house next door to the palace. The Czar visited them several times for the *smotriny* and exchanged a few words with them. On the day appointed for the choosing, the postulants—who had been up since dawn and were scrubbed, polished, coiffed, painted, and dressed in their finest gowns—presented themselves one by one before the sovereign seated on his throne. Each dropped a deep curtsy and watched fearfully for a spark of desire in the master's eye. Ivan, solemn and motionless, revealed nothing of his feelings. But at the end of the procession he rose, unhesitatingly approached Anastasia Romanovna Zakharina-Yurieva, and offered her a handkerchief embroidered with gold and silver and pearls. The lucky girl flushed with happiness, while her unfortunate rivals choked back their tears. There was nothing left for them but to go home again in disappointment, bitterness, and jealousy.

Anastasia Romanovna belonged to a family of ancient nobility whose ancestors had left Prussia to settle in Russia in the fourteenth century.* By good fortune, her relatives had not been compromised in any of the intrigues hatched by the Shuiskys and Belskys. However, it was neither because of the girl's high birth nor because of the political innocence of her family that the Czar had chosen her. From the first glance, he had found her singularly beautiful. Also, talking with her during the *smotriny,* he had been impressed by her intelligence, gentleness, modesty, and piety. He had thought he was taking a wife because it was necessary to ensure the dynasty; suddenly he discovered he was in love with the one he had singled out. It was an entirely new feeling for him and it astonished him. Was he not going to lose in authority what he gained in affection? With amusement, he called Anastasia his "little heifer."

The Czar's marriage was celebrated on February 3, 1547, in the Cathedral of the Assumption. The ceremony was exactly the same as his parents', twenty years earlier. It was all done over: the hymns, the prayers, the tapers decorated with marten skins, the showering of the couple with hops. After the blessing, Metropolitan Macarius addressed the bride and groom sententiously: "Now you are united forever by virtue of the mysteries of the Holy Church. Prostrate yourselves together, therefore, before the Almighty and live in virtue. Those virtues which should chiefly distinguish you are love of truth and kindness.

---

*The Romanov dynasty, descended from this family, was to take power in 1613.

Czar, love and honor your wife. And you, truly Christian Czarina, obey your husband, for as the holy Crucifix represents the head of the Church, so man is the head of woman."

When the divine service was over, the sovereign couple appeared before a cheering people. With her own hand the Czarina distributed alms to the many beggars, who fell to the ground facedown before her. Young Prince Yuri Glinsky prepared the nuptial bed, laying upon it the traditional sheaves of wheat, and accompanied Ivan to the bath. At last the newlyweds, heavy with too much feasting, deafened by the ovations of the boyars, and stiff from standing for hours in the church, came together in the bedchamber feebly lit by lamps burning in front of the icons. According to custom, the Grand Equerry, Prince Mikhail Glinsky, spent the night on horseback, sword in hand, under the Czar's windows. No one must disturb the sovereign in his lovemaking.

IV

Reforms

Following the Czar's wedding, both the common people and the boyars continued to carouse daily, with much drinking and shouting, until the beginning of Lent. Then the ringing of a thousand bells called the faithful to prayer and penitence, the festivities abruptly came to an end, and a gray dullness settled over the city. Ivan and his wife donned the garb of simple pilgrims and set out on foot in the snow for the Monastery of the Holy Trinity. There they spent the first week of Lent fasting, taking communion, and meditating every day on the tomb of St. Sergius the miracle worker.

Anastasia was as pious as Ivan, but her religious feeling was composed of charity and indulgence, while for him mysticism in no way implied the love of humanity. The young woman, who had been brought up modestly by a widowed mother, lived on an equal footing with her fellow creatures and tried to sympathize with their sufferings, but her husband considered himself to be placed so high that his nearest neighbor was not man but God. Down below swarmed the anthill; he could crush it beneath his heel without compunction. It was not the opinion of insects that mattered to the Czar but the opinion of the Heavenly Father. And the Heavenly Father had often given him to understand that his position as Russian sovereign authorized him to indulge in all kinds of excesses. Intoxicated with this unlimited power, Ivan paid no attention to the work of administration, and devoted himself exclusively to the joys of hunting, drinking, and lovemaking.

Back from his pilgrimage to the Monastery of the Holy Trinity, Ivan took pleasure in disconcerting his entourage with the absurdity of his whims. Nothing amused him more than to order an unjust punishment or to grant an undeserved reward. Choosing a new favorite for a few days, he relished the despair of the one he had sent away and whose goods he had confiscated. The more arbitrary his judgments were, the more he felt they affirmed his independence. He confused authority with omnipotence, strength of character with cruelty. As for day-to-day politics, let others worry about that! The Glinskys were used to it. It was they who ran the country, in the name of the Czar. Loaded with honors and riches, they oppressed the people, shamelessly took money for their smallest interventions, pitilessly punished those who complained. The Czar needed them for the everyday dirty work, and he was grateful to them for taking charge of it, even if they filled their pockets in the process. The common people and most of the boyars, however, nursed a silent hatred for these oppressors whom Ivan protected. For the whole nation the Glinskys became the symbol of tyranny, dishonesty, and vice.

In their distress, the inhabitants of the city of Pskov soon decided to appeal directly to the Czar, sending him a delegation of seventy prominent men to complain of their governor, Prince Turuntai-Pronsky, a favorite of the Glinskys. This daring step may be explained by the fact that the Pskovians, whose city had been annexed by Muscovy only in 1510, did not yet have any clear understanding of the sovereign's character. They had learned that for the moment he was living in his country house at Ostrovka, near Moscow, and thither they went on June 3, 1547, as one goes to see a father. Furious at being disturbed for trifles, in his retreat, Ivan insulted the delegates, had their hands tied behind their backs, poured boiling alcohol on their heads, and, going from one to the next with a candle, ignited their hair and beards. Then, having made the seventy men undress, he ordered them to be stretched out naked in rows on the ground. While he was planning a final torment for them, a messenger galloped up with news that the great bell of the Kremlin had fallen, for no apparent reason, and that the handles had broken in the crash. The Czar was stricken, and wondered if it was not a bad omen. Forgetting the people of Pskov, he had a horse brought up and rode off at once for his capital. His victims were released and took to their heels, blessing the providential bell whose fall had saved their lives.

In Moscow the Czar had a moment of terror. The incident of the bell was not the first that had troubled his mind. On April 12, fire had destroyed many houses, some churches, and a few shops in the central quarter, Kitaigorod. A week later, a second conflagration had devoured all the streets on the other side of the Yauza, where the potters and tanners lived. On June 20, flames rose again in the city. Fanned by winds of unprecedented violence, they seized upon the many wooden buildings, which collapsed in showers of sparks. They leaped over the crenelated walls of the Kremlin and attacked the roofs of the churches and palaces there. Enormous explosions echoed through the continuous roar of the fire, for Ivan's munitions depots were blowing up, one after another. In the blazing furnace iron glowed red, copper melted. Inside the stone churches flames licked the frescoes; the icons roasted, the relics burned. The sky was a roof of purple smoke rent with exploding plumes of light.

Inside the Cathedral of the Assumption, old Metropolitan Macarius, half asphyxiated, was desperately praying. Priests begged him to flee. He found himself with them on a wall looking down over empty space. Despite his protests, they obliged him to climb down a knotted rope. Toward the end of the descent his strength gave out; he let go, fell, and was injured. He was carried unconscious into a nearby monastery. On all sides the inhabitants of the city were running, jostling each other, dazed, weeping, not knowing what to do to stop the disaster. The city had no means of fighting the fire; it could only count on God's mercy. Women looking for their children screamed with terror. Old men stood sobbing and crossing themselves in front of the wreckage of their homes. Shrieking figures ran past, their clothes afire. Some threw themselves into the river to escape the flames. Cows and horses died of suffocation in the cattle sheds and stables. Dogs barked pitifully around corpses. In gardens the trees were nothing but black skeletons bristling with sparks. A cloud of hot soot whirled in the air.

As soon as the conflagration had begun, the Czar, Czarina, and their retinue had taken refuge in the village of Vorobievo, which overlooked Moscow.* From this vantage point Ivan watched the sheet of fire and coldly estimated the damages. While Anastasia, horrified, plunged into interminable prayers, he had messengers bring him hourly reports on the progress of the disaster. The cupola of the Cathedral of the Assumption, the palaces of the Czar and the Metropolitan, two monasteries, several churches with all their wealth, the residences of dignitaries, the arsenals, the treasury fell prey to the flames. There were said to be 1,700 victims—"without counting the children."

---

*It was from this same spot, called the Sparrow Hills, that two and a half centuries later Napoleon would also look down upon Moscow in flames.

Toward evening, at last the wind subsided, and in the middle of the night the fire died out for lack of fuel. But in the smoking desert menacing gleams still flickered here and there. The next day the inhabitants, with blackened faces and singed hair, came back to the ruins to search the ashes for their disfigured dead and the remains of their fortunes. From time to time, says the chronicler, one of the tragic ragpickers would stoop down, stand up again, and utter lamentations like the cries of "wild animals." Fantastic rumors circulated among the droves of people searching through the rubble. From mouth to mouth the word flew that the Moscow fire was not an accident but the result of witchcraft. "The Glinskys, the Glinskys!" They alone were responsible. According to those who were best informed, old Princess Anna, the mother of Yuri and Mikhail Glinsky, had torn the hearts out of corpses, plunged them in water, and sprinkled the streets with the diabolical liquid. "That is why our city burned!" The Shuiskys, open enemies of the Glinskys, shrewdly sent their agents among the people to spread this version of the event. The Czar's own confessor, Feodor Barmin, deliberately supported the absurd accusation. Some of the boyars joined in. Impressed by their certainty, Ivan ordered an investigation. On June 26, five days after the fire had ended, a crowd of homeless persons was ordered to assemble in the Kremlin square. Many witnesses declared on oath that the Glinskys had indeed had recourse to black magic to destroy the city.

During this time Princess Anna Glinsky, Ivan's maternal grandmother, was with her son Mikhail on his estates in Rzhev, but her other son, Yuri, was present among the assembly of boyars facing the crowd. At first, he shrugged his shoulders at the idiotic allegations put forward by ignorant yokels. Then, realizing that certain high dignitaries were lending a ready ear to the shouts of the rabble, he was seized with fear. Slipping quietly between the rows, he sought refuge in the Cathedral of the Assumption. Despite his precautions, this retreat did not go unnoticed. Furious, the crowd surged after him, and the nobles gave way. A frenzied, shouting band rushed into the cathedral with its sooty walls and charred iconostasis and, profaning the holy place, seized Yuri, knocked him down, strangled him, and dragged his body out of the Kremlin to the place of execution. Their appetite whetted by this first murder, the raging mob poured into neighboring streets, looted and burned the palace of the Glinskys, and massacred the relatives and servants of the detested family. The rioters had stolen arms from the arsenal, banners and icons from the churches. They brandished these over their heads—one carrying a cross, another a saber.

Three days later, in obedience to a mysterious impulse, the crowd headed for the village of Vorobievo and demanded that the sovereign's uncle, Prince Mikhail Glinsky, and his grandmother, Princess Anna, be delivered up to their wrath. They weren't there. But no matter! They would be dragged from their estates! Ivan, terror-stricken in the face of this popular uprising, nevertheless refused to give in. Even if he had believed the Glinskys guilty, it would have been degrading for him to let anyone dictate his conduct. It was on him, and on him alone, that life and death should depend in his country. Without hesitation he commanded his guards to fire into the crowd. A few men fell, others fled, still others prostrated themselves and asked for mercy. Several of the demonstrators were arrested at random and executed on the spot, in front of their petrified comrades. Order was reestablished, and the Czar came out of the adventure with enhanced authority. But he had been in mortal fear, especially because during the revolt he had received a visit from a priest, Sylvester, a native of Novgorod, who was in charge of the Church of the Annunciation.

Unlike Ivan's confessor, who considered the Moscow fire to have been the effect of black magic, Sylvester had declared that the city had been destroyed by the Almighty as a punishment, just as Sodom and Gomorrah had been destroyed in ancient times. He was not afraid to repeat this firmly before the Czar, raising a finger in denunciation. Ivan was shaken by the force of his voice and the prophetic light in his eyes. Suddenly, the master of Russia doubted the infallibility of his decisions. For the first time he accepted criticism. Yes, he had been wrong to abandon the affairs of state to the Glinskys; yes, he had heavy sins on his conscience; yes, on many occasions he had shown how little love he had for his neighbor. Sylvester opened the Bible before him, reminded him of God's commandments, and urged him to purify his soul if he wanted to avoid an even more fearful catastrophe. Sylvester went so far as to reveal that he had had visions and received signs condemning the Czar. At these words, Ivan fell on his knees. He had always imagined that God and he were a pair of friends—and now here was a divine messenger, clearly well informed, who swore the opposite. Perhaps God really was turning away from His representative on earth. Perhaps there was a misunderstanding between them, a quarrel such as sometimes occurs in the best of families. Perhaps he had to change his conduct before it was too late. Holding back his sobs but stammering with terror, the Czar agreed with Sylvester, promised to mend his ways, and, as proof of his good intentions, removed from power the Glinskys, whom the people wanted to be rid of.

To replace these servitors who had damaged his reputation, Ivan formed a new type of council, the Izbrannaya Rada (Chosen Council), composed of members of the nobility and the clergy who were distinguished for their wisdom, sober judgment, and devotion. Among them were the Metropolitan of Moscow, Macarius, who had recovered from his accident, the priest Sylvester, Prince Alexei Adashev, and Prince Andrei Kurbsky. This assembly was dominated by two men: Macarius, the most cultivated man in Russia, by now author of several works of piety and history, and Sylvester, the mystical preacher who dared to speak to the Czar as to a simple penitent. This parish priest of modest origins gained such a hold over his sovereign by threatening him with the wrath of heaven that he was soon given near-complete responsibility for the administration of ecclesiastical and civil affairs; everything passed through Sylvester's hands, and all around he was praised for his competence in so many fields.

At Sylvester's side stood the young boyar Alexei Adashev —an excellent officer, good-looking and with a keen mind. Not long since, he had been one of the gentlemen of the bedchamber "making the bed." Now, by the will of Ivan and with the blessing of Macarius and Sylvester, he became an adviser and even confidant of the Czar. The contemporary chroniclers compared him to a "heavenly angel" and praised the purity and sensitivity of his intentions. The nineteenth-century historian Karamzin wrote, "Inclined to do good without any sordid motive, he had sought Ivan's favor more in the interests of the country than in his own." Sylvester's exhortations had awakened in the Czar's heart a desire to do good, declared Andrei Kurbsky, and Adashev had given him the means to carry out that desire.

To these beneficent influences was added that of the Czarina Anastasia. More than once, her husband's character— violent, scheming, sadistic, yet cowardly—had caused her deep anxiety. To her he was like a wild animal that she loved, feared, and was trying to tame. He loved her too, for her beauty and her submission. Through her weakness she obtained from him what he would have refused had she been less vulnerable. And then, they often communed in prayer. These joint prayers expressed, for her, faith in a God of Mercy; for him, fear of a God of Vengeance.

After the burning of Moscow and the formation of the Rada, Ivan distributed money to the victims of the catastrophe and ordered the city to be rebuilt. Workers gathered from all sides. The capital's sister cities sent icons and relics to replace those that had been destroyed. Moscow was transformed into a vast construction site, echoing with the grind of saws and the thud of axes. The roofs of houses were now covered with earth, so that sparks from chimneys would not set fire to them another time. A few shops opened again amid the rubble.

But this was not enough to erase the horror of heaven's punishment. Ivan felt the need to rebuild both the ruins of his capital and the ruins of his soul. He wanted to win God back with a demonstration of his repentance, and to show his people the ardent desire for virtue that burned inside him. All the provinces of Russia were ordered to send to Moscow representatives of the different races and of different social conditions to hear the voice of the Czar. In fact, only members of the clergy, boyars, and official functionaries were ultimately designated for this mission to Moscow. The assembly thus gathered together in 1550 took the name Zemsky Sobor. Its only role appears to have been to register the decisions of the sovereign.

After the first meeting of the Zemsky Sobor, Ivan heard mass, received communion, and, followed by all the notables and the clergy, proceeded to the Kremlin square, which was black with people.* There he stopped on the Lobnoe Mesto, the raised platform where executions were carried out. He faced the silent crowd. The priests said one more prayer and in the multitude innumerable hands made the sign of the cross, like birds fluttering from branch to branch. When it was over, the Czar spoke. His young, firm voice passed over their heads. First, he addressed Metropolitan Macarius: "Holy Father, your zeal for virtue, your love for the motherland are known to me. Help me in my good intentions. I lost my parents too young and the great nobles, who only aspired to rule, took no care of my person; in my name they usurped offices and honors; they enriched themselves through injustice; they oppressed the people without anyone's daring to bridle their ambition."

This complaint was one that those who knew the Czar well had already heard a hundred times on his lips: To excuse his faults he had always invoked the fact that he had been orphaned

---

*It was only in the last half of the seventeenth century that this square was given the name Krasnaya Ploshchad, which may be translated as either Red Square or Beautiful Square. Before that, it was called Pozharnaya Ploshchad, or Square of the Conflagrations.

young and that instead of raising him like their son, the great lords had robbed him and robbed the people. But never yet had he accused the boyars in public, at the same time beating his breast like an ordinary sinner. Raising his voice, he continued his speech in theatrical, bombastic style. He was an actor intoxicated with his lines, addressing a captive audience. He loved grandiloquent language, skillfully calculated silences, tragic facial expressions. Before his eyes, in the place of execution, men who had been hanged at his orders swung on a gallows. Did he see a reproach in these desiccated puppets the crows were picking at? No, he was carried away by his rhetoric, in which the boyars alone were responsible for his mistakes. He addressed the next part of his harangue to them: "I was as if deaf and mute in my deplorable childhood, for I heard not the lamentations of the poor and my words did naught to alleviate the ills they suffered. You did as you pleased, rebellious subjects, corrupt judges! How can you justify yourselves now? How many tears have you not caused to be shed! How many times have you not made blood flow, blood of which I am guiltless! But fear the judgment of God!"

At these words the Czar bent over, bowing to the four sides of the square. Then he resumed, speaking this time to his humble subjects: "Oh you, the people, whom the Almighty has entrusted to me, today I invoke both your religion and the attachment which you have for me: Be magnanimous! It is impossible to undo the evil that has already been done. But I can promise you that henceforth I shall preserve you from pillage and oppression. Forget, therefore, what was and will never be again. Banish from your hearts all cause for hatred and enmity. Let us all be united in fraternal Christian love. Starting from this day, I shall be your judge and your defender!"

The people could not believe their ears. This extraordinary orator who, dressed in gold and spangled with jewels, stood glittering in the sun like a scarab, was their czar. And a czar cannot lie. An era of happiness was dawning for Russia! To inaugurate this wise policy, Ivan announced that he granted pardon to all the guilty boyars, and invited his subjects to embrace each other like brothers. The crowd shed tears of gratitude and exchanged triple kisses, as at Easter. They all but cried, "Christ is risen!"

Satisfied with the success of his oration, Ivan turned to Adashev and instructed him to receive the petitions of the poor, the orphans, and "all the afflicted." "Alexei," he said to him, "you do not have the titles accorded by birth and fortune, but you are virtuous. . . . Without regard for rank or power, rectify the injustices of those who, having won honors, would forget their duties. Be careful also not to let yourself be moved by the false tears of the poor man when he slanders the rich out of envy. Examine all affairs carefully in order to report to me faithfully upon them, and have no other fear but that of the Supreme Judge."

After these last words, Ivan received the congratulations of his entourage, starting with Anastasia, who looked upon her husband's moral regeneration as a miracle. He himself thought that God must be vindictive indeed if He did not relent after such a fine speech. But how sincere was he in his intention to pardon the boyars who had served him ill? True, he did not condemn the guilty ones to death. He contented himself with dismissing a few courtiers; sending his confessor, Feodor Barmin, who after the Moscow fire had roused the rabble, to a monastery; and exiling Mikhail Glinsky with permission to choose his place of residence. Fearing for his life, Glinsky tried to flee to Lithuania with his friend Turuntai-Pronsky; they were arrested, an investigation was undertaken, and only a magnanimous decision by Ivan saved them from the scaffold. New boyars entered the Council, including Zakharin, the Czarina's uncle; Khabarov, a friend of the unfortunate Ivan Belsky; and Dimitri Paletsky, whose daughter Juliana was judged worthy to become the bride of Prince Yuri, the monarch's own brother.

Yet despite these auspicious measures, Ivan grimly nursed

the memory of the wrongs he had suffered in the past. It was his nature to be capable of showing momentary indulgence for an injury, never of forgetting it completely. The enemies he had forgiven did not enjoy absolute safety but a reprieve that could be revoked at any time. Even as they strutted about reveling in their impunity, he watched them out of the corner of his eye, hating them in silence.

For the time being Ivan's model was his illustrious grandfather, Ivan III, who had given Russia its first written laws. Ivan IV wanted to be an equally inspired legislator. The Rada surrounding him included some men versed in the science of civil law. As for Sylvester, he had written with his own hand passages in the famous household guide the *Domostroy*, a veritable handbook of manners of the time. This work, which was divided into sixty-five chapters, set forth rules of conduct in religious and social matters, ostensibly for the guidance of a wealthy bourgeois who was the father of a family and master of many servants.

From the *Domostroy*'s jumbled instructions one learned that a pious man always held his breath when kissing holy images, so as not to place them in contact with bodily impurities; that a woman attended services only to the extent that her household occupations allowed, and that she was careful not to sing or laugh while working, so as not to awaken the demon that slept within her; that a father chastised his children severely but without anger. "If you love your son, beat him frequently; in the end he will be a joy to you. . . . Do not laugh with him, do not play with him, for if you weaken in small things you will suffer in great ones. . . . Break his heart while he is growing up, for if it hardens, he will not obey you."

Furthermore, a wife also should be punished often, so as to remain malleable. But this required some delicacy. Thus, one did not strike the guilty female on the head or "under the heart," and one avoided using a stick or an iron object. Only the whip was recommended—in Russia at the time the whip was a true instrument of civilization. But one did have to know how to use it. The husband should lead the sufferer far from prying eyes and there, having removed her blouse so as not to tear it and having tied her hands, he should lash her methodically as long as he judged necessary; after which, he should speak affectionate words to her so as not to compromise future conjugal relations. In general, every day the wife should seek the advice of her husband, not only regarding household matters but also regarding the visits she planned to make, the guests she intended to receive, and even what she proposed to talk about with them. "The house of a woman who has a sense of order should be clean and orderly," the *Domostroy* continued. "One should enter there as into paradise. . . . At the entrance straw should be placed so that one can wipe one's feet. . . . In each bedroom the Christian will place icons on the walls, honoring them with lamps, decorations, and candles. After prayers, curtains should be drawn over the icons to protect them from dust." The house should also contain provisions for the entire year. Thrift should rule domestic life, even in a wealthy household: "When bread is baked, the clothes should also be washed; that makes only one piece of work and does not waste wood."

The master of a house should have among his servants tailors, bootmakers, and carpenters, so that all tasks could be accomplished cheaply under his own roof. In case he was unfamiliar with domestic matters, the *Domostroy* provided instructions for cooking, making liquors, doing laundry, slaughtering and salting pigs. It also described the way in which a servant should behave when sent on an errand to another house: On arriving at the door, the model servant was to wipe his feet, blow his nose in his fingers, spit, clear his throat, and say, "In the name of the Father, the Son, and the Holy Ghost." If no one answered, "Amen," he was to repeat his prayer somewhat louder and, lastly, to knock gently on the shutter. "If he is admitted into the room," continued the *Domostroy*, "he will take care not to put his finger in his nose, not to blow his nose, not to spit. He will stand respectfully, will not look all around, and will execute his orders without touching anything. He will return as quickly as possible to report the answer to his master."

In the last part of the book, Sylvester exhorted his son Anthemius to practice the Christian virtues. When the young man had himself become the head of a family, he should refrain from getting drunk when it was time to go to vespers, summon a priest often to conduct services under his roof, distribute alms without excess, love his neighbor sincerely, attack no one, keep his door open, obey the Czar, and fear God. "When you travel, share your meal with the passersby. . . . Offer them drink. . . . If you act thus, you will not be betrayed at the relay station, you will not be killed on the road. . . . If your men happen to quarrel with someone, scold them. If the affair becomes serious, strike your servant, even if he is in the right!"

Such pieces of advice, delivered in a grave and authoritative tone, revealed in their author (or authors, for it is not certain that Sylvester was the sole author of the *Domostroy*) a curious mixture of mysticism and opportunism, of charity and cynicism. Their narrow-mindedness and strict materialism were accentuated by constant references to the Bible. Indeed, in the *Domostroy*—a work that was at once a manual of deportment and a breviary, a cookbook and a statement of evangelical principles, a horticultural almanac and a treatise on civility—the sacred and profane were inseparable, like wine and water in a cup. According to this half-pagan, half-Christian catechism, God loved thrift, cleanliness, wealth, work, summary justice, and the submission of the slave to the master, the wife to the husband, the son to the father. All of society was founded on the family unit, at the center of which stood the master of the house, his influence radiating outward in all directions. Everything started from him and everything came back to him. In his clan, he was the equivalent of the czar in his empire.

Such as it was, the *Domostroy* served—and was to serve for a long time—as indisputable dogma in the daily life of Russia.

Ivan, for his part, was well satisfied with it. But the good order that the *Domostroy* instituted in the private domain he meant to impose in the public as well. Accordingly, with the help of his advisers he set about drafting the *Tsarski Sudebnik,* or Czar's Code, of 1550, to replace the legal code of his grandfather, which dated from 1497. This new code did not overturn the earlier provisions but made them consistent and adapted them to the current fashion. Until the mid-sixteenth century, a law that was in effect in Moscow might have been unknown in Novgorod or Pskov, which had their own customs. Ivan, the centralizer, could not tolerate this chaos.

Notwithstanding his extreme youth—he had just turned twenty—Ivan now demanded that in all the territories under his authority the judges should apply the same laws. He restored former local jurisdictions at this time and ordered that magistrates elected by the communes should sit on the tribunals beside his appointed functionaries. There were three levels of tribunals, the highest being the Supreme Court in Moscow. Rates of pay were now fixed for the judge, the notary, the scribe. Minor offenses were punished with the knout. Repeated offenses, treason, sacrilege, murder, highway robbery, and arson were punishable by death. Sometimes the judge called witnesses, on whose testimony he would base his sentence, but the accused had the right to reject them and to ask for a duel. For this judgment by God, both accuser and accused could choose combatants to replace them. The champions of the two parties were not allowed to use the bow and arrow: "Their offensive weapons," the law stated, "are the javelin, the lance, the ax, and the dagger. Their defensive weapons are the cuirass, the buckler, and the coat of mail. The testimony of a noble has more weight than that of six persons of low degree." Lastly, in big trials nothing could equal torture for unmasking the guilty person.

Ivan's code condemned corruption. But bribery, the plague of Russian society, continued to exist at all levels of the administration, to such an extent that it was impossible to win one's case without greasing a few palms. According to custom, before a trial both parties laid an offering before the holy images—"for the candles." And at Easter, magistrates of every sort received "red eggs," accompanied by a well-filled purse. A German, Heinrich von Staden, interpreter for the *prikaz,* or department, of ambassadors, wrote in his memoirs: "There were two doormen at every chancellery or law court. They opened the doors for those who gave money. The doors remained closed to those who had nothing to give. . . . It was always found . . . that the man who was in the right and had sworn an oath was not in the right if the other party had more money. Even if the latter was in the wrong, he was still found right and the right was found wrong. . . . And if one had robbed, murdered, or stolen, and lived with the money and goods in a monastery, he was as free in the monastery as in heaven. . . ."[1]

These imperfections were of small consequence: Ivan was obsessed with the idea of unifying his country and taking judicial, administrative, and fiscal powers away from the local nobility. To help in his task he looked for assistants not among the unruly aristocrats, this time, but among the humble people. It was new men, men of modest backgrounds, who were placed in all the key positions of the empire. Posted far apart, they supported the vast spiderweb whose center was Moscow. Little by little, the people realized that they were no longer governed by boyars but by the Czar himself, through agents who carried out his orders. They wondered if the change had been to their advantage: One could hate a lord, but not the sovereign. Giles Fletcher, the English ambassador to Russia, wrote: "A great people, inert and silent, regarded with a mixture of love and terror this father of the great Russian family, this living law, this representative of God on earth, whose very crimes were accepted as a punishment sent by God to his people and to whose cruelty they must submit, for it created martyrs and opened the doors of heaven."

While Ivan was concerned about the morality of his people, he was no less concerned about the morality of his church. To exalt the glory of the Orthodox faith at a time when the tide of the Reformation was sweeping over western Europe, he had called together two councils, one in 1547 and another in 1549. These councils canonized thirty-nine remarkable Russian personages, who were added to the twenty-two saints already existing. Heartened by this arrival of reinforcements for the haloed ranks, the clergy thought themselves safe from all criticism.

Two years later, on February 23, 1551, Ivan convoked a third ecclesiastical council. The prelates, led by Metropolitan Macarius, were received in the Kremlin by the Czar and the entire Council of Boyars. They believed that they had been summoned to bless the Czar's new code of laws. And indeed, that formality was soon taken care of. But then, turning toward the Metropolitan, the nine bishops, the archimandrites, and the abbots, Ivan reminded them in moving terms of the misfortunes of his childhood and the disasters of his country. It was the Moscow fire, he said, that had made a new man of him: "At that moment my soul was seized with terror; a sudden trembling took hold of me, my spirit was subdued and pity entered my heart. Now that I have as much horror of vice as love of virtue, I crave to be instructed by your zealous faith. O Christian pastors, you holy guides of princes, worthy representatives of the Church, do not spare me in my errors; reproach me boldly for my weaknesses, and thunder forth the word of God so that my soul make keep its purity."

Needless to say, none of the ecclesiastics dreamed of reproaching him for anything whatsoever. Thinking the ceremony was ended, they were already preparing to withdraw when Ivan called them back. To their great surprise, he delivered to them a document on the reforms he had in mind to purify the Church. With the help of Sylvester and Adashev, he had composed a questionnaire and proposals which together made up the *Stoglav*, or "Collection of the Hundred Chapters," no doubt a reference to the Hundred and One Grievances of the Diet of Worms. Point by point, the *Stoglav* dealt with the property belonging to the monasteries, the misconduct of monks and priests, the scandalous traffic in relics, the mistakes the copyists made in reproducing holy books. Some of these reproaches were so vehement that they shocked the assembly, as did the seventh: "There are monks and priests who have themselves tonsured in order to lead a merry life and who stroll through the villages for pleasure." And the seventeenth: "In all the monasteries, the abbots and monks get drunk, the priests of ordinary churches drink until they lose their senses. In the name of God, reflect carefully upon these scandals." And the eighteenth: "Why is the prohibition against widowed priests' and deacons' being attached to a church no longer observed?"

After a moment's stunned silence, the prelates promised that in future they would check on the conduct of the clergy and that abuses would be severely punished. Other grave questions were also discussed and resolved by the learned men of the faith. The council ordered that every Orthodox Christian should cross himself with the thumb and first two fingers of the right hand together, as a symbol of the Trinity, and that these fingers should be placed first on the forehead, then on the chest, then on the right shoulder, lastly on the left shoulder. Anyone who did not proceed in this manner "deserted the Cross of Christ and gave himself up to the Devil." He would be damned forever. Damned likewise was anyone who danced in the cemeteries on Trinity Saturday; who jumped up and down and made merry on Midsummer Night, Christmas Eve, or Twelfth Night; who cried, "Hallelujah!" three times, in accordance with the Latin heresy (whereas a good Orthodox Christian should say it twice and add "Glory to thee, Lord!"); who imitated the indecent gestures of clowns or who indulged in sodomy. Perverts were forbidden to enter churches, for: "Neither those who are debauched, or adulterous, or effeminate, nor those who practice pederasty, bestiality, or onanism, nor public officials who extort money, nor thieves, nor sorcerors, nor drunkards shall inherit the Kingdom of God," said the document. "They are excluded from the Church until they are cured."

The *Domostroy* had already recommended that decency should be maintained in merriment. The *Stoglav* went further: It condemned to hell all those who played the rebec, the zither-like gusli, the tambourine, or the trumpet; all who danced or jumped up and down and clapped their hands at public gatherings; persons who liked the company of dogs, birds, or trained bears; those who played dice, chess, or backgammon; and anyone who dared to cut his beard or mustache or to wear foreign dress. "The sacred rules forbid Orthodox Christians to shave their beards and mustaches," decided the council in reply to a question asked by the Czar. "It is a Latin heresy. . . . This custom was instituted by the heretical emperor Constantine Caballinos;* it is well known that he had the beards of his heretical servants cut. Therefore, you who, following their example, violate the law to satisfy your own wishes, shall be hateful unto God, who made you in His image."

There were directives to the painters of icons too. These artists, sometimes inclined to drink and steal, were ordered in future to be "full of humility, gentleness, and piety" and to conform to the rules for the representation of "the heavenly powers and the saints." They were to prepare themselves for their work with fasting and prayer, copy the traditionally prescribed images, thin their paints with holy water and thus become not creators proud of their works but modest, anonymous instruments of the will of the Almighty. And, since copyists made too many mistakes in transcribing holy texts, it was decided to stop copying liturgical works by hand and to set up a printing press in Moscow to reproduce these books on the basis of the most correct models. Nevertheless, for the simple folk an

---

*Constantine V, Byzantine emperor (718–775), notorious for his tyranny in religious matters.

error consecrated by time had more value than a modern correction. Furthermore, they regarded the first printing press as a machine of the devil, and they promptly destroyed it during a riot. Besides, few priests knew how to read; they knew by heart all the words of the different services.

Ivan, who had a passion for reading, was pained at the ignorance all around him. He persuaded the members of the council to make instruction obligatory for priests. Throughout the country the parish priests would be placed under the supervision of their hierarchical superiors. Each town would have a school run by educated priests and *diaki,** who would teach reading, writing, arithmetic, singing, religion, morality, and the abomination of "infamous sodomy." However, when Ivan put forward the notion that monks, who were theoretically dead to the world, could not own land and that their holdings should revert to the crown, Macarius, supported by the entire clergy, rejected the blasphemous suggestion. The Czar had to be satisfied with a half-measure: In future, it was decided, the bishops and monasteries could make no acquisition of land without the consent of the sovereign. (In fact, this decision was never observed and business went on as usual.) Also, the monasteries were forbidden to lend money at usurious rates. Such measures were designed to put a stop to the Church's staggering accumulation of wealth.

At the same time Ivan was bringing the priests and monks to heel, he was permanently reorganizing the nobility of the country. Below the chief officers of the crown and the members of the Council of Boyars came the boyars known as "service men": the thousand young noblemen who were highest born and most capable. Listed in the *Book of the Thousand* (though actually they numbered 1,078), they supplied the officers for the Czar's Regiment and were sometimes given administrative or diplomatic missions. Lands were allotted to them to enable

---

*A *diak* was an educated man; e.g., an official or secretary.

them to perform their service. Each spring when a "mobilization" took place, the service men were required to report to appointed places, armed, on horseback, and accompanied by a number of peasants determined by the extent of their arable land (one peasant for every 135 acres); they were irrevocably bound by this obligation all their lives. A few of them, instead of joining the army, were appointed to high posts in Moscow, but in general the military destiny of the men in the "service" class was decreed from the time they were born.

Similarly, workers and tradesmen were now all catalogued and enrolled in guilds. In addition, they were divided into categories according to the amount of taxes they paid. The wealthiest merchants were called to Moscow, where they formed an upper class, the *gosti*. In exchange for certain privileges, they had to take personal responsibility for the city's supplies and finances.

At the bottom of the social scale were the peasants. The majority of these worked six days out of seven for a landowner, paid very heavy taxes, and did not have the right to move away or change masters. Others were considered free farmers and, in theory, could leave when their lease ran out and they had carried out all the provisions of the contract. But in practice, most of them were unable to pay back the enormous debts they had contracted in order to pursue their farming, so they remained attached to the soil in fact if not in law. Although serfdom was not officially proclaimed, it spread insidiously throughout Russia. In desperation many peasants fled to the forests. More and more lands were left uncultivated. Ivan did not care.

There was a brilliant logic to Ivan's plan. To ensure the cooperation of the nobles, he had tied them permanently to their task. To enable them to perform that task free from other cares, he had given them estates. To cultivate those estates, he had forced the peasants who lived on them to work for the benefit of the nobles. Thus, he had created a Russia subjugated from top to bottom, in which each man, according to his rank and capacities, contributed to the greatness and prosperity of the country. At the summit of this pyramid of slaves was the czar.*

The money Ivan needed he derived from taxes and duties. According to the English ambassador Giles Fletcher, Ivan IV's system of fiscal oppression demanded of his exhausted people four times what Henry VIII of England had asked of his. The vast sums, gathered by tax collectors, went into the Great Treasury. But the Czar also had at his disposal his personal patrimony: Thirty-six towns, with their dependent villages, supplied him not only with rents in money but also with cattle, wheat, fish, honey, and fodder—which he sold. Of course, most of the expenditures supported by the Great Treasury related to the maintenance of the army. The taxes were increased every year, but even so the coffers were often empty. Fletcher cited various means used by Ivan to "draw the wealth of the land into the emperor's treasury": Let the tax collectors enrich themselves, then make them cough up; require a city to deliver products that cannot be found and fine it heavily because it has not executed the order; and so on. Ivan and his service men didn't let themselves be hampered by a foolish sense of fairness. Still, the Czar wanted to keep the appearance of legality. He governed with the help of the Duma of boyars. In serious cases he even convoked the Zemsky Sobor. But neither the Duma nor the Zemsky Sobor encroached on the monarch's prerogatives. These assemblies had only a consultative voice, and most of the time they restricted themselves to recording the wishes of the Czar.

Thus, from the first years of his reign Ivan demonstrated a sense of order and a will to dominate that confounded his entourage. How had this young man—deprived of affection and guidance in childhood, educated haphazardly by palace scribes, pushed toward mysticism by Macarius—managed as soon as he

---

*Peter the Great was to perfect this hierarchical organization of Russia by instituting the Table of Ranks, with its categories, classes, and equivalencies among the different ranks.

ascended the throne to acquire such a firm conception of his role as sovereign? Even those who secretly criticized his violence, cruelty, and despotism were forced to agree that they had before them a leader of peoples. While they might tremble for themselves, they no longer trembled for Russia.

V

Kazan

Even before Ivan began reorganizing the country internally, he was worrying about its borders. He had three causes for concern: the Swedes, the Poles, and the Tatars. He was particularly angry about the Tatars, who made frequent incursions into Russian territory. To resist them he had a line of forts built south of Muscovy, and he now organized regular troops supplied with firearms. Soon he could count on six regiments of foot soldiers, harquebusiers who were recruited among the freemen and signed up for life. These troops, known as *streltsy,* or shooters, were armed and equipped in European style and were given wages, uniforms, powder, and flour. They were supported by 80,000 cavalry and a permanent corps of artillery. But the main body of the army was made up of the service men and of recruits levied outside the military class. These latter conscripts, supplied by the towns and villages, were neither trained nor disciplined; they were therefore used chiefly for building earth-works. As for the service men—boyars, sons of boyars, courtiers —these were divided into five regiments. A few foreign merce-naries were enrolled to enhance the army's overall effectiveness. The high command was no longer entrusted to officers of noble lineage but to qualified leaders who had distinguished them-selves in combat. Thus, for the first time in the military in Russia, professional merit outweighed birth.

The mainstay of battles was the cavalry. The weapons of the mounted troops were many and varied, and included the curved Turkish-style saber, the bow, the ax, the lance, and sometimes a pistol. There were few cuirasses, but some helmets; no spurs, but a whip. The small, strong horses were not shod; they had extraordinary endurance, as did their masters. The Muscovite cavalrymen camped in the snow, lit a small fire, dined on a handful of flour mixed with boiling water, and went to sleep rolled up in their cloaks. Their bravery was confirmed by the testimony of foreigners. On attack, they began by shooting ar-rows, then charged en masse without order, saber in hand, to the sound of drums and trumpets and shouting at the top of their lungs to frighten the enemy.

Ivan had no doubt that with men of this stamp he would drive back the Tatars once and for all. He set out on campaign in December 1547, reached the Volga, and decided to use the deeply frozen river as a route to Kazan, the city from which the chief raids on Russian territory were mounted. But when the army had launched itself onto the ice, a great cracking was heard, water gushed up along the banks, and wide fissures opened in the hard white surface, swallowing up men, horses, cannon. From this disaster Ivan concluded that God had not yet pardoned him for his sins, and he returned to Moscow to prepare a second campaign, with prayer and fasting. Meantime, Prince Dimitri Belsky was sent out with a small detachment, not to conquer Kazan but to bar the route to the Tatars, who would now be tempted to attack Russian villages to procure captives of both sexes.

On November 24, 1549, the Czar left again for the army, accompanied by his brother, Yuri. On February 14, 1550, he was under the wooden ramparts of Kazan. Gabions were hurriedly set up to protect the attackers. Cannon fired, catapults launched stones, battering rams smashed in the gates of the Tatar city. For the first time Ivan, saber in hand, directed operations on the spot, though without exposing himself: According to Muscovite tradition, a sovereign did not fight but exhorted others to fight. Sixty thousand Russians poured through a breach, spread throughout the city, and massacred without distinction all the inhabitants who fell into their hands. Nevertheless, they were unable to take the central fortress. The following day, operations were disrupted by a sudden thaw accompanied by torrential rain. The Muscovites' powder became wet, the cannon wouldn't fire, the ice on the rivers broke up, roads turned to mire, supplies couldn't reach the hungry troops, and Ivan grew afraid that flooding would soon cut off his retreat. With rage in his heart, he ordered an immediate withdrawal. He was sure the Tatars would pursue him and that he would have to engage in rear-guard action, but the Kazan Tatars contented themselves with collecting the arms and equipment he had left behind.

Relieved to have gotten off so lightly, Ivan decided to build a fortified town near Kazan, in enemy territory, and to use it as a base from which to mount another attack. This town, at the confluence of the Volga and the Sviaga, was given the name Sviazhsk. It quickly became a center of attraction for the mountain tribes of the vicinity—the Cheremiss, Chuvash, Mordvinians—and an intolerable provocation for the Tatars of Kazan. With the success of this Russian settlement in the Khan's zone of influence, Ivan tried to mask the failure of his military expedition. In reality, neither the boyars nor the people were deceived. The most hostile among them muttered that everything the Czar undertook seemed to turn out badly; the most indulgent explained this new reversal by the sovereign's extreme youth; but all agreed in condemning the conduct of Dimitri Belsky, who was even accused of treason. The general, however, had not betrayed the Russian cause, he had simply proved incompetent. Ivan, who believed the commander loyal but inept, could have struck him down. Instead, he spared his life. With excellent timing, Dimitri Belsky died of an illness shortly after the army returned to Moscow.

At Sviazhsk, meanwhile, the garrison was being weakened by the plague and by a lack of discipline. According to a chronicle of the period, the men of Sviazhsk were "shaving their beards and debauching the youths." So, to raise the morale of the troops there, the boyars in Moscow sent a flask of consecrated water to purify the border fortress—along with an edifying sermon by Metropolitan Macarius. And they would not hear of another armed expedition against Kazan: the preceding ones had cost too dear.

Meanwhile, in the border regions every month there were further skirmishes, incursions, and fruitless negotiations. Unlike the service men, who advised Ivan to wait until the situation came to a head, the high clergy, led by Macarius, encouraged the Czar to resume the struggle against the infidels, who were "spilling the blood of Christians, desecrating and ruining the churches." The Czar himself was eager to take revenge on the Tatars, who had made him look ridiculous. It was not only his personal prestige that was at stake, but his whole foreign policy. He must either vanquish the hereditary enemy gnawing at Muscovy's flank or accept increasingly daring attacks like the progressive inroads of a fatal disease. A holy war was inevitable. On June 16, 1552, Ivan entrusted the conduct of internal affairs during his absence to his brother, Yuri, begged the Metropolitan to bless his action, and took leave of the despairing Anastasia. She was pregnant and fell sobbing upon her husband's breast. Undisturbed, he recommended that she look after the poor, keep the keys to the prisons, and free those inmates whom she judged most deserving. Then, having kissed her, he passed between two banks of boyars and walked toward his horse.

A Russian army composed of 100,000 men—cavalry, artillery, *streltsy*—left Moscow preceded by holy banners. At its head rode the Czar, flanked by Adashev and Prince Andrei Kurbsky. Five days later Ivan learned by messenger that Devlet-Guirey, the Khan of Crimea, was marching on Tula. He immediately changed his route and, instead of continuing east toward Kazan, rushed south. When he reached Tula, the Tatars had already been repulsed by the garrison of the town and had lifted their siege. Kurbsky pursued them and hacked them to pieces. Weapons, baggage wagons, and many camels fell into the hands of the Russians. Prisoners revealed that after laying siege to Tula, the Tatars had intended to advance upon the capital while the Czar was detained in Kazan. Ivan sent all the booty back to Moscow, where the citizenry spat upon the swarthy, black-haired captives who dared to believe in Allah, and went into raptures at the sight of the camels.

Emboldened by this first success, Ivan quickened the advance of his troops toward Kazan, the true goal of the expedition. At every stop, he invoked another of Russia's patron saints. In the cathedral of Kolomna he bowed before the icon of the Mother of God that Dimitri Donskoy had carried in the victorious battle against the Sultan Mamai. In Vladimir he learned from a messenger that the epidemic that had ravaged Sviazhsk had come to an end and that after many disorders discipline had been reestablished in the garrison. Didn't this show that at long last God had allowed Himself to be moved by the Czar's piety and goodwill? The news from Moscow was also excellent: Anastasia was well, the people were praying for the safety of their sovereign, and Macarius wrote to Ivan, "Let your soul be pure and chaste. Be humble in good fortune and courageous in adversity. The virtues of a monarch are the salvation of his empire."

During this long expedition the Czar went sometimes on horseback, sometimes on foot. He endured fatigue with a cheerfulness that amazed his entourage. They camped on the banks of streams or in the forests, and lived by hunting and fishing. The chieftains of a few rebel tribes, impressed by the deployment of Muscovite troops, came to submit to the Russian sovereign and assured him that the right bank of the Volga was entirely loyal to him. They offered to help him conquer Kazan. On August 11, the voivodes, or military commanders, of the Sviazhsk garrison came to meet Ivan. Officers and men were all invited to a festive repast under open tents. The inhabitants of the neighboring villages supplied the guests with bread and mead. As it was during Lent, the menu was frugal, but the splendor of the landscape under an intensely blue, cloudless sky made up for the simplicity of the meal. On one side stretched undulating grasslands like green velvet and, in the distance, the dark mass of the forest; on the other side rolled the Volga—broad, majestic, and slow, scattered with islands.

But Ivan did not want to linger. Quickly the dishes were picked up, the fires put out, the tents folded, and the Muscovites resumed their march. On August 13, the army came in sight of Sviazhsk, the new town founded by the will of the Czar. He entered it on horseback, received the blessing of the clergy, attended a mass at the cathedral, inspected the fortifications, the arsenal, the newly built houses, the many shops, and declared himself satisfied. Peddlers, attracted by this great concentration of unlooked-for customers, arrived by boat from Nizhni-Novgorod, Moscow, and Yaroslavl to offer their merchandise at open-air bazaars.

By order of the town authorities, the finest residence in the place had been set aside for the monarch. He refused to set foot in it, declaring, "I am on campaign now," and rode off again to his tent, which had been pitched in a meadow at the gates of

Sviazhsk. From there, having taken counsel with his advisers, he sent Yadigar-Mohammed, the governor of Kazan, a message written in Tatar, inviting the inhabitants to surrender and promising them the clemency of Russia. Actually, he had little hope of avoiding a battle, for the sacred character of this war of the Cross against the Crescent made any compromise impossible. Accordingly, without waiting for an answer, he set his troops in motion again. The reply came on August 20. It was negative and insulting: Kazan spat on Ivan, on Russia, and on Christianity. "All is ready here," declared Yadigar-Mohammed. "We await you to begin the festivities."

During the night, a Moslem nobleman who had escaped from the city came to Ivan to confirm that the defenders, numbering 30,000, were fanatic warriors and that they were plentifully supplied with food and ammunition. The task would not be easy. Ivan knew that. But he also knew in his heart that he could count on the help of God. He rode toward Kazan with the feeling that he was the champion of Christianity. At sunrise on August 23, he came in sight of the city—with its mosques, its high towers, its double walls of oak with gravel and clay crammed between. Then, to the sound of trumpets and drums, he had his standard-bearer unfurl the banner of the faith, portraying the face of Jesus Christ. A mass was celebrated beneath the flags. Priests dressed in liturgical garments blessed the soldiers, who were kneeling on one knee. The wind dispersed the fumes of incense and carried afar the rough voices of the choirs. Fixing his eyes on the sacred banner, Ivan crossed himself and cried, "Lord, it is in Thy name that we march against the infidels!" Then, turning toward his soldiers, he summoned them to combat, exalting the heroism of those who would fall in defense of the faith, promising to assist their widows and orphans, and swearing to sacrifice his own life, if necessary, for the triumph of the Orthodox church.

Immediately afterward, the cannon and powder were unloaded and timbers were made ready for the erection of the siege towers; the army gathered in a slow and powerful flood under the walls of Kazan. But the city appeared abandoned. Not the least sound. No one on the ramparts. Was it a trap? Cautiously the *streltsy* entered upon the silent, deserted streets. Doubtless the population had taken refuge in the central fortress, the kremlin. And indeed, all of a sudden the iron gates of the citadel clanged open. The Tatars who poured out through them were not men but grimacing, screaming devils. Some on horseback, others on foot, they formed a solid mass in which light flashed from glittering eyes, teeth, and scimitar blades. Hell was vomiting forth its legions against Christianity. Terrified, the Russian harquebusiers retreated in disorder; some fell and commended their souls to God. With great difficulty their officers regained control of them outside the city. After hand-to-hand fighting, next came artillery fire and exchanges of flights of arrows. When at last the Tatars withdrew into their fortress and the gates closed again, calm returned and Ivan pretended to believe that this first assault had turned to his advantage.

The night passed quietly, but next day a violent storm beat down upon the region. A number of tents, including the Czar's pavilion, were torn from their stakes by the high winds; field churches collapsed while frightened priests snatched up icons, banners, and relics; the river, suddenly swollen, overflowed its banks, smashing the boats, flooding the food and ammunition depots. In next to no time, the army's supplies were almost completely destroyed. In the midst of the general consternation Ivan stood firm. While his generals were already considering a retreat, he summoned the merchants and ordered them to re-provision the troops by boat and caravan.

The following days were spent in skirmishes. The Tatars rained down upon the Russians a hail of bullets, arrows, and cannonballs as they tried to scale Kazan's walls. And, as they retreated, the Russians drew after them pursuing Tatars, whom they then fought on open ground. As soon as Ivan's army had taken a few prisoners, they were tied to stakes facing the walls of the city so that their groans might persuade their comrades to surrender. A herald shouted to the besieged, "Ivan promises them life and liberty and to you pardon for the past, if you surrender to him!" From the top of a tower the enemy spokesman replied in a thundering voice, addressing the prisoners themselves: "It is better for you to receive death from our clean hands than to perish at the hands of the evil Christians!" And the Tatar archers loosed flights of arrows at their brothers.

At the end of August, the Czar ordered a German engineer to tunnel under the ramparts in order to blow up the city's main source of drinking water. The sappers worked underground for ten days. Overhead they could hear the comings and goings of the passersby. Having located the site of the fountain, they rolled casks of powder up to the spot. On September 5, Ivan climbed onto a mound surrounded by gabions and ordered the fuse to be lit. An enormous explosion shook the city, part of the wall crumbled, and beams, stones, and mutilated corpses were thrown high into the air. The Russians rushed into the breach. But the Tatars, momentarily stunned, soon collected their wits and, urged on by the shrieking of their women, once again repulsed the assailants.

This fierce resistance was disconcerting to the Russians. It was said in the ranks that every night just before dawn Mongolian witches climbed up onto the ramparts, tucked up their skirts, and made obscene gestures, insulting the Christian enemy and casting spells on him. It was they who summoned up the wretched weather that was such a trial to the Muscovites. It rained unceasingly. The soldiers, soaked and blinded, floundered through the mire: impossible to find shelter under the leaking tents. Desperate ills called for desperate remedies: Ivan had a miraculous cross brought from Moscow, and the waters falling from heaven were blessed with it; then a religious procession wound through the camp, the priests sprinkling holy water every few steps. At once the rain stopped, the sun reappeared, and the army took heart again. "Allah is retreating!" the attackers shouted.

Two versts* away from the camp they built a huge wooden tower some forty feet high, mounted on wheels, and at night they rolled it up to the walls of the city near the Royal Gate. This tower was fitted with ten heavy guns and fifty light cannon, and it was manned by many gunners. From their elevated position they could see a whole district of the city. In the first light of dawn the bombardment began. While the panicked inhabitants sought refuge in cellars and trenches, the defenders replied with musket fire that killed a great many Russian cannoneers. The bloody affair was inconclusive. Meanwhile, the mining went on, casks of powder were exploded, hand-to-hand fighting continued in the outer sections of the city. The generals urged Ivan to order the final assault. He insisted that the whole army go to confession and take communion first. As Soldiers of Christ, they should go to death with pure souls.

At last everything was ready. The priests had done their office, dawn rose in a cloudless sky. The archers with hands on their quivers, the gunners with matches lit awaited the signal to commence the carnage. They all knew that a great explosion was to open the way for the attackers. But for the moment the silence was broken only by the chanting of the priests, who were celebrating mass a short distance away. As if to show that he was counting more on God than on himself to obtain victory, the Czar at this moment was not with his men but was in the main church of the camp. Just as the deacon, reading from the Scriptures, uttered the words "There shall be but one fold and one Shepherd," a tremendous explosion made the earth tremble beneath the monarch's feet. The biggest mine had just blown up. The Czar, delighted, left the sanctuary and watched from a distance as debris and earth fell back to the ground amid the smoke. Then, having shaken the dust from his clothes, he re-

---

*A verst is about two-thirds of a mile, or slightly more than one kilometer. (Trans.)

turned to his prayers. Shortly afterward, while he was thus engaged, a second explosion resounded, answered by a sound like rolling thunder as 100,000 soldiers shouted, "God is with us!"

The Russians surged forward to attack. From the top of the ramparts the Tatars hurled beams, rocks, and boiling water down upon them. Despite enormous losses the assailants scaled the walls with ladders, clung to the embrasures, hoisted themselves onto the shoulders of their comrades to climb through the openings and, saber in hand, confronted the defenders, who soon lost ground and fell back. The clash of blade striking blade, the shouts and groans did not reach the retreat of the Czar, who was kneeling before the icons. Several times his generals begged him to break off his prayers and show himself in the midst of his sorely tried troops. But whether from cowardice or from piety, he refused to come out before he had finished the liturgy.

Meanwhile, in Kazan the massacre continued. The fighting was carried to the very rooftops. In their rage the Russians spared neither women nor children; when they did not slit their throats, they bound them and gathered them together to be sold as slaves. On reaching the bazaar they were dazzled by the riches displayed there—objects of gold and silver, furs, silks—and, forgetting their warlike fury, abandoned themselves to looting. The Tatars took advantage of this disorder to counterattack, but the Russians recovered themselves in time. The battle resumed, with fierce fighting of uncertain outcome. Again the boyars begged Ivan to show himself. He hesitated a while longer. Then, having run out of excuses, he kissed the miraculous picture of St. Sergius, drank some holy water, swallowed a piece of the host, received the good word from his chaplain, and mounted his horse. When he appeared on the plain, the Russian flag was already floating over the ruins of Kazan. The besiegers, outnumbering their adversaries, had overcome them. So the Czar had been right to pray instead of exposing his life. Ivan rode into the city picking his way among heaps of corpses and pools of blood.

In the meantime, Yadigar-Mohammed had retreated into

his palace with the remnant of his troops. When the Russians broke down its doors, they found a group of richly dressed women who fell weeping at their feet. But Yadigar-Mohammed had fled. They came upon him in a tower that had remained intact. It was the end. He surrendered, kneeling before his conqueror and asking for mercy. Magnanimously, Ivan granted him pardon, saying, "Unhappy man, you did not know the power of Russia!"

Having congratulated his generals, Ivan gathered the army together in camp and indulged in his favorite pleasure: public speaking. Standing opposite his soldiers with their bloodstained uniforms and faces blackened by smoke and gunpowder, he cried with the look of one inspired: "Valiant warriors, boyars, voivodes, officers, all of you here on this solemn day have suffered for the greatness of God, for the faith, for the motherland and for your Czar; you have acquired immortal renown. Never has a people displayed so much bravery and achieved such a brilliant victory. . . . You have shown yourselves to be worthy descendants of those heroes who, on the orders of Grand Prince Dimitri, exterminated the infidel Mamai. . . . And you who remain on the field of honor, noble sons of Russia, you are already in the celestial halls, amid the Christian martyrs, resplendent with glory."

Thus, on October 2, 1552, Kazan became Russian. The twenty-two-year-old czar took legitimate pride in this first conquest, yet not once had he brandished a saber or shouldered a harquebus during those heroic days, not once had he visited the forward positions of his soldiers exposed to enemy arrows. His role had consisted of praying—protected by a large escort—and of appearing in camp from time to time magnificently dressed. To all his fighting men he was nonetheless the symbol of Russian power, Russian courage, Russian faith. Yadigar-Mohammed, having recognized him as sovereign, promised to become a Christian when he arrived in Moscow, and at the Tatar's urging many of his followers converted. The harem women and the widows of Tatars fallen in battle were invited to a great feast. They too soon abjured the Moslem faith. As concubines of the victors, the women would give them superb sons, Ivan thought, combining in their blood the warlike virtues of the two races.

Meantime, he must help Kazan to rise again. Ivan had the ruins sprinkled with holy water to purify them and laid the cornerstone of the Cathedral of the Visitation. Then, going about the streets surrounded by members of the clergy, he indicated places where other churches should be built. His dream was that the whole Tatar population of Kazan should be replaced by Russians, but notwithstanding the privileges to be granted to merchants from Moscow and Nizhni-Novgorod who might wish to settle in the region, very few volunteers presented themselves. Kazan, a city founded by the Bulgarians, descendants of the Huns, and later dominated by the Mongols, had been since ancient times an important commercial center, famous for its fairs and for its trade with China, Persia, and Samarkand. This ideal meeting place could not be allowed to fall into decay. Therefore, to continue profitable trade with foreign lands, Ivan found himself obliged to call upon all the Mohammedans of the country, no longer requiring them to convert—it would be enough for them to swear allegiance to the Czar and to pay taxes to the designated collector. So, having recovered from their terror, the Tatars came back, shops opened their doors again, and a hybrid population, part Russian and part Mongol, part Orthodox and part Moslem, undertook to rebuild the city's ruins and to live in harmony despite their quarrels of the past.

Deaf to the remonstrances of his generals, who wanted him to stay with them, Ivan decided to return to Moscow. He left a garrison of 5,000 men in Kazan and named Alexander Shuisky governor of the city, with Prince Peter Serebriany as his deputy. Their task would be to continue to subdue the region, which was still roamed by rebellious bands. He himself had better things to do than to supervise these police actions. Impatient to see his wife again and to present himself in Moscow in all his glory, he took ship on the Volga on October 14.

A splendid reception awaited him in Nizhni-Novgorod. The cheers of the crowd were so loud that they drowned out the voices of the clergy. The people rejoiced all the more because, until then, the Tatars' incursions had been a grave danger to the city's famous fair. It was also to be hoped that the destruction of the bazaars of Kazan would bring more business to Nizhni-Novgorod. God had eliminated a formidable commercial rival. Let Him be praised! Ivan delivered another ringing address, and continued on his way to Moscow on horseback. Near Vladimir he met a boyar sent by Anastasia to inform him that she had given birth to a son, Dimitri. Ivan was overcome with ecstatic joy. He wept, leaped down from his mount, and, not knowing how to thank the messenger, gave him his horse and his cloak. To be sure, his wife had already given him two daughters (one of them, Anna, had died at twenty months; the other, Maria, was still living). But the births of female children were merely incidents in the life of a prince, while the birth of a male heir transported the father in a single bound to the steps of the Throne of God.

It was this feeling of having been reconciled with heaven that, strangely enough, kept Ivan from rushing to the bedside of the mother. Rather than press on night and day to see her as soon as possible, he stopped in Vladimir to pray for a long time. Then came another halt at Suzdal and more prayers. Finally, when he was only a few versts from the capital, instead of galloping the last stretch of the way to the Kremlin, he stopped at the Monastery of the Holy Trinity, performed his devotions at the tomb of St. Sergius, and took communion with the monks. At last, on the morning of October 29, he entered Moscow, where he was given a triumphal welcome. So many people crowded around him as he passed that the soldiers had difficulty containing them with their halberds. Breaking through the ranks of guards, stammering men and weeping women kissed the sovereign's stirrups, shouting "God grant long life to our pious czar, conqueror of the barbarians and savior of the Christians!"

Once again, Ivan indulged in the satisfaction of making his voice heard above the crowd. He addressed Metropolitan Macarius and the clergy: "You have sent up to heaven prayers which God has answered. . . . Sustained by the visible influence of your prayers, we advanced against Kazan and achieved the desired goal. . . . That populous city fell before us: Celestial justice caused an infinite number of infidels to perish in a single moment; their leader was taken prisoner and the standards of the Crescent, now replaced by the holy Cross, have disappeared forever from its walls. And we, full of health and joy, have returned here before the image of the Holy Virgin, in the bosom of our dear motherland. . . . Continue to intercede zealously before the Throne of God and to support me with your wise counsel so that I may consolidate faith and justice and make morality reign inside the empire, and so that Russia's new subjects, abjuring their errors, may recognize the true God and join us in glorifying the Holy Trinity."

Old Macarius replied in a broken voice: "What a change has taken place in the destiny of the country! The perfidious men of Kazan spread terror throughout Russia; they slaked their thirst for the blood of Christians, dragged them into slavery, desecrated and destroyed the temples of the Lord. . . . But heaven made the rays of its grace shine upon you, as once they shone upon Constantine the Great, St. Vladimir, Dimitri Donskoy, Alexander Nevsky. . . . You have set your name beside these illustrious names and your glory is equal to theirs. . . . Kazan, a sovereign city which was like a nest of serpents that ceaselessly threatened us with their poisonous tongues, has fallen at your feet. . . . Abandon yourself to joy, Czar beloved of heaven and of the motherland! The Lord has not only granted you victory but He has also caused to be born unto you a much longed-for son! . . . As for us, O Czar, in witness to our gratitude for your difficult labors and glorious exploits, we prostrate ourselves before you!"

At these words the Metropolitan, the members of the clergy, the dignitaries, and the people fell facedown before the monarch. Ivan tasted the intoxication of seeing a sea of heads undulating at his feet. Then he changed his heavy armor for the caftan of a sovereign, placed around his neck a necklace from which hung a cross, and put on the Cap of Monomakh. The priests, bearing icons, crosses, banners, censers, and lanterns, surrounded the Czar and accompanied him to the Kremlin. It was only after he had bowed before the holy relics and the tombs of his ancestors that Ivan went into the palace to be reunited with the Czarina, who was still in bed. On seeing him, she forgot how weak she was, rushed to meet him, and, laughing and crying, embraced her master's knees. He raised her up, kissed her on the forehead, and had his son brought to him.

On November 8, the prelates and boyars gathered at the palace for a gigantic banquet. On this occasion Ivan presented each guest with a gift proportionate to his rank and courage: sable furs, brocades, gold cups, garments, horses, full purses, carpets, weapons, estates . . . The feasting lasted for three days, during which the guests drank steadily, laughed heartily, boasted of their exploits, and listened as the Czar's singers celebrated the Russian victory to the sound of guslis—and all of Russia rejoiced.

To commemorate the capture of Kazan with a lasting monument, Ivan ordered that there be built on the great square of the Kremlin a church of the Intercession of the Holy Virgin, which would later come to be called the Cathedral of Basil the Blessed. Macarius encouraged him. Together they drew up the first plans for the edifice. In their opinion it should not look like anything else, but was to be an act of mystical madness, an explosion of joy, a delirium of forms and colors. Who would be the master architect? They thought of various Italians, the Italians having already proved themselves in Moscow. But no, the architect of this symbol of triumphant Russia must be a Russian. In the end it was Posnik Yakovlev who was chosen. To him would fall the task of building this curious monument reflecting all the contradictions of the Czar. Little by little, there rose from the earth an exuberant, sublime basilica with eight unequal cupolas dominated by a tall pyramid whose point was topped with a gilded onion. The multicolored bulbs—ribbed, covered with scales, or cut in facets—stood out hard and glittering against the sky. It was like a basket of fantastic fruits prepared for an ogre. The construction was to go on for six years.* As for the cost, it was only right that it should be borne by the inhabitants of Kazan as a war indemnity.

---

*This cathedral stands on the site of a cemetery where Basil (Vasily) the Blessed, whom Ivan held in great veneration, was buried. According to a legend that has never been confirmed, the architect of Basil the Blessed had his eyes put out at Ivan's orders, so that he might never build so beautiful a cathedral elsewhere.

VI

Illness and
Its Consequences

As soon as Anastasia had recovered from childbirth, the Czar went with her to the Monastery of the Holy Trinity. There Nicander, the Archbishop of Rostov, baptized the Czarevich Dimitri at the shrine of St. Sergius. The Czar then made preparations for the baptism of two princes of Kazan: the child Utemish-Guirey and the former governor of the town, Yadigar-Mohammed. Remembering his own childhood as an orphan, Ivan decided that little Utemish-Guirey, having received the Christian name Alexander, would live in the palace and be brought up in a manner befitting his high rank. When it came to setting a date for Yadigar-Mohammed's baptism by immersion, the Czar could think of none better than February 26, in the dead of winter. The ice on the Moskva River had to be broken so that the new convert, wrapped in a linen sheet, could be plunged in. After celebrating an outdoor mass, the Metropolitan asked Yadigar-Mohammed if it was not in response to outside pressure that he had decided to change his religion. "No," replied the Tatar in a firm voice, "I am persuaded to do so only by my love for Jesus Christ and my hatred for Mohammed." This being said, he stepped toward the hole in the ice, entered the freezing water, and emerged again at once, a shivering but happy Christian. Henceforth he would be known as Simeon. The Czar gave him a spacious house in the Kremlin, allowed him to have a personal court, and encouraged him to marry Maria Kutuzova, the daughter of a Russian dignitary.

Ivan's joy over these three remarkable baptisms was soon overshadowed by news of an epidemic of ulcerous plague in the city of Pskov. In a few months the number of dead reached 25,000. In Novgorod-the-Great, for fear of contagion, all the merchants from Pskov were expelled and their personal belongings burned. But it was no use, the disease spread and the inhabitants of Novgorod perished by the thousands. The terrified survivors no longer dared bury the corpses. Archbishop Serapion, who risked his own life to bring the comfort of religion to the dying, likewise succumbed. His pious functions were to be taken over by the monk Pimen; Ivan and the Metropolitan prayed with Pimen for a long time before he set out. The man of God took with him a considerable quantity of holy water with which to purify Novgorod. And indeed, not long after the sprinkling of the water, the plague receded.

It was followed, however, by another, no less deadly evil.

In the newly conquered territory of Kazan the wild tribes of Mongolian origin—the Cheremiss, Mordvinians, Chuvash, Votyaks, and Bashkirs—revolted against the Russian tax collectors. They massacred Muscovite functionaries and merchants and built a redoubt seventy versts from Kazan. The voivode Boris

Saltykov marched against them in the depths of the winter, but his foot soldiers and cavalry sank heavily into the snow. The Tatars, meanwhile, had tied boards to their feet and were gliding toward the enemy as if on solid ground. They surrounded the detachment of *streltsy* and exterminated it. Few Russians managed to escape; Boris Saltykov was taken prisoner and had his throat cut amid wild rejoicing. In Kazan it was feared that the city would fall into the hands of the infidels again.

Ivan was worried: He regretted not having listened to the boyars, who had advised him to remain on the spot with his army until the region had been entirely subdued. There was such discouragement at court that certain members of the council dared suggest to the Czar that he abandon to the Moslems a city so remote and apparently impossible to hold. Ivan was indignant and refused to listen to them, but then suddenly his strength gave way. In March 1553, a few days after having received the bad news from the province of Kazan, he fell gravely ill. It was not the plague, for Moscow had been spared that scourge, but an inflammatory fever of unknown origin, which the physicians declared incurable (it was doubtless pneumonia). Ivan thought he was lost, and prepared for death with meditation and prayer.

On learning that their czar was at death's door, the common people were struck with consternation. Ivan's evident piety had made him a kind of saint in their eyes—a demanding, frightening saint who gave orders, fought, punished, but whose brow was free from all stain. If God called him back to Him, at the age of twenty-three, it was because He considered him too perfect for sinful Russia. "We must be very wicked," they said in Moscow, "since God takes such a sovereign from us!" Night and day, a weeping crowd waited in front of the palace for news of the patient. In all the churches prayers were offered for his recovery.

Among the boyars, however, it was not despair that reigned but perplexity. Most of them nursed a secret resentment against the Czar, who had brushed them aside and chosen advisers among men of low birth. They were worried about the succession. Mikhailov, the Czar's secretary, approached the monarch's bed and dared suggest that he draw up a will. Ivan acquiesced, and then and there dictated his last wishes: After his death his son Dimitri, a few months old, should assume the crown. Mikhailov immediately went to read the testament to the boyars gathered in the next room. A lively discussion broke out between those who agreed to swear allegiance to the Czarevich and those who refused. Everyone put forward decisive arguments. Voices were raised.

Hearing the sounds of quarreling on the other side of the door, Ivan summoned the dignitaries, who came in hot from the angry debate. "Whom, then, do you want to choose for czar, since you refuse to accept my son?" he asked in a faint voice. "Have you forgotten your oath to serve me, me and my children? I am too weak to speak long. Although Dimitri is yet in the cradle, he is nonetheless your legitimate sovereign. If you are deaf to the voice of your conscience, you will answer for it before God." Then Feodor Adashev, the father of Ivan's favorite, declared to the Czar that he would never consent to submit to the Czarina's brothers, the Zakharin-Yurievs, who would no doubt govern the country for a long time in the child's name. "That," he cried, "is the true cause of our anxiety! To how many evils, how many torments were we not exposed when the boyars governed before you reached the age of reason? We must avoid such calamities in future." Ivan was too weak to reply. From the depths of his torpor and nausea he looked at the boyars, inflamed by ambition and fighting over his inheritance like thieves after a robbery. Overcome by so much tumult, he begged them, with a groan, to leave the room.

Two diametrically opposed parties were forming. One, led by the Czar's secretary, Mikhailov, favored the infant in swaddling clothes with a regency entrusted to the Czarina's family. The other wanted to give the crown neither to the baby nor to Ivan's brother, Yuri, whom nature had not favored with any judgment, but rather to Vladimir Andreyevich, Prince of Staritsa and cousin germane to the Czar, an intelligent man skilled both in war and in politics.

The following day, mastering his infinite lassitude, Ivan again adjured the opposing boyars to bow to his will. "For the last time," he murmured, "I demand your oath. Kiss the cross. Do not allow the traitors to approach the Czarevich. Save him from their wrath. . . ." Despite this solemn injunction, the quarreling went on around the dying man's bed. Only a few took the oath and kissed the cross. Sylvester and Alexei Adashev, notwithstanding their attachment to the monarch's person, maintained a prudent neutrality. Anxious for their future at court, they placed their bets on Vladimir Andreyevich, supposing that once he was installed on the throne he would reward them for having supported his cause. Ivan guessed that his close advisers had executed an about-face and was pained by it. Now it was clear to him that after his death his decisions would not be respected. The two clans would tear each other apart as in the old days, during his childhood. Once again Russia would be given over to the bloody rivalry of the boyars.

In a last burst of hope, Ivan made a vow that, if God spared his life, he would take his wife and son and make the long and difficult pilgrimage to St. Kirill's (St. Cyril's) Monastery, near Kirillov in the far north country. Praying with eyes closed, he lay so motionless that the men gathered around him believed he had fallen into a coma. But the fever soon reached a peak, and then abated. Ivan felt an almost immediate relief and understood that he was saved. The doctors spoke of a "favorable crisis" that had hastened the recovery by shaking up the "humors." As for the boyars, they followed the rapid progress of the convalescence with anxiety. Those who were most compromised wondered what vengeance the miraculously resuscitated czar would take upon them for their treachery. Would they be beheaded, imprisoned, ruined, or merely exiled?

Ivan, who had hated them in his youth, had somewhat forgotten his animosity in these last years. And now here he was again, facing the same enemies as before: the boyars, always the boyars, more arrogant and scheming than ever. Yet when he had implored God on his deathbed, he had promised that if he were cured he would forgive those who had speculated on his death, like a true Christian. Now that he had recovered, he contented himself with enjoying the spectacle of their fear and baseness. When the chief pretender to the throne, Vladimir Andreyevich, bowed before him with humble eyes and an obsequious look on his face to congratulate him on being restored to health, Ivan stroked his head and spoke a few pleasant words to him. Emboldened by so much clemency, the other boyars also assured the monarch of their joy at seeing him look so well. He listened to them, thanked them, and detected nothing but lies on all their lips and in all their eyes. Even honest Sylvester and the devoted Alexei Adashev had a false look of happiness when they approached him. He had by now lost confidence in them, and their defection left him alone, disillusioned, embittered, icy. Besides, Anastasia, who had formerly encouraged her husband's friendship for these two remarkable men, now advised him not to take them into his confidence any more. Had they not more or less openly come to terms with those who wanted to sacrifice her and her son to the ambitions of Vladimir Andreyevich? The Czar nevertheless continued to ask the advice of Adashev and Sylvester. But the tone of their conversations was no longer the same, and their meetings were marked by coldness.

Meanwhile, Ivan never relaxed. He kept a watch on himself and he kept a watch on others. Now and then a cruel gleam would appear in his eyes. Of course he had sworn to God that he would spare the guilty—but after a reasonable amount of time had passed, oaths could be transgressed without heaven's taking offense. In any case, there was one vow that Ivan meant to honor as soon as he had strength to set one foot in front of the other: the vow to make a pilgrimage to the north with his family.

Ivan's advisers in the Rada tried to persuade him that he was not yet sufficiently recovered, that the strains of the journey might be dangerous for his infant son and that he would do better to remain in the capital to settle the worrisome situation in Kazan, where there were more and more revolts. Sylvester and Adashev, particularly, urged him to give up the journey. Perhaps they were afraid that the many prelates exiled to the monasteries would complain to the sovereign of his closest collaborators. All they could make him agree to was that before leaving for Kirillov, he would go to the Monastery of the Holy Trinity to seek the opinion of the pious hermit there, Maxim the Greek. This very learned monk, who had been born in Albania and raised in a monastery on Mount Athos, had been called to Russia by Grand Duke Vasily III, Ivan's father, and then banished for having disapproved of his sovereign's remarriage with Elena Glinskaya. Imprisoned for twenty-one years, the old man had been freed by Ivan himself and transferred to the Holy Trinity. There he had become a symbol of asceticism, wisdom, and holiness.

When he entered the cell of Maxim the Greek, Ivan did not know that emissaries from Sylvester and Adashev had begged the holy man to make the Czar give up his plan. After a few words of welcome, the old monk said to his visitor, "Is it right for you to undertake a difficult journey with your young wife and your son, to wander afar from monastery to monastery? Can vows that are condemned by reason be agreeable to God? There is no need to seek in the wilderness Him who is everywhere!" And he assured the Czar that the best way for him to thank the Almighty would be to undertake a new campaign against the Tatars.

Ivan remained unshakable. He wanted to go to Kirillov not merely because he had promised God that he would do so but also because his mother had made the same pilgrimage when she was pregnant with him. In the confusion of his thoughts, he needed this return to the source of life. To frighten him, Alexei

Adashev told him it had been predicted that if he persisted in his absurd intentions, he would not bring the Czarevich Dimitri back alive. This threat angered the monarch. He thought it was inspired solely by Adashev and Sylvester's personal concerns. How long did they mean to keep him tied to their apron strings? God could not disapprove of the Czar's desire to do homage to the relics of martyrs of the faith. After the celebration of the Easter holidays, Ivan waited for the thaw and then departed with his brother, Yuri, his wife, and his son under the guard of a large escort. They traveled chiefly by boat.

In a distant monastery the Czar met an elderly, vindictive monk by the name of Vassian, the former Bishop of Kolomna. Vassian had been banished by the boyars during Ivan's minority and had retained a fierce hatred for the nobility. Deferentially, the sovereign questioned him as to the best way to govern the country. Vassian's eyes glittered with spiteful cunning as he bent toward the Czar and whispered in his ear, "If you wish to be an autocrat, do not keep beside you a single counsellor wiser than yourself, for you yourself are better than all; thus you shall be firm in the realm and you shall hold all men in your hands. And if you keep near you men wiser than yourself, then perforce you will be subject to them." These words corresponded so well with Ivan's private thoughts that he grasped the monk's hand, kissed it piously, and murmured, "O, even if my father had been alive, he would not have given me such useful advice!"[1] He was never to forget this exhortation to seek power amid solitude.

The next day, he continued his journey northward by the Dubna, and then later by the Volga and the Sheksna. Crowds gathered to stare in wonder wherever he passed. He visited all the monasteries he came to on the way. When he reached Kirillov, the child, who had caught cold during the exhausting journey, suddenly died. Anastasia herself was ill. Stunned with grief, Ivan ordered an immediate return.

Thus, the terrible prediction had been fulfilled. Heaven, which the Czar had wanted to thank for having saved his life, had

taken in exchange that of his son. Was this just? Was it accept-
able? No, no, there was dirty work behind it. Unable to tolerate
the idea that God had struck him just as he was asking His
blessing, Ivan thought of witchcraft: A spell had been thrown
upon the unfortunate Czarevich. And the persons responsible
could only be the ones who had advised against the journey:
Adashev and Sylvester. Lacking proof, he hesitated to punish
them as they deserved, but his anger fed on his despair.

Having returned to Moscow with the coffin of his son, Ivan
pulled himself together. Dimitri was buried in June 1553 in the
Cathedral of St. Michael the Archangel, at the feet of his grandfather, Grand Duke Vasily III. Nine months later, on March 28,
1554, Anastasia gave birth to another son, Ivan. The bereave-
ment was forgotten. Hope was born again at court and among
the people. Ivan said to himself that after an incomprehensible
quarrel, God had decided to be reconciled with him. Under
these conditions, he could do no less than appear likewise generous and patient with his entourage. Hiding his resentments,
he again listened graciously to the advice of Adashev and Sylvester, behaved affably toward his cousin, the would-be usurper
Vladimir Andreyevich, and took no reprisals against the boyars
who had conspired against him during his illness.

Ivan was still constantly concerned about the pacification of
the Kazan region. To subjugate the rebel Tatars he raised a
large army and gave command of it to Mikulinsky, Peter
Kurbsky, Peter Morozov, and Sheremetev, all energetic, capable
men. This time he did not participate in the expedition himself.
The troops went into action during the winter of 1553–54, in
bitter weather. Acting with dispatch, the Russians pitilessly attacked the refractory tribes, destroyed some Mohammedan
strongholds, killed thousands of men, captured a great number
of women and children, and compelled all the inhabitants of the
region to recognize the sovereignty of the Czar and agree to pay
taxes. In 1555, the newly Christian region was established as a
diocese. Conversions increased. Ivan sent gold medals to all his

commanders. He was aware that for the first time in centuries he had reversed the relation between the Orient and Moscow. Formerly, it had been the Tatars who humiliated Russia by repeatedly invading the country and laying it waste. Now it was Russia that was pressing with all its weight against the borders of the Moslem world and directly threatening Crimea.

But while the Czar was contemplating with satisfaction his conquests in the East and South, an incredible event took place that reminded him of the existence of a western Europe lying beyond the bounds of his political horizon. A messenger from the St. Nicholas Monastery on the White Sea came to inform him that on August 24, 1553, a foreign ship of great size had dropped anchor at the mouth of the Dvina,* that men speaking an unknown language had come ashore, that they seemed to have come with peaceful intentions, but that no one knew what to do with them. On further investigation the ship proved to be an English vessel, the *Edward Bonaventure,* commanded by Captain Richard Chancellor. It was the sole survivor of Sir Hugh Willoughby's expedition to discover a northeast passage to India; the two other ships had been destroyed by a storm and their crews had frozen to death. Chancellor said that he bore a message from his king, Edward VI, for the Czar. Ivan ordered the travelers to be furnished with horses and sleighs at his expense.

The mission arrived in Moscow in December 1553 after several weeks of an exhausting journey across deserts of snow. Wishing to impress the foreigner with the magnificence of his court, Ivan received Chancellor in solemn audience. Dressed in a long robe decorated with gold and purple, with a conical sable-trimmed hat on his head, he sat immobile on a gilded throne amid an assemblage of nobles waiting in respectful silence. The captain handed him the letter from his sovereign, which had been drawn up in Latin, Greek, and other languages,

---

*It was at this spot that the city of Arkhangelsk was to rise thirty years later.

as well as English. An interpreter translated the most important passages: "Edward the sixth, by the grace of God, King of England, France etc. To all Kings, Princes, Rulers, Judges, and Governors of the earth . . . in all places under the universal heaven: peace, tranquility, and honor be unto you and your lands and regions. . . . Forasmuch as the great and Almighty God hath given unto mankind, above all other living creatures, such an heart and desire that every man desireth to join friendship with other, to love and be loved, also to give and receive mutual benefits: it is therefore the duty of all men . . . especially to show this good affection to such as, being moved with this desire, come unto them from far countries. . . . And if it be right and equity to show such humanity toward all men, doubtless the same ought chiefly to be showed to merchants, who wandering about the world, search both the land and the sea, to carry such good and profitable things as are found in their countries to remote regions and kingdoms, and again to bring from the same such things as they find there commodius for their own countries. . . . We therefore desire you kings and princes . . . to permit unto these our servants free passage by your regions and dominions. . . . If therefore they shall stand in need of any thing, we desire you . . . to aid and help them with such things as they lack. . . . Show yourselves so toward them as you would that we and our subjects should show ourselves towards your servants, if at any time they shall pass by our regions. . . ."[2]

Responsive to these words, Ivan honored the English with a feast for one hundred persons. The food was served on gold dishes by one hundred and fifty servants, who changed livery three times during the meal. The guests remained at table for five hours. The menu included spiced elks' brains, cocks with ginger, stuffed fish . . . The Russians, animated by the wine, tried to communicate with the English seafarers in sign language. Everyone smiled and clinked glasses, with greasy lips and moist eyes. Richard Chancellor visited the palace with much curiosity. He found the decor sumptuous and yet rustic at the same time:

scant furniture, benches, chests studded with nailheads, bare wooden tables, earthenware stoves rising to the ceiling, and beside these a profusion of carpets, brocades, velvets, furs. . . . Not one picture, not one mirror, but icons everywhere. Sometimes you might have thought you were in a caravansary, sometimes in a church. The air smelled of incense, beeswax, the hot oil of lamps. Ivan, for his part, observed with astonishment these Englishmen who might have fallen from the moon, so strange were their dress and manners.

In February 1554, he gave Richard Chancellor a reply to his "brother and cousin Edward," in Russian and in German. He assured him that English merchants would be "protected, free and treated like friends" in Russia. This letter would be read not by Edward VI but by Mary I, the new Queen of England and Ireland.

After Chancellor had left, Ivan remained obsessed with the thought of England. That unreal country from which merchants and seafarers set out seemed to him to be the end of the world. Meeting its representatives, he felt as if he were abolishing space. But he had no time to dream. The Russian reality was there with its demands, of which Sylvester and Adashev reminded him every day. To complete the operation against Kazan he must push south and subdue the region of Astrakhan, whose prince was inspired with a holy hatred for Russia. As the Khan of the Tatars of Crimea had not yet reorganized his troops following his defeat by the Russians in 1552, the moment seemed well chosen.

Prince Yuri Shemiakin took command of an army of Cossacks, *streltsy*, Votyaks, and young nobles. They boarded boats and were rowed down the Volga, singing as they went, for there was not the shadow of an enemy. Arrows remained in their quivers and the bold adventurers regretted the lack of action. At last, there before them lay Astrakhan. However, the Tatar garrison had fled. The Muscovites pursued it, exterminated it. In the abandoned city they found the prince's five wives, who were sent to Moscow. A Tatar, Derbish, was named governor of the city. The inhabitants swore allegiance to the Czar, promising to send him a heavy annual tribute of silver together with 3,000 sturgeon.

By this easy conquest Russia obtained an outlet on the Caspian Sea. Henceforth, she controlled the length of the Volga, from its source to its delta. The subjugation of the nomadic tribes consolidated her eastern borders. Persia and central Asia opened to her trade—and feared her army.

The Czar received news of this success on August 25, 1554, his twenty-fourth birthday. On learning that Astrakhan, a city founded two centuries earlier by Tamerlane and the capital of a Tatar khanate, had fallen into his hands, he was exultant. A Te Deum was celebrated at once. The most distinguished of the captives were baptized. And Ivan adopted a new formula for the beginning of his edicts and letters: "In this the twenty-first year of our reign over Russia, the third over Kazan, the first over Astrakhan . . ." Now he felt that his glory was so assured that he no longer feared anyone in his entourage.

After having shown his mistrust of his cousin Prince Vladimir Andreyevich, he became friendly toward him again and made a new will appointing him regent and governor of the country in case he should die. Andreyevich, moved to tears by so much benevolence, swore to be faithful to the Czarevich and the Czarina. With this decision the Prince turned his back on his former supporters, the boyars, and even on his mother, the scheming Princess Euphrosyne; and now that he had dropped them, some of the former plotters tried to flee to Lithuania. Princes Simeon and Nicholas Rostovsky were arrested at the border. Simeon was condemned to death. However, on the intervention of Sylvester, Metropolitan Macarius, and Alexei Adashev, he saved his head and was merely exiled. The other members of the family were judged irresponsible "by reason of idiocy" and were left free under surveillance. But opprobrium was attached to the name of the unfortunate defectors.

In the next year, 1555, the Englishman Richard Chancellor returned to Russia with two ships chartered by the Fellowship of English Merchants for Discovery of New Trades, commonly called the English Company or the Russia Company. The company's agents had been empowered to conclude a trade treaty with the Czar. Ivan received them at his table, thanked them for the kind letter from his "very dear sister Mary" (Tudor), and signed a charter authorizing English subjects to trade freely in all the towns of Russia without being molested and without paying any duties. The products imported would be chiefly arms, cloth, and sugar.

On July 21, 1556, Richard Chancellor left again for England at the head of five richly laden ships. An ambassador of the Czar, Osip Napeia, accompanied him. But a violent storm struck the flotilla and scattered the boats, smashing them on reefs. Chancellor perished, drowned in sight of the Scottish coast. Only the *Edward Bonaventure* reached London, with Napeia on board, more dead than alive. The warm welcome given him by the Queen and her husband, Philip II of Spain, consoled the ambassador for the loss of his baggage. He visited London with wondering admiration, stood on the platform next to the Queen during the solemn ceremony of the Order of the Garter, received from the Russia Company a gold chain valued at one hundred pounds sterling, and accepted as a gift for his master iridescent fabrics, costly weapons, a lion and a lioness. But above all, in accordance with instructions from the Czar, he hired craftsmen, miners, and doctors to take back to Moscow. For despite an unbounded national pride, Ivan recognized that the Russians—a rough, slow people—needed to receive a few foreigners so as to steal some scraps of knowledge from them.

All these embarked on one of the company's ships, commanded by Anthony Jenkinson. This time the voyage was uneventful. Napeia reported to the Czar the exceptional marks of esteem he had been accorded, confirmed the reciprocity of the commercial advantages granted to the English, assured him that though those people did not speak Russian they were Russia's most precious friends, and delivered to him letters from Mary and Philip in which he was referred to as "august Emperor." Ivan was flattered. Already he foresaw a possible alliance between his own country—vast, powerful, and barbarous—and this distant island that was the home of navigators, scholars, and adventurous merchants.

VII

Livonia and Anastasia

Whereas the sovereigns of England honored Ivan with the title "august Emperor," Sigismund Augustus, Grand Duke of Lithuania and elective King of Poland, did not. To justify his refusal he proclaimed haughtily that he "did not like novelties" and that to his knowledge only the master of the German Holy Roman Empire and the Turkish Sultan had a right to that prestigious appellation. Furthermore, he considered that Poland, a Catholic country that was humanistic, prosperous, and civilized, did not have to bow before Orthodox, primitive Russia. Disdaining Ivan's claims to superior status, he accredited his ambassadors not to "His Majesty the Czar of Russia" but to "His Majesty the Grand Duke of Moscow." Ivan was nettled, and addressed his missives to the "Grand Duke of Lithuania," purposely omitting to call Sigismund Augustus "King of Poland."

This exchange of incivilities soured relations between the two courts. In 1553, when new ambassadors from Sigismund Augustus arrived in Moscow, the Czar rejected their credentials, did not invite them to his table, and declared that he saw no necessity of signing—as he was asked to do—an eternal peace treaty with a country that failed to recognize the greatness of Russia and its monarch. Over the next few years, in support of his claims he would cite the letter from the English sovereigns, who, for their part, acknowledged his right to the title of emperor and his lightning conquest of Astrakhan. Sigismund Augustus wrote to congratulate Ivan upon his victory over the infidels, but he stubbornly persisted in calling him Grand Duke of Moscow. At the same time he sent another ambassador, a nobleman by the name of Tishkovich, to urge Ivan to conclude a just and permanent peace between the two states. The Czar did not even receive the gentleman. In reality, Ivan's hostility was not based merely on a question of protocol. Like all the Russian people, he had an ancestral antipathy for the Poles, and like his forefathers, he dreamed of delivering Kiev from Polish domination. But he hesitated to launch a new war while the Tatars were still making trouble in the East and South.

It was only when Ivan learned that the troops of Devlet-Guirey, the Khan of the Crimean Tatars, had been driven back that he returned to his old plan of acquiring ice-free ports on the Baltic. He felt the need for these outlets almost like a physical necessity, as if without them he could not breathe: Russia's borders had to be pushed to the sea, for in effect they were pressing in upon his own chest. To him, Poland, Lithuania, Sweden, and Livonia were all obstacles to the Russians' rightful expansion toward navigable waters.*

---

*This plan was to become an obsession with Peter the Great and dictate his entire foreign policy. Livonia was a territory composed of what is now eastern Prussia, Estonia, and part of Latvia.

Livonia, with its rich cities of Reval, Dorpat, and Riga, was a tempting prey. The population, made up of Finns, Latvians, and Germans, was governed by a chivalric order, the Knights of the Sword, headed by a Grand Master. But the doctrines of the Reformation had spread among these knights and caused serious dissension among them. Furthermore, they had long since lost their character as a formidable military force and, living in luxury, idleness, and depravity, had degenerated into a band of effeminate, gluttonous lords. Their country was the key to the Baltic. These arguments, which Ivan laid before the Rada, were violently opposed by Sylvester and Alexei Adashev, both of whom were in favor of pursuing operations against the Tatars of Crimea. Sylvester was so carried away by his conviction on this point that he even threatened the Czar with the wrath of God if he gave up the fight against the infidels in order to attack Livonia. Ivan, furious at his advisers, unceremoniously dismissed them. Nothing would persuade him to abandon his idea.

In 1554, Ivan demanded that the Bishop of Dorpat pay 50,000 crowns, representing an alleged annual tribute that the city owed the Czar and that had not been paid since 1503. At the end of three years, delegates from the Order of Knights of the Sword presented themselves in Moscow to ask for an extension, because it had not yet been possible to gather together the sum demanded. The Czar told them straight out, "If you refuse to carry out your promises, we shall find the way to take what belongs to us," and sent them away. They returned shortly afterward with fair words but still no money. Then Ivan invited them to dinner and had only empty plates set before them. They rose from table having eaten nothing, and returned to Dorpat with heads hanging.

On January 22, 1558, a Russian army of 40,000 men entered Livonia. These troops were composed chiefly of Tatars and men from Novgorod and Pskov, and were under the command of Shig-Aley, the former Khan of Kazan, who had gone over to the Russians. They ravaged the defenseless country, burned, massacred, pillaged, despoiled tombs, raped women and then tied them to trees and riddled them with arrows.

On May 12, Narva was taken by assault. Most of the inhabitants had their throats cut as the Russians went from house to house amid a whirlwind of flames and smoke. The survivors swore an oath of fealty to the Czar. An Orthodox archpriest was despatched to the site to purify the city with processions, prayers, and sprinklings of holy water. It was rumored that the burning of Narva had been started by some drunken Germans who had broken into the house of a Russian merchant and thrown his icon of the Holy Virgin into the fire. The sacred effigy itself had not burned but had given rise to a huge conflagration. The attackers had taken advantage of it to surprise the defenders and hack them to pieces. As soon as the icon had been recovered—intact—the fire had gone out of its own accord. It was immediately ordered that a church be built in which the miraculous image would be displayed for the worship of the faithful. At last Narva, "purged of the Latin and Lutheran religions," was given the privilege of carrying on free trade with Russia.

Two months later, on July 18, Dorpat capitulated to the regiments of Princes Peter Shuisky, Peter Serebriany, and Andrei Kurbsky. Shuisky entered the city in triumph and ordered his soldiers to spare the population. This great clemency won him the hearts of the Livonians. "Even the women," wrote a chronicler, "have recovered from their fright and are no longer afraid to show themselves." The extraordinary treatment with which Dorpat had been favored induced a score of secondary towns to surrender to the Russians.

Old Johann Fürstenberg, Grand Master of the Knights of the Sword, now relinquished his post. Young Gotthard Kettler, his successor, tried in vain to revive the patriotism of his fellow citizens. But they had lost confidence in the forces of the Order and their only thought was how best to negotiate with the enemy. It was with great difficulty that Kettler was able to raise a few thousand men. In despair, he begged his neighbors for help. Emperor Charles V, who might have come to his assistance, had abdicated and withdrawn from the world, and his successor, Ferdinand I of Hapsburg, was then too much concerned with the power of the Turks to take an interest in poor Livonia. Other sovereigns were also loath to take direct action. Poland, Sweden, and Denmark restricted themselves to seizing the ships that used the port of Narva. When Kettler suggested a truce, Ivan replied with icy irony, "I await you in Moscow, and the mercy you receive will depend on the number and humility of your genuflections." The Grand Master of the Order could not accept such degradation. The war went on, carrying fire and the sword to the very outskirts of Riga.

In September 1559, Kettler, a pleasant and persuasive man, at last obtained the protection of Poland. Sigismund Augustus undertook to defend the Order of the Knights of the Sword for a consideration of 700,000 florins to be paid as tribute after the victory. Having signed the agreement, he wrote to Ivan demanding imperiously that he evacuate Livonia, a country which was henceforth under his protection. "Livonia is a province that was formerly a tributary of Russia and not of your sovereign," Ivan answered the ambassadors who had brought him the letter. "I am punishing it now for its faithlessness, its guilty plotting, its crimes, and the destruction of our temples." Nevertheless, he promised a few months' truce.

Actually, Ivan needed this respite because the Tatars of Crimea, under the orders of Devlet-Guirey, had resumed their incursions. In the Czar's eyes they represented a more serious threat than the Poles and Livonians. The latter would never venture to besiege Moscow, while Devlet-Guirey was aiming for the capital. Fortunately, during the summer of 1559, Prince Dimitri Vishnevetsky won a series of signal victories over the Tatars, who once again fell back. Meanwhile, Kettler, believing that the Poles were preparing to march against the Russians, laid siege to Dorpat and other fortresses. This treacherous violation of the truce brought the main body of Russian troops back to Livonia. In vain did Ferdinand I remind Ivan that this country was a part of the German Empire and that no one had the right to trample it underfoot—in his letter he made the mistake of not mentioning the title "Czar," and Ivan sent the messenger back with a negative reply. The yelps and howls from Europe left him cold: He conducted his politics without worrying about treaties, traditions, or contradictory friendships. Andrei Kurbsky and Daniel Adashev, the brother of Ivan's adviser, Alexei, now pursued the Knights of the Sword from castle to castle, crushing them at Ermes, seizing the fortress of Fellin, and capturing Fürstenberg. Impressed by the efficiency of these operations, Sigismund Augustus made no attempt to come to the aid of the nation he had sworn to protect. Once again Ivan noted that violence paid off. God was on the side of bold Russia; all her undertakings were blessed.

As if military triumphs were not sufficient cause for happiness, Ivan could now boast of a second living son, Feodor, born on May 31, 1557. The baptism festivities were of a magnificence worthy the event. But this sixth delivery* had considerably weakened the Czarina. Still as gentle, loving, and self-effacing as always, she found comfort only in prayer. In November 1559, she went with Ivan to the Monastery of Mozhaisk. There, ill-lodged in a cold cell, she was seized with a sudden indisposition. Sylvester, who had accompanied her on this pilgrimage, immediately began talking about a sign of the Almighty's displeasure. Was it possible that the poor woman had been poisoned? There was no doctor at hand, no medicine. In panic, Ivan ordered that preparations be made for an immediate return, and she was brought back to Moscow on a sleigh. Her condition improved, but in July of the following year the illness returned. She grew rapidly worse.

While the Czarina was in bed, a fire broke out in a district near the Kremlin. Fanned by a raging wind, the flames licked the walls of the palace. From her room Anastasia could hear the

---

*Anastasia's children were: Anna (1548–1550), Maria (1551–?), Dimitri (1552–1553), Ivan (1554–1582), Eudoxia (1556–1558), and Feodor (1557–1598).

roaring of the fire, the cracking of burning beams. She thought she was back in the year she was married. In a fit of hysterics she left her bed. Neither the doctors nor the priests could calm her. Ivan had her carried on a litter to his residence in the village of Kolomenskoye, ten versts from Moscow. Then he went back to the city and organized the fight against the fire. Sparks flew in his face; he shouted orders over the crackling blaze; around him his boyars were wielding axes, climbing on rooftops, passing buckets of water. When the fire was under control, Ivan returned to Anastasia and found her shivering with fever. In her delirium she imagined that the flames were closing in upon her on all sides, upon her and her children. No potion, no powder could bring her relief, and she was surrounded by the murmur of priests. Ivan, on his knees, threw the weight of his empire into the scales of fate: If only God would listen to him, at that moment he, the Czar of Russia, was ready for any sacrifice. He would almost give up Livonia—if that would ensure his wife's recovery! She died on August 7, 1560, at five o'clock in the morning.

Ivan's despair verged on madness. The people of Moscow wept for their charitable Czarina; as the funeral procession passed, their lamentations drowned out the chanting of the priests. The poor refused the alms that were distributed to them according to custom, not wanting to have any kind of consolation on this day of national mourning. The sovereign walked bareheaded behind the coffin. His brother, Yuri, and his cousin Vladimir Andreyevich supported him. He staggered, groaned, beat his breast with his two fists. Metropolitan Macarius, on the verge of tears himself, entreated him to submit to the will of heaven. Ivan was not listening. Shut up within himself, he was trying to comprehend the reasons for this undeserved punishment.

Anastasia, the Czar's "little heifer," was buried in the convent of the nuns of the Ascension, within the walls of the Kremlin.

VIII

Sorrow and Violence

For thirteen years, thanks to the advice of his wife, Sylvester, and Alexei Adashev, Ivan IV had governed the country with relative wisdom. Even foreign observers had acknowledged that he was an outstanding sovereign. "This Emperor," wrote one of them, "doth exceed [his predecessors] in stoutness of courage and valiantness, and a great deal more, for he is no more afraid of his enemies, which are not few, than the hobby* of the larks. . . . [He] useth great familiarity, as well unto all his nobles and subjects, as also unto strangers, which serve him

---

*A small falcon, formerly used for hawking. (Trans.)

either in his wars, or in occupations. . . . And by this means he is not only beloved of his nobles and commons, but also held in great dread and fear through all his dominions, so that I think no prince in Christendom is more feared of his own than he is, nor yet better beloved. For if he bid any of his [boyars] go, they will run. . . . He delighteth not greatly in hawking, hunting, or any other pastime, nor in hearing instruments or music, but setteth all his whole delight upon two things: first, to serve God, as undoubtedly he is very devout in his religion, and the second, how to subdue and conquer his enemies."[1]

Without question, these admirable characteristics underwent a change for the worse during the Czar's illness, when he observed that his closest confidants, Adashev and Sylvester, had joined the opposition instead of supporting him in the quarrel over the succession. But when he recovered he had not visited his wrath upon them. In reality, it had been a great effort for him to play the strong, just monarch when inwardly he was boiling with resentment. When Anastasia died, a bolt had been sprung in his heart, loosing all the base instincts of his childhood. Suddenly, he discovered he was alone. His guardian angel had flown.

Ivan's contact with God had been broken. Or, more precisely, by striking him without reason God had dispensed him from obeying His holy precepts. Ivan believed in God more than ever. But he no longer attempted to find any logic in their relationship; the convenient system of reciprocity had ceased to exist between them—virtue was no longer rewarded with happiness. The Almighty was temperamental: One day He overlooked everything, the next He hurled thunderbolts because of a peccadillo. Unpredictable and disordered, He had, in fact, the same character as Ivan. God was another Ivan, a super-Ivan. They were two of a kind, both exempt from the moral laws that governed ordinary mortals. Now, because the Czar had lost his wife, he was allowed to do anything. Since God had offended him, he had the right to offend God. Besides, he was secretly convinced that God could not be angry with him for long over anything. No doubt even his excesses were pleasing to the Almighty, who appreciated violent natures and detested those that were lukewarm, timorous, and calculating.

Having buried his wife, Ivan, wild with rage, abandoned himself to drunkenness and consoled himself with a mistress. This did not prevent him from weeping for Anastasia in public. At court everyone feigned despair, but most of the boyars did not regret the Czarina. They blamed her for having persuaded the Czar to turn his back on the nobility in favor of the people. Furthermore, the princes of high birth regarded the family of the deceased, the Zakharin clan, as dangerous parvenus. Alexei Adashev and Sylvester were, likewise, political parasites to be gotten rid of. Eliminating those two would be easy, since Ivan had not forgiven them for shifting their loyalty at the time he was ill. Some even dared whisper in the Czar's ear that his two advisers might have poisoned Anastasia, who had been cool to them of late. Others, more cautious but no less malevolent, were content to declare that Adashev and Sylvester must have used witchcraft to make themselves indispensable to His Majesty for so long. Adashev soon left for the army in Livonia as a voivode and Sylvester withdrew into the solitude of a monastery. But their absence from court did not save them. Ivan ordered Sylvester to be taken from his pleasant retreat and exiled forever to a harsher monastery, on one of the Solovetsky Islands in the White Sea. He was to die there in obscurity and prayer.

In a letter to Kurbsky, Ivan revealed his feelings toward this pious, devoted man: "For the salvation of my soul I had attached to my person the priest Sylvester, in the hope that by his character and merit he could guide me toward the good. But this cunning, hypocritical man, who managed to deceive me with his sweet eloquence, thought only of worldly greatness. He joined with Adashev to govern the State in the name of a sovereign whom they despised. They aroused the spirit of insubordination in the boyars. . . . I was the slave on the throne. . . . Will I ever be able to describe all that I suffered during those days of shame and humiliation? . . . They invented childish causes for fear in order to plant terror in my soul. . . . They opposed my wish to visit the monasteries and to punish the Germans [of Livonia]. . . . Traitors to their conscience and their oaths, did they not try, when I was on my deathbed, to choose another czar, excluding my son from the succession? . . . They hated and slandered the Czarina Anastasia and were always the friends of Prince Vladimir Andreyevich. . . ."

Thus, as was his habit, Ivan claimed to have been scorned and betrayed by ingrates. The able and affectionate Alexei Adashev was now nothing but a mangy, snarling, false-hearted "cur" that should be punished. With no regard for the services that had been rendered him by this great administrator, the Czar ordered him to be tried. But for greater security, the accused would not be permitted to present his defense. "Poisonous as a basilisk," he might cast a spell over his judges. In vain did the venerable Metropolitan Macarius intercede in favor of the unfortunate man; the boyars assembled in judgment considered that "the tranquility of the Czar and of the country requires an immediate decision on this important matter." After deliberation, Adashev was imprisoned in Dorpat. Two months later he died in his cell, some said of a fever, others said of poison.

At the time, the Czar was satisfied. He had swept off his doorstep. But he was soon unable to be content with this limited punishment. The traitors had left behind them accomplices, or at least relatives, sympathizers. Having rid himself of Alexei Adashev, Ivan ordered the arrest and execution of his adviser's brother, the gallant Daniel, hero of several campaigns, and of Daniel's twelve-year-old son. The three Satins, whose sister had married Alexei, and Alexei's kinsman Shishkin (together with his wife and children) met the same fate. A Polish friend of Alexei's, old Maria, who was living in quiet piety, was assassinated by order of His Majesty, together with her five sons. When young Feodor Basmanov, the sovereign's favorite, complained that Prince Ovchina-Obolensky had dared to call him, Feodor, a sodomite, Ivan, trembling with rage, stabbed the slanderer with his own hand.

The Czar soon failed to observe fasts, and ridiculed the pious. One night in the palace, drunk on mead, he was dancing with some masked companions. Catching sight of Prince Repnin, who was the only one present with his face not hidden, he tried to force a mask on him. Repnin indignantly threw the mask on the floor, trampled it underfoot, and cried, "Is it fitting for a monarch to play the clown? As for me, a boyar and a member of the Council, I should blush to act like a madman!" Ivan made him leave the room. But that was too mild a disgrace. A few days later, on the parvis of the church where he was going to pray, Repnin fell under the daggers of hired thugs.

In this atmosphere of terror, the most innocent boyars wondered if they did not have something to reproach themselves for. From every side informers were flocking to the palace, eagerly pandering to Ivan's suspicions. He listened to all of them. No denunciation was to be disregarded—the more outrageous the calumny, the more it aroused his curiosity. No sooner was he informed of it than he ordered investigations, sent out spies. A man no longer dared to speak freely among his friends, was careful what he said within the family, and kept silent at public gatherings, with fear in the pit of his stomach. To oblige the monarch, judges no longer required any genuine evidence: Conviction or acquittal no longer depended on facts but on Ivan's whim. Thus it was that for no valid reason, and without any form of trial, Prince Yuri Kashin, a member of the Council of Boyars, was executed with his brother. Prince Kurliatev, a friend of Alexei Adashev's, was first forced to become a monk and then soon after condemned to death with all his family. Prince Mikhail Vorotynsky, the conqueror of Kazan, was exiled with his wife, son, and daughter. The illustrious Ivan Sheremetev, terror of the Tatars of Crimea, was thrown into a dungeon, loaded with chains, and put to torture in the presence of Ivan, who asked him coldly, "Where are your treasures? You were supposed to be rich!" At the Czar's orders the victim's brother, Nikita Sheremetev, another great voivode who had been wounded several times in battle, was strangled.

The prisons and monasteries overflowed with victims. The harder Ivan struck, the more he wanted to strike. The blood that was shed, far from quenching his thirst, whetted his appetite for fresh excesses. To kill his neighbor became a necessary pleasure for him, the sight of suffering a drug he could no longer do without. As a child he had smashed puppies to pieces by throwing them from the top of the palace walls down to the courtyard below. At the age of thirty he improved on the game by applying it to men. As always, he justified his cruelty by the wrongs that had been done him by those around him. "If that dog of an Alexei Adashev, whom I picked out of a dunghill, had not separated me from my little heifer, Saturn would not have had so many victims," he exclaimed. The principle was clear: At the least doubt, one had to strike out vigorously, without wasting time verifying suspicions. Better to cut the throats of ten innocent men than to leave one guilty man alive. And one should not be content to sacrifice the chief suspect. As a matter of sound policy, it was important to excise a wide circle of flesh around the point of infection: Punish the family, the close associates, all those who might have been subject to the pernicious influence of the head of the clan. Make rivers of blood flow to cleanse the body of the state.

To replace those boyars who were guilty of having displeased him, Ivan chose men of the petty nobility with narrow minds and supple backs, men who never contradicted him and who encouraged him in debauchery. Some, like Alexei Basmanov and his son Feodor, as well as Maliuta-Skuratov and Vasily Griaznoy, became both his drinking companions and his political advisers. "What!" they would say to him, "will you weep for your wife eternally? You'll find another just as beautiful. Remember that too much sorrow may endanger your pre-

cious health. God and your people require that for an earthly
woe you also seek earthly consolations." These words indulged
the taste the Czar had always had for women. His wife was hardly
buried before he thought of consoling himself with a fresh bed-
mate. It was not that he had forgotten the gentle Anastasia, but
he could not make up his mind to abstinence. To Ivan, making
love and killing were the two highest expressions of manhood.
Besides, God appeared to agree. In any case, to be on the safe
side, Ivan had distributed a few thousand rubles to the churches
and the poor in memory of Anastasia.

Old Metropolitan Macarius, who by now could hardly stand
on his feet, proclaimed that the Czar should indeed open his bed
to a new Czarina. It was unthinkable that he should oppose the
matrimonial intentions of His Majesty. But whom to choose?
Ivan would not have been displeased with a foreigner. Why not
one of the sisters of the King of Poland? Of course, that country
was theoretically at war with Russia, since Sigismund Augustus
had declared himself the protector of Livonia and had called
upon the Russians to evacuate the occupied territories. But the
two armies had not yet confronted each other. If he had any
judgment at all, Sigismund Augustus would forget his hatred for
the man whom he refused to call "Czar" and in the interest of
concluding a durable peace would deliver to him a young lady
after his heart—beautiful and submissive. Immediately, Ivan put
an end to the mourning at court and sent ambassadors to Poland
with instructions to assess personally the physical and moral
charms of the best candidate.

When the Muscovites reached Vilna, they met the King's
elder sister, Anna, and the younger, Catherine. For reasons of
"face, figure, and health," they chose Catherine. Although Sigismund Augustus was dumbfounded by the effrontery of the proposal, he did not categorically reject it. He merely stated that he
could not consent to the marriage without having obtained the
approval of his protector, Emperor Ferdinand I, adding that if
the marriage did take place his sister would have to remain in

the bosom of the Roman Catholic Church and that in any event, he would prefer to marry off the elder, Anna, before the younger, Catherine. Furthermore, before he would grant his permission, the Polish king insisted on certain border rectifications. Marshal Simkovic was sent to Moscow to inform Ivan of these demands. They were exorbitant: If he wanted to marry a sister of Sigismund Augustus, the Czar must abandon the cities of Novgorod, Pskov, and Smolensk, as well as the territory of Seversk.

Ivan took offense, gave up the idea of becoming the brother-in-law of the intractable Sigismund Augustus, sent Simkovic back, and sighed over the portrait of Catherine that his emissaries had brought him from Poland. Since he could not obtain the hand of this charming girl, he would make war on her country. As a preliminary, he wrote to inform Sigismund Augustus that he had ordered a hole dug in the earth so that he could bury the King's head in it when he had cut it off.

The persons around the Czar tried to soften his disappointment by pointing out that while the Polish ladies doubtless made good wives, they were not the only ones who knew how to please a man in bed. Since he had a taste for the exotic, why not choose a Circassian princess? There was one who was said to be of rare beauty: the daughter of Prince Temriuk. She was brought to Moscow. She appeared at the palace in national costume, and when she raised her veil, Ivan was so dazzled that he decided on the spot to wed her. Metropolitan Macarius baptized her and gave her the name Maria. The wedding was celebrated on August 21, 1561, four days before Ivan's thirty-first birthday. But they were no sooner united than he regretted his choice. Illiterate, spiteful, and uncouth, the little barbarian could not forget her tribe. Her Asiatic upbringing had not prepared her to be the stepmother of the Czar's children. Assuredly, the Polish Catherine would have been a better match.

Now Sigismund Augustus was more determined than ever to occupy dying Livonia. The inhabitants of Reval had given themselves up to the King of Sweden, Eric XIV, who had succeeded his father, Gustavus Vasa. And by an act of November 21, 1561, Kettler, Grand Master of the Order of Knights of the Sword, had ceded Livonia to the King of Poland, becoming his vassal. The King hastened to conclude a matrimonial alliance with Sweden. His sister Catherine, whom he had refused the Czar, was given in marriage to the heir to the Swedish throne, John, Duke of Finland. This fresh insult made Ivan advance the opening of hostilities.

Having exiled or put to death some of his best generals, the Czar replaced them with Circassian and Tatar princes. At their head he set his cousin Vladimir Andreyevich and Andrei Kurbsky, who had so far been spared. A formidable army of 280,000 men, half of whom were Orientals, swept into Lithuania. The Czar rode among these heterogeneous troops, who, in spite of the holy banners, resembled a Mongol horde. He had an empty coffin carried in front of him, which was destined, he said, for Sigismund Augustus.

At the orders of the Polish monarch, his kinsman Nicholas Radziwill set out with 40,000 soldiers mobilized in Minsk and twenty cannon. The disproportion between the two forces was so great that as soon as they made contact with the Russians, the Lithuanians fled. On February 15, 1563, the great commercial city of Polotsk, scarcely defended, fell into Ivan's hands. He wrote Metropolitan Macarius, "Today is fulfilled the prophecy of the holy Metropolitan Peter, who said that Moscow would raise her arm above the shoulders of her enemies"; and he sent Macarius a cross set with diamonds. The booty was immense. Quantities of gold and silver confiscated from the richest citizens were sent on their way to Moscow. The many Jews who lived in Polotsk were baptized by force. Those who resisted were drowned in the Dvina. "The Jews," said Ivan, "turn my subjects away from Christianity and in addition they commit murders with poisonous herbs." The Tatar soldiers also put to death a few Catholic monks; the Latin churches were purified or simply razed. A Te Deum was sung in the Cathedral of St. Sophia in the middle of the conquered city, and Ivan added to his numerous titles that of "Grand Prince of Polotsk." He ironically proposed peace to the King of Poland, on condition that the latter surrender to him all of Livonia and, as a bonus, his sister Catherine. It did not matter, he explained, that she was the wife of the Duke of Finland and that he himself had remarried, for he would keep her as a hostage, maintaining the most profound respect for her person.

Sigismund Augustus did not answer, but while the Russian army continued to ravage the country, even threatening Vilna, he sent a messenger to Devlet-Guirey, Khan of Crimea, advising him to take advantage of the opportunity and throw his Tatars against Moscow, which was left defenseless. The Khan was amused by this proposal made by a Christian king to a Mohammedan, but all things considered, he decided against the adventure. Very fortunately for Sigismund Augustus, Ivan, who was fatigued from the campaign, decided not to press his advantage but to return to Moscow, leaving garrisons in the conquered cities. The belligerents signed a six-month truce. On the way home, the Czar met a beaming messenger: The Circassian Czarina had just given birth to a son, Vasily.

In Moscow the clergy welcomed Ivan with crosses and banners in front of the Church of Sts. Boris and Gleb and the people cheered him, but he had the impression that his subjects' enthusiasm was not so sincere, so warm as after the fall of Kazan some ten years before. In the midst of the victory celebrations he sent a letter to the mother of Prince Vladimir Andreyevich, the ambitious Princess Euphrosyne, to congratulate her on the successes her beloved son had achieved in Lithuania. Then, changing his mind, he obliged the old woman to take the veil, banished her to Belozersk, and had her drowned in White Lake. Had she not once desired a change of dynasty? No one protested. There was talk of a natural death.

For the Czar, other deaths marked this year of 1563. Early

in May he lost his youngest son, Vasily, only a few weeks old. Then it was his own younger brother, Yuri, who succumbed to illness. The simpleminded Yuri had never interfered with Ivan's career, and he had been a faithful friend to Anastasia. His wife, Juliana, was a self-effacing, pious woman whose virtues recalled those of the late Czarina. Ivan was much moved, organized a grandiose funeral for his brother, and arranged luxurious accommodations for his sister-in-law in a convent. Not long afterward, in a fit of fury because she was leading too retired a life and not showing him sufficient gratitude for his benefactions, he was to have her murdered. Another victim of his resentment was Prince Vladimir Andreyevich himself. The brilliant service record of this warrior and adviser could not make Ivan forget the conspiracy of ten years before, when, near death, he had heard the boyars quarreling around his bed over his succession. After a long respite, anger rose up in the Czar again; he accused the Prince of treachery, exiled him to his estate in Staritsa, and surrounded him with spies. The reports he received from them should have reassured him, but he insisted on checking up on the exile in person. From time to time he went to visit Andreyevich on his estate. And there, with strange inconsistency, he became as affectionate as in the old days, feasting and jesting with the man whom he had banished without compunction.

At the close of the year 1563, the sovereign was saddened by one more death, that of the venerable and illustrious Metropolitan Macarius. Too old to oppose the Czar's will or even to rebuke him for the disorder and cruelty of his conduct, Macarius had long contented himself with praying for the future of Russia. Did he sense in Ivan a supernatural force disguised in human shape? Did he wonder whether the Lord's anointed was not, in reality, the Devil's envoy? He had been used to saying, in a quavering voice, "I only know about the affairs of the Church. Don't talk to me about affairs of state!" His death left a great void in Ivan's life. The Czar's last link with the past had broken. When he looked around, he no longer saw anyone who had been a witness to his childhood.

All the bishops of Russia came to Moscow to participate in the election of a new pastor of the Church. It was Athanasius, Abbot of the Chudov Monastery and the Czar's confessor, who was chosen. When the divine service was completed, the prelates removed the sacerdotal garments of the new metropolitan, laid on his breast a gold image of the door of the sanctuary, dressed him in a cassock, and placed a white mitre on his head. Athanasius received the Czar's congratulations, gave him his blessing, and prayed the Almighty to grant Ivan health and victory. In his speech he did not dare mention virtue.

The Czar was grateful for the omission. He could no longer bear having a priest nag him about his conduct. His new spouse, the Circassian Maria, was wild and cruel by nature and applauded all his excesses. She herself, it was said, was sensual, depraved, vindictive, a liar, and something of a witch. The blessings brought by the baptismal water had not penetrated to her soul. Ivan did not love her; he still thought of Anastasia and his regrets increased his rage. For some while now he had taken to carrying with him at all times a long wooden staff with a steel point at its end. This heavy spear had a carved handle that he would caress lovingly with his fingertips while staring at his interlocutor. When seized with anger, he would strike people with it. Often he was content to wound them and, with quiet pleasure, watch the blood flow. Sometimes he killed them. According to his contemporary Daniel Printz von Bruchau, he was so violent that he "foamed at the mouth like a horse." After each of his crimes Ivan would hurry to confession. He would even accuse himself publicly before the boyars, calling himself "stinking cur," "damned soul," and "assassin." But coming from him, these words of repentance were more frightening than threats. The persons who were close to him knew that he was merely going through an exercise good for his mental health and that by humiliating himself he was getting ready to start all over again. He was like a man who habitually overeats and, having stuffed himself with an undigested meal, sticks two fingers down his throat, vomits to empty his stomach, and returns to the table with renewed appetite. If he crouched in mortification, it was only because he was preparing to spring upon the next victim. Woe to any man who had heard the Czar humble himself before him!

It was at about this time that some of the common folk were already beginning to call him "Ivan the Terrible."*

---

*In Russian the word *grozny*, which is used to designate Ivan IV, does not mean "terrible," exactly, but rather "threatening" or "dread" or "formidable"—with a connotation of power and majesty. Yet it is as Ivan the Terrible that he is known in English . . . and in truth, the name is fitting enough.

IX

The Kurbsky Affair

The Czar's senseless rages were such that some of the boyars, fearing for their lives, were driven to seek refuge abroad. Thus, the very pious Prince Dimitri Vishnevetsky refused to expose himself to the whims of a tyrant and fled to Poland. Sigismund Augustus received him kindly but demanded that he serve in the Lithuanian army against the Russians, his erstwhile comrades in arms. As a man of honor, Vishnevetsky refused. He was turned over to the Sultan of Turkey, who had him beheaded.

Other, less scrupulous boyars found safety and profit in exile. A great number of Russians betrayed Ivan and made their way to the court of Sigismund Augustus. The most famous of them was Andrei Kurbsky. A descendant of the reigning family of Vladimir Monomakh, Prince of Smolensk and Yaroslavl, he had distinguished himself in battle at Tula and Kazan, in the deserts of the Bashkirs, and in Livonia. But in 1562, after an ill-advised maneuver, his army, 40,000 strong, was crushed at Nevel, near Vitebsk, by 15,000 Poles. Ivan was angry with him for this humiliating defeat. Kurbsky, in disgrace, became convinced that his life was in danger. And while he was willing to die in combat, he could not bear the idea of execution. Having embraced his wife and his nine-year-old son, he slipped out of his house under cover of darkness, left Dorpat without being seen, and rode to Volmar, a town occupied by the Poles. Welcomed by Sigismund Augustus with open arms, he was given villages, lands, and money and accepted without qualms the command of the Polish troops who were to fight the Russians. At the time it was not unusual for a man to change sides in this way, because the notion of patriotism had not yet become sacred. Nevertheless, Andrei Kurbsky's disloyalty was as revolting to Ivan as if the man had spat in the face of Christ. To crown all, once he had reached safety the turncoat had the audacity to write to the Czar to justify his conduct. Educated, devout, and full of hate, he dipped his pen in vinegar. His equerry, Shibanov, was instructed to deliver the letter to the Czar in Moscow.

When Ivan received the messenger, he drove the iron point of his staff through the unfortunate man's foot, nailing him to the ground. Then, leaning on the handle of the spear with both hands, he fixed his eyes on the face of the servitor, whose blood was flowing on the floor but who stood with clenched teeth, not uttering a cry. A clerk read the letter aloud in a shaky voice: "Monarch who was once illustrious and blessed by the Lord, but who now, as a punishment for our sins, is consumed by an infernal fury, corrupt to the depths of his conscience; tyrant for whom the most faithless sovereigns in the world provide no precedent, hear me! . . . Why have you destroyed amid terrible torments the strong men of Israel, the illustrious warriors whom heaven had given you? Why have you shed their precious, sacred blood in the temples of the Almighty? Were they not burning with zeal for their sovereign, for their motherland? Cunningly inventing calumnies, you call the faithful traitors, you call Christians sorcerors; in your eyes virtues are vices, light is only darkness; and wherein had these worthy protectors of Russia offended you? Are they not the heroes who destroyed the realm of the Tatars? Have they not covered your reign and your name with glory by bringing down before you the German fortresses? What is the reward of these unfortunates? Death! What! do you think yourself immortal? Is there not a God and a supreme tribunal for kings? In the disorder of my heart I cannot express all the evil you have done me. I will say only one thing: You have forced me to abandon holy Russia. My blood that I have shed for you cries out for vengeance to the Almighty, who reads in the depths of hearts. I have tried to discover what I can have been guilty of, either in my actions or in my most secret thoughts; I have scrupulously examined my conscience and I do not know what crime I have committed against you. Never, under my leadership, have your battalions turned their backs to the enemy. My glory has been reflected upon you. I served you not for just one or two years filled with hardships and deeds of war, but for a great many years, suffering privation and illness, far from my mother, my wife, my country. Count my battles and my wounds. I do not wish to boast of them, but God knows all. It is in Him I trust, full of hope in the intercession of the saints and of my ancestor, Prince Feodor of Yaroslavl. . . . Farewell! We are now separated forever and you will not see me again until the day of the Last Judgment; but the tears of the innocent victims are preparing terrible punishment for the tyrant. Fear the very dead! Those whom you have massacred are nigh the throne of the Almighty and ask for vengeance. Your armies will not save you. Vile flatterers, those ignoble boyars who are now the companions of your feasts and your debauchery, the corruptors of your soul, bring you their children to satisfy your lewd appetites; but they will not make you immortal. May this letter, stained with my tears, be placed in my grave, so that I may appear with it at the Judgment of God.

"Written in the city of Volmar, in the domain of King Sigismund Augustus, my sovereign, from whom, with the grace of God, I hope for favor and consolation."

Having listened to the reading of the letter with a face of stone, Ivan ordered the messenger taken away and put to torture to obtain further information from him. Under the red-hot pincers, Shibanov revealed the names of no accomplices and continued to praise his master. The Czar admired the victim's fortitude but had him put to death, along with a few of Kurbsky's servants who were suspected of having helped him to escape. The traitor's mother, wife, and son were thrown into prison, where they died a few years later.*

Ivan's long-contained wrath burst out in the answer he made to the missive from his former general. Fond of fiery discourse, he mingled in his indictment insults, mockery, accusations, solemn oaths, and fake biblical quotations. His hatred and his learning, his piety and his cruelty all spilled onto the paper in a river of words. He spoke of Moses, Leo V the Armenian, John Chrysostom, and Isaiah. Clearly this epistle, like Andrei Kurbsky's, was not intended only for the addressee. Its contents would be widely circulated in court and among the people. It was an open letter, testimony offered for the judges of posterity. Across the borders a literary duel began between the autocratic czar and the prince who had betrayed him.

"Why, unfortunate wretch, do you want to sell your soul like a traitor by fleeing to save a perishable body?" Ivan wrote. "If you are truly just and virtuous, why were you not willing to

---

*Kurbsky himself died in 1583 in Poland, where he was to be remembered as a cruel, brutal, and ungrateful man.

die at your master's orders and thus win the crown of a martyr?
. . . The conduct of your servant Shibanov should make you
ashamed. . . . Faithful to his oath, he did not betray his master
even at the gates of death. And you, for a single word I breathed
in anger, bring down the curse due to traitors not only upon
yourself but also upon the souls of your ancestors, who once
swore to my illustrious grandfather that they would serve us
faithfully, not only they themselves but also their descendants.
The venom of the asp is in the mouth of him who is forsworn.
. . . You complain of the persecutions I have inflicted upon you,
but you would not be with our enemy now if I had not been too
merciful toward you all, ungrateful as you are."

Further on, to show how shamefully Kurbsky had conducted himself, Ivan reminded the brilliant general of all the
occasions when he had failed to live up to his reputation: When
the Khan had been beaten at Tula, the Prince had celebrated the
victory instead of pursuing the fleeing enemy; under the walls
of Kazan when the storm had dispersed the ships and swallowed
up the munitions, his only thought had been to flee "like a
coward"; when the Russian troops had taken Astrakhan, he had
not participated in the battle; when the time had come to conquer Pskov, he had feigned illness. "But for your insubordination, Adashev's and yours," wrote Ivan, "Livonia would be in
our power. You conquered in spite of yourselves, acting like
slaves, only under compulsion."

Then the Czar came to the justification of his own crimes
against humanity. According to Ivan, a sovereign was not answerable to anyone. He had divine impunity: "What you say
about my alleged cruelties is an impudent lie. I do not put to
death the strong men of Israel; I do not shed their blood upon
the peoples of the Lord. . . . I deal severely only with traitors.
But in what place are traitors spared? . . . I have inflicted many
punishments, and that painful duty has rent my heart. Yet everyone knows that the number of betrayals has only increased.
. . . *Until now, the sovereigns of Russia have been free and independent.*

They have rewarded or punished their subjects as they have seen fit, without being answerable to anyone. Never will this change. I am no longer a child: I need the grace of God, the protection of the Virgin Mary and of all the saints, but *I ask no instruction from men.* Thanks to the Almighty, Russia is prosperous; my boyars live in peace and friendship; your friends, your advisers are the only ones plotting in the shadows. You threaten me with the judgment of Christ in the other world. Do you think, then, that divine power does not also govern this world? That is a Manichean heresy! According to you, God reigns in heaven, Satan in hell, and men on earth. Error! Lie! The power of the Lord reaches everywhere, in this life and in the next. You announce to me that I shall never see your black face again! Oh heavens! What a misfortune for me! . . . You surround the throne of the Almighty with those whom I have put to death. Another heresy! No one, says the apostle, can see God. . . . To crown your treachery, you claim that Volmar, a city in Livonia, belongs to King Sigismund, and you await the effects of that prince's favor, after having abandoned your legitimate sovereign, the master whom God had given you. . . . Your great king is the slave of slaves. Is it surprising, then, that he should be praised by slaves? But I shall say no more, for Solomon forbids us to waste words on fools, and you are one."

Kurbsky replied contemptuously that the Czar demeaned himself by stooping to the lies and insults with which his letter was crammed: "You should be ashamed to write like an old woman, to send so badly written an epistle to a country where there is no lack of people who know grammar, rhetoric, dialectics, and philosophy. . . . I am innocent and I groan in exile. . . . Let us wait, the time of truth is not far off."

In another letter from the Czar to Kurbsky, he called him a "cowardly deserter": "I know my iniquities, but the divine mercy is infinite; it is that which will save me. . . . I do not boast of my glory. That glory belongs not to me but to God alone. . . . how, then, have I been guilty toward you, friends of Adashev and Sylvester? Is it not you yourselves who, taking from me a beloved wife, have become the true causes of my human weaknesses? It becomes you well to talk about the cruelty of your sovereign, you who wanted to take away his throne and his life! . . . This Prince Vladimir Andreyevich, whom you so love, did he have some right to the crown by reason of his birth or his personal qualities? . . . Look with wonder upon Providence! Turn in upon yourself, reflect upon your actions. It is not pride that prompts me to write to you, but Christian charity, so that this remembrance may serve to mend your ways and that you may save your soul."

This absurd exchange of correspondence was to continue, with long interruptions, from 1564 to 1579. In each successive letter the two writers laid out the same arguments and the same recriminations. Kurbsky, the illustrious representative of the boyars, considered that aristocratic caste as having been chosen by God to advise the Czar. Apart from this oligarchy surrounding the throne, there could be no salvation for Russia. By exterminating the friends of Alexei Adashev and Sylvester, who had always given him wise counsel, Ivan had exceeded the rights of the sovereign and asserted a criminal despotism from which the country would never recover. Ivan, for his part, declared that his mission was divine, refused to recognize the essential role of the boyars of the Rada, and held himself responsible only to God: "All the Russian sovereigns are autocrats and no one can find fault with them," he decreed. "The monarch can exercise his will over the slaves whom God has given him. . . . If you do not obey the sovereign when he commits an injustice, not only do you become guilty of felony* but you damn your soul, for God himself orders you to obey your prince blindly." In short, the czar, the elect of God, had unlimited power, which it was blasphemous to rebel against or even to criticize. His most senseless, cruel, iniquitous decisions were to be respected by his subjects as emanating, through him, from God—who had placed

---

*In the feudal sense: a vassal's violation of his oath of fealty to his lord. (Trans.)

him on the throne. To revolt against the sovereign was to commit not a political crime but a mortal sin against the Almighty. Writing to the "elected" and not "hereditary" King of Poland, the Czar signed his letter: "We, humble Ivan, Czar and Grand Prince of all the Russians by the grace of God, and not by the restless will of men."

In the meantime, Andrei Kurbsky had become the intimate adviser of Sigismund Augustus. So bitter was his hatred for the Czar that he pushed his new protector to tighten his alliance with the Tatars. Kurbsky was not greatly troubled by the thought that the infidels, thus encouraged, might invade his native land and profane the churches in which he had been used to praying. He was guided by a single hope: that a Russian defeat would incite some boyar to assassinate Ivan, thus ridding the country of the tyrant and making it possible for the defectors to return with heads held high.

At last the Khan of Crimea, Devlet-Guirey, went on campaign and laid siege to Ryazan. The city heroically resisted his assaults, and the boyars Alexei and Feodor Basmanov, who had come to the rescue with fresh troops, hastened the rout of the Tatars. Danger had scarcely been warded off in the south, however, when it appeared again in the west. A joint Polish-Lithuanian army, commanded by Radziwill and Kurbsky, sought to recapture Polotsk, a city recently conquered by the Russians. This attempt likewise ended in failure.

Ivan should have rejoiced over the double victory of his voivodes. And to be sure, he sent gold medals to his brave captains. But ever since Kurbsky's betrayal he had been prey to a vague fear that grew more pronounced from month to month. Despite the execution or exile of the chief friends of Adashev and Sylvester, he had the feeling that he was the object of a dark conspiracy. He anxiously scrutinized the faces of his boyars. If they spoke volubly, they were lying to him. If they said nothing, they were plotting some treachery against him. He hoped for fresh denunciations and complained that he did not receive

enough of them. Metropolitan Athanasius had neither the energy nor the authority required to admonish and comfort him.
The current favorites—Alexei Basmanov, Mikhail Saltykov,
Athanasius Viazemsky, Ivan Shibotovy—thought only of encouraging his mistrust, cruelty, and lechery.

Suddenly, early in the winter of 1564, Ivan decided to leave
his capital to wander aimlessly, without a fixed destination, leaving it to God to choose his route. On December 3, a great
number of sleighs were assembled on the snow-covered Kremlin square. Palace servants loaded them with chests full of gold
and silver together with icons, crosses, precious vases, dishes,
clothes, furs. Ivan was not simply leaving on a trip, he was
moving out. In the Cathedral of the Assumption, in the presence
of the dumbfounded boyars, Metropolitan Athanasius blessed
the Czar for a journey to a destination unknown to any of them.
Ivan, the Czarina, and his two sons, aged ten and seven, climbed
into the first sleigh. The court secretaries, high functionaries,
favorites, and a number of servants likewise installed themselves
in the vehicles and wrapped themselves up against the cold. The
common people who had gathered in the square asked each
other, "Where is the Czar going? Why is he abandoning us? And
for how long?" Finally, the endless column began to move off,
leaving in its wake a frightened crowd. A thaw obliged Ivan to
stop for two weeks in the village of Kolomenskoye. Then, as
soon as road conditions permitted, he proceeded to the Monastery of the Holy Trinity. On Christmas Eve, he arrived with his
retinue and baggage in Alexandrovskaya Sloboda, north of
Vladimir.

For thirty days the boyars of the Duma, who had stayed in
Moscow, received no news of their sovereign, who had left town
without leaving a forwarding address. At last, on January 3,
1565, the officer Konstantin Polivanov brought Metropolitan
Athanasius two letters from Ivan. In the first the Czar listed the
disorders, betrayals, and crimes of the service nobility, high
functionaries, and generals, all of whom had looted the Trea-

sury, mistreated the peasants, and refused to defend the nation's soil against the Tatar, Polish, and German enemies. "And when," he continued, "guided by a sense of justice, I show my resentment to these unworthy servants, the Metropolitan and the clergy come to the defense of the guilty, to displease us and importune us. Therefore, with a heart filled with sorrow, no longer wishing to endure your perfidies, we have given up governing the country and have left to settle in whatever place God may lead us to."

The second letter was addressed to the "foreign and Russian merchants and all the Christian people of Moscow." In it the Czar stated that while he "laid his wrath" on the boyars, churchmen, and high functionaries, he felt paternal benevolence toward the common people of his empire. His Majesty's secretaries read this missive aloud in the public square before a crowd in consternation. No more czar! Was it possible? Wasn't tyranny better than chaos? Shouts rose from the multitude: "The Czar has abandoned us! We are lost! How can the sheep remain without a shepherd?" Then very quickly the people's distress turned to rage. If the Czar had stepped down from his throne, it was the fault of the nobles, who had betrayed him. Shops were closed, houses were emptied, a surging mass of demonstrators swept spontaneously toward the Kremlin, screaming with despair and demanding that the guilty be punished. Terrified by the echoes of the riot, Metropolitan Athanasius held an emergency meeting with the clergy and the boyars. "The state cannot remain without a master," they decided. "We will prostrate ourselves before him with our faces on the ground. We will move him by our tears."

A delegation made up of princes, bishops, officers, and merchants, and headed by Archbishop Pimen of Novgorod, left at once for Alexandrovskaya Sloboda. The long procession, whipped by the wind, straggled over the snowy track in an extraordinary assemblage of sacerdotal garments, brocade robes, pelisses, banners, censers, and crosses. They were not deputies going to visit their leader but pilgrims making their way toward a miraculous icon. They reached their destination two days later, on January 5, 1565. The Czar received them with an angry and distant mien. After having blessed him, Archbishop Pimen said with tears in his eyes, "Do not forget that you are not only the guardian of the state but also the guardian of the Church, the first monarch of the Orthodox world. If you go away, who will preserve the truth and purity of our faith? Who will save millions of souls from damnation?"

Thus, by the clergy's own admission, the Czar's power extended not only over the perishable bodies of his subjects but also over their eternal souls. He reigned on earth and in heaven. The Church resigned in the face of his power. All of them, prelates and boyars, had knelt before him; he alone was left standing, the iron-pointed spear in his hand. He enjoyed his victory to the full; the trick of the sudden departure had been a complete success. Frightened at the idea of losing their master, the great men of the empire were crawling at his feet. Once again he had risked everything in front of cowards. If they had taken him at his word, at this moment he would no longer be anything but an abdicated sovereign. But by abasing themselves before him they strengthened him, they raised him up. In a ringing voice Ivan addressed the ambassadors of repentance, speaking, as usual, eloquently and at length.

He rebuked them for their spirit of revolt, their greed, their cowardice, and even claimed—a new complaint, this—that they had tried to murder him, together with his wife and eldest son. Although they were struck by the enormity of this accusation, not one of the boyars present dared protest. Better to be blamed unjustly than to displease the monarch by denying his facts. While he was speaking vehemently, with glittering eyes, each of them felt the threat of increased tyranny weighing upon him. Then, at last, Ivan revealed his true intentions: "Out of regard for Metropolitan Athanasius, out of consideration for you, venerable archbishops and bishops, I am willing to consent to resume my scepter under certain conditions." These conditions were simple: Henceforth, the Czar would be entirely free to punish traitors by disgrace, death, or the confiscation of their property, without having to put up with any criticisms from the clergy. Obviously this arrangement stripped the Church of its ancestral right to intercede on behalf of the innocent and of guilty persons deserving of clemency. But the delegates were so happy to have overcome the Czar's alleged repugnance to ascend the throne again that they thanked him with sobbing voices. Satisfied by their humility, he invited some of them to celebrate the feast of Epiphany with him in Alexandrovskaya Sloboda. Notwithstanding the people's impatience, he was in no hurry to return to Moscow. The longer he made them wait, the more demanding he could be.

X

The Oprichniki

On February 2, 1565, Ivan made his entrance into a Moscow buried in snow. A huge crowd of people who had been gathering since dawn fell to their knees and wept as he passed, thanking heaven for having returned their sovereign to them. But those who humbly raised their eyes to him were struck by his gloomy, haggard look. According to all witnesses, the thirty-four-year-old Czar had the appearance of an old man. His face was gray and wrinkled, his eyes were dull, his hair scanty, his lips thin and clenched, his forehead deeply furrowed. As he was in the habit of tearing out his beard in fits of anger and despair, he had only a few hairs left on his chin. He was stoop-shouldered and hollow-chested, and as his eyes wandered over the crowd they held a demented look. Did he even see the people who were cheering him? Did he hear the church bells in full peal overhead? He was so accustomed to being praised, flattered, worshiped, that he could no longer take pleasure in any demonstration of enthusiasm.

When Ivan arrived at the palace he told the assembled boyars that he no longer wanted to live within the walls of the Kremlin, near the remains of his ancestors, and that a vast fortified residence must be built for him without delay in the middle of the city. Then, after having once again enumerated his grievances against the nobility, he demanded that the Church confirm in advance its absolute approval for all measures he would see fit to take against traitors. Since it was their fault that he had had to undertake the journey, he would receive a sum of one hundred thousand rubles for travel expenses and the cost of his stay in Alexandrovskaya Sloboda. In addition, the country would be divided into two parts: the *oprichnina*, constituting the Czar's private domain, which he would administer as he pleased and over which he would have total power, and the *zemshchina*, comprising the rest of the territory, which would also be placed under the sovereign's power but would keep its Duma of boyars and its former functionaries.* By unilateral decision of His Majesty, the *oprichnina*, Ivan's personal property, a sort of state within the state, would include several quarters of Moscow, twenty-seven cities, eighteen districts, and the major communication routes. This gigantic expropriation operation would be carried out under the supervision of a new militia chosen by the monarch and devoted to his orders: the *oprichniki*.

When the plan was set forth, the boyars realized that by

---

*Oprichnina, a word popularized by the Czar, comes from *oprich* (separate or apart) and, according to S. and E. Milioukov, originally designated "a special military organization separate from the general Russian organization and maintained by the revenues from a detached territory." *Zemshchina*, from *zemlya* (land), means the country, all the communes taken as a whole.

confiscating their villages, peasants, and property the Czar meant to break their power permanently. But they could no longer rebel against the man whom they had begged to return and in whom the people placed a fanatical confidence. On pain of being thrown into prison for insubordination, they had to abandon their hereditary domains, which would become fiefs of the crown. The right to exploit these lands—not to own them —would be given as a reward to *oprichniki*, but only conditionally and only for their lifetimes. As for the former owners, they would receive in exchange a few poor and distant lands belonging to the *zemshchina*. Thus began a vast movement of "sorting out" and exile, ruining all the old families of appanaged princes and driving their representatives to the far confines of the Russian state. Twelve thousand aristocratic families were deported to remote regions and thus stripped of their fortunes and influence. Wrenched from the soil which had been theirs for centuries, cut off from their roots, deprived of their dependents, these nobles newly transplanted by administrative decision became men without a past, without support, without defense. In short, the formation of the *oprichnina* in 1565 was only a sudden extension of the program for bringing the nobility to heel that had been initiated by Ivan and his advisers as far back as 1550. By this redistribution of wealth and power throughout Russia, he hoped to consolidate his throne forever.

In place of the arrogant boyars, proud of their birth, Ivan was establishing a new nobility consisting of paid servants. A privileged class was to arise, the *oprichniki*, closely tied to the Czar and assured of impunity for all the crimes they would commit in his name. Among the *oprichniki* the right of precedence would disappear; all that would count was devotion to the central cause. The few princes of high birth who belonged to this Praetorian Guard were submerged in the mass of new men who came from modest families and owed their rise to Ivan alone. The others, those who were dispossessed, left their homes in the middle of winter and traveled in slow caravans to the places of residence that had been assigned to them. Some died of cold along the way. No matter—Ivan was not concerned with the tears and sighs that accompanied this necessary upheaval. As a first stage he had chosen from among the young men of the petty nobility 1,000 *oprichniki* to make up his personal guard and to unmask traitors. Soon they would number 6,000. Maliuta-Skuratov, Viazemsky, and Basmanov, the Czar's favorites, saw to it that all the members of this militia were men known for the crudeness and cruelty of their ways. The "chosen legionnaires" took an oath of allegiance to Ivan: "I swear to be loyal to the Czar and to his empire, to the young Czarevich and the Czarina, and to reveal everything that I know or can find out about any enterprise directed against them by any person or persons. I swear to deny my family and to forget my father and mother. I also swear not to eat or drink with the people of the *zemshchina* and never to have any relations with them. In witness whereof, I kiss the cross."

The *oprichniki* lived apart in houses allotted to them and received a substantial income. Poor men the day before, overnight they became lords vested with immense power. They dressed in black and bore on their saddles a dog's head and a broom, the symbols of their mission, which was to hunt down their master's enemies and sweep them away. Their function placed them above the law. To insult one of them was to commit an act of treason punishable by death. The *zemshchina* was their field of operations. There they could impose fines, torture the men, rape the women, put out the eyes of the children, loot the houses, burn the forests and the harvests without anyone's having anything to say about it. The Czar encouraged their violence, and after each of their high deeds rewarded them with property taken from traitors. "The more the people detested them, the more confidence the sovereign showed in them,"[1] wrote Taube and Kruse, two Livonian German noblemen, in their *Memoirs.* And indeed, Ivan was reassured by the hatred his *oprichniki* aroused in the country. If they were so feared and loathed, it was because they were faithful to him. In a way, he had become incarnated in them: 6,000 little Ivans who extorted money and bled the people in his stead. What he dreamed of in his palace, they executed with their hands in Moscow and in the provinces.

On February 4, the very day on which he instituted the *oprichnina,* the executions began. They took place in the great square of the Kremlin next to the Church of the Intercession of the Virgin (today's Cathedral of Basil the Blessed), which had just been completed and whose elaborate colored domes glittered gaily in the winter sun. Among the first victims were the illustrious Prince Alexander Shuisky, hero of the fall of Kazan, and his seventeen-year-old son, Peter. Both were accused of having conspired with Andrei Kurbsky against the life of the monarch, the Czarina, and their children. The son was to be beheaded first, but the father asked the favor of dying before him. The executioner made no objection and Alexander Shuisky placed his head on the block. The ax fell. The son picked up his father's head, kissed it tenderly and kneeled in turn to receive the blow. Six other boyars were decapitated the same day. A seventh, Prince Dimitri Shevirev, was impaled. It took him twenty-four hours to die; during this time, the lower part of his body pierced, and his face twisted with pain, he sang hymns to the glory of God. Other boyars escaped the ax and were merely locked up in monasteries or exiled afar. For some of them Ivan demanded 25,000 rubles in bail, so as to be sure they would not leave the country. Finally, wanting to manifest that he was able to pardon as well as punish, he recalled to Moscow the boyars Mikhail Vorotynsky, exiled to Belozersk, and Yakovlev, a close relative of Anastasia. This act of clemency was celebrated by the clergy as a boon from heaven.

Meanwhile, the more Ivan oppressed the country, the more he felt he was hated; and the more he felt hated, the more fiercely determined he was to discover those who were plotting against his life. A morbid anxiety prevented him from sleeping.

If he heard a clock strike at night, he was seized with terror as at an evil omen. If he saw a shooting star in the sky, he fell to his knees and trembled before his icons. The new fortified castle he had had built in Moscow no longer seemed a safe refuge from his enemies. Taking an aversion to his capital, he moved to Alexandrovskaya Sloboda, to a palace surrounded by moats and ramparts. The interior decor of this sinister structure reflected four different aspects of the sovereign's personality. Some of the rooms were superbly decorated; others were crammed with precious books and parchments; still others, with low-vaulted ceilings, were of monastic bareness; lastly, others underground were divided into a series of dungeons, where prisoners rotted. Thus, the Czar's favorite residence combined splendor, study, prayer, and torture. In each of these compartments he felt at ease. The officials of his court occupied separate houses. Whole streets of the little town were set aside for the *oprichniki*. Alexandrovskaya Sloboda, buried in the depths of dark forests, swarmed with armed men; houses and churches were built in haste; merchants streamed in, attracted by the rich customers. In the Church of the Mother of God, Ivan had relics installed and the altar decorated with gold, silver, and precious stones. At his orders a cross was engraved on every brick in the building.

But this demonstration of piety was not enough to give the Czar an easy conscience. Abruptly, he decided to transform his palace into a monastery and his *oprichniki* into monks. Choosing three hundred from among the most depraved, he granted them the name "brother." He gave himself the title of abbot, while Prince Athanasius Viazemsky became treasurer and Maliuta-Skuratov sacristan. Each brother wore a black cassock over his gold-embroidered coat trimmed with marten. What might have been only a masquerade took on, in Ivan's mind, the value of an homage paid to God. He sincerely believed he had created a new monastic order. He drew up its rules and saw to it that they were observed.

At three o'clock in the morning, Ivan would go with his sons to the belfry to ring matins. All the brothers would immediately hurry to the palace church. Anyone who failed in this duty was punished with a week in prison. During the service, which lasted a good three or four hours, the Czar would sing, pray, and prostrate himself, striking his forehead against the paving stones. Now he wore a long black robe tied at the waist with a friar's girdle, a frock of sackcloth, and a wooden cross on his breast. Sometimes he would replace his spear with a crook. At eight o'clock, all would gather again to hear mass, and at ten they sat down to a copious repast that the Czar did not touch. Standing in the presence of his brothers, he would read aloud to them from a religious text. Then he would take his midday meal apart, alone, listening to the reports of his favorites. After a short nap, he liked to visit the dungeons to witness the torture of a few prisoners.

Ivan knew all there was to know about the various instruments, from the knout to the stake, from the needles to the pincers, from the burning coals to the rope that could saw a body in two. He had a connoisseur's appreciation for the skill of the torturers and the endurance of the sufferers. Coming away from mass, his head still filled with angelic music, he enjoyed the contrasting pleasure that came from following the slow death of his victims. The spurts of blood, the cracking of bones, the screams and rattles of drooling mouths—this rough cookery smelling of pus, excrement, sweat, and burnt flesh was pleasing to his nostrils. In some strange way, every time one of the human rags breathed his last, Ivan felt the delights of sexual climax. He took such joy in the bloodbath that he had no doubt, in these moments of horror and ecstasy, that the Lord was at his side. The habit he had acquired of identifying himself with God was enough to persuade him that the holocaust was as pleasing to heaven as to himself. To him, prayer and torture were but two aspects of piety. According to witnesses, he would leave the chambers of suffering only reluctantly, his countenance "beaming with contentment." Thereafter, he would jest with those around him and talk "more cheerfully than usual." It was the relaxation after nervous tension, the rest after lovemaking.

At eight o'clock in the evening, the Czar-abbot would go with all his people to vespers. Afterward, their dinner together generally turned into a drinking bout. They would eat until ready to burst: pikes' heads with garlic, hares in sunflower-seed oil, kidneys with ginger, chickens with pepper, all washed down with mead, wine, *kvas,* and vodka. Before each dish or drink was presented to the Czar, it was tasted by one of his companions, as insurance against poisoning. Tumblers enlivened the meals with their performances. Trained bears were displayed. Some evenings, the false monks would bring women of humble station and amuse themselves undressing them, whipping them, raping them in front of the Czar. Maliuta-Skuratov, the most cruel and debauched of the brotherhood, would force naked peasant girls, with hair flying and breasts swaying, to chase after hens while the *oprichniki* shot arrows at the terrified, screaming victims.

After these orgies Ivan would retire to his room, where he was awaited by three blind old men. Their task was to take turns recounting legends to him until he fell asleep. Stretched out on his bed, in the room dimly lit by the lamps in front of the icons, he would listen with delight to the stories of paladins, sorcerors, and far-off princesses. The storyteller, with his long beard and empty eyes, would talk quietly. His monotonous voice would make the Czar drowsy, make him think he was a child again. Finding momentary solace, Ivan would close his eyes. He did not sleep long. At midnight he would go to the church to pray again. Lifting up his soul, he would hear God whispering in his ear the names of new victims to sacrifice. It was on his knees, between two prayers, that he would give his bloodiest orders. Just as for deep-sea divers there is an intoxication of the depths, so for monarchs by divine right there in an intoxication of absolute power. In some, it is not serious; in others, like Ivan, it leads to delirium.

Rumors of this strange life quickly spread abroad, and Sigismund Augustus concluded from them that the Czar had gone mad. Was this the beginning of Russia's downfall? The

King of Poland ardently hoped so, and he asked the Russian ambassador to Warsaw to tell him precisely what the *oprichnina* was. Following the orders he had been given, the diplomat replied categorically, "We don't know what you mean. There is no *oprichnina*. The Czar lives in the residence he has been pleased to choose, and those of his servants who have given him satisfaction are with him; the others are a little farther off. That's all! If ignorant peasants talk about an *oprichnina*, you should take no account of their words." But every day more fugitives from Ivan's tyranny arrived in Poland. Their accounts confirmed Sigismund Augustus's impressions.

Through secret messengers the Polish king corresponded with a few boyars in the *zemshchina* who had been robbed of their lands. They scarcely dared reply. Exiled, their goods expropriated, they lived in fear of the morrow. The Church also was silent, gagged. Metropolitan Athanasius, having promised in advance not to criticize the Czar's actions or intervene on behalf of his victims, was no longer a spiritual leader but merely a distinguished officiant. By placing Ivan above the Church he had mocked the Scriptures and merged the things that were Caesar's with the things that were God's. Although the Metropolitan was informed of all the crimes committed by the *oprichniki,* he never raised his voice on behalf of the innocent sufferers. By the same token, he never protested against the establishment in Alexandrovskaya Sloboda of the caricature of a monastery, with its frocked fornicators, bloody masses, and orgies.

Around the Czar there was nothing but weakness and cowardice. His taste for theological discussions brought him closer to Protestantism. Questioning German prisoners from Livonia, he was greatly taken with the freedom of their religious thinking. He took into his service the Germans Kalb, Taube, Kruse, and Eberfeld.* The latter demonstrated to him, in conversation and

---

*The memoirists Taube and Druse, who were close to Ivan for a time, were to betray him and enter the service of Poland.

in writing, the purity of the doctrines of the Augsburg Confession. The Czar was apparently shaken; he wondered if the Orthodox religion was indeed the one that suited Russia. A mad idea crossed his mind: What if, with a stroke of the pen, he were to convert his country to Protestantism? He soon gave up the notion, frightened by his own audacity, but he gave the Lutherans permission to open a church in Moscow. Metropolitan Athansius was appalled by this decision. He allowed himself to raise his voice in the presence of one of the heretical foreigners. Ivan immediately condemned him to a large fine. The Metropolitan fell ill over the incident and withdrew to a monastery.

But the Czar's infatuation with German craftsmen and thinkers was as nothing to his infatuation with English merchants. The daring Anthony Jenkinson, who was negotiator, businessman, and explorer all at once, traveled across Russia, visiting Astrakhan, Bokhara, and even Persia. Braving a thousand dangers, he returned to Moscow, recounted his journeys to Ivan, brought him presents from the Sultan and shahs, and drew a map for him of the countries he had traversed. Captivated by this man of many talents, Ivan treated him like a friend, granted his company an extension of the monopoly, even authorized him to mint money and placed him and the merchants of his group under the direct protection of the *oprichniki*. From then on, Russia exported to England fish, salt, furs, skins, tar, wood for the shipyards, hemp, flax, tallow, and wax, and imported from England (at high prices) silk, dishes, copper, lead, spices, arms, and ammunition. This double current of commercial exchange was so powerful that Ivan came increasingly to think of England as a natural ally of Russia.

During one of his nocturnal terrors, another idea came to the Czar. Always obsessed with the notion of a conspiracy against his person, he thought of asking for asylum in England in case he should have to flee for his life. This humiliating request from the master of Russia seemed to him a divine inspiration. In 1567, he instructed Jenkinson to carry a secret message to Queen Elizabeth I. The Queen, who had succeeded her half sister Mary, was reported to be a beautiful, intelligent woman, cultivated and strong-willed. Her relations with Ivan had always been extremely courteous. She was thirty-four years old and not married. He was thirty-seven and his wife, the Circassian, had long since ceased to please him. Why not repudiate her and marry the Queen of England? Jenkinson was ordered to submit to Her Majesty this second proposal. In short, Ivan presented himself to her simultaneously as a possible political refugee and a definite suitor, asking for her hand today and her potential protection tomorrow. To be sure, he was aware that she had already shown the door to innumerable marriage candidates. But, he thought, none of them could match the Czar in political power. If she were forced to answer yes or no, she could not refuse.

Jenkinson left for London to plead these two preposterous causes. As soon as he arrived, he had a long private conversation with his sovereign. The stakes were high. As an essentially commercial nation, England could not allow herself to disappoint the Czar, who had granted her merchants so many privileges—especially since the representatives of other states were pressing him to abolish the favored treatment he had given the island nation. On the other hand, Elizabeth had no intention of marrying. Always the prudent businesswoman, she played for time. What she did not realize was how impetuous her new suitor was. Receiving no answer to his advances, Ivan became angry and opened the port of Narva to other foreigners. The Company grew anxious and turned to the Queen. Since Jenkinson himself was unable to return to Russia at the moment, she immediately sent as her ambassador Thomas Randolph, Master of the Queen's Posts.

The new envoy landed in St. Nicholas on the White Sea and reached Moscow, by way of Kholmogory and Vologda, in October 1568. His mission was to "re-establish order in British trade" by assuring the Czar of the right of asylum but avoiding, if possible, the question of marriage. So far as the promise of sanctuary was concerned, Ivan posed as a condition that it be made reciprocal. In other words, since honor forbade him to receive anything without offering something in exchange, he demanded that the Queen agree to settle in the Kremlin in case conspirators should place her life in danger. Needless to say, the daughter of Henry VIII could not agree to this curious bargain and had no reason or desire to leave her country.

When Thomas Randolph arrived in Moscow, he was subjected to the ill humor of the monarch, who was irritated by the Queen's overlong silence. The Englishman was held prisoner for four months in the house that had been designated as his residence. Sentries prevented visitors from approaching. At last he obtained an audience, but contrary to custom, horses were not sent to bring him to the Kremlin. He was obliged to borrow a horse for the trip, while his followers waded through the snow. At the palace he was given an unceremonious reception. Offended, he kept his hat on in the presence of the Czar. The dignitaries foresaw an explosion of wrath. But Ivan, whose reactions were always unpredictable, addressed Thomas Randolph kindly and assured him of the friendship he bore his "dear sister" Elizabeth. On dismissing him without having invited him to dinner he said, by way of compensation: "I will send you dishes from my table." Shortly afterward an official of the court, followed by five servants, presented himself at the ambassador's house with all sorts of wines and victuals. To prove that they were not poisoned, the official tasted them all before having them served to Randolph.

Some while later, Randolph was invited to come to the palace at night, alone, and "dressed in Russian style." Doubtless during this mysterious interview, which lasted nearly three hours, Randolph made substantial promises to the Czar, for he obtained new advantages for the Company: exclusive rights to trade with Persia, to extract iron from certain mines, and to give chase to foreign ships on the White Sea.

In August 1569, Randolph returned to England accompanied by a Russian nobleman, Savin, whose mission probably was to persuade the Queen to sign a treaty of military alliance, offensive and defensive. After a stay of ten months on the banks of the Thames, Savin brought the Czar back only a letter from Elizabeth couched in vague and friendly terms: "If at any time it so mishap that you, Lord, our brother Emperor and great Duke, be by any casual chance either of secret conspiracy or outward hostility, driven to change your countries, and shall like to repair into our kingdom and dominions, with the noble Empress, your wife, and your dear children, the Princes, we shall with such honors and courtesies receive and [treat] Your Highness and them as shall become so great a Prince; and shall earnestly endeavor to make all things fall out according to Your Majesty's desire, to the free and quiet leading of Your Highness' life, with all those whom you shall bring with you; and that it may be lawful for you, the Emperor and great Duke, to use your Christian religion in such sort as it shall like you. . . . Besides, we shall appoint you, the Emperor and great Duke, a place in our kingdom fit upon your own charges, as long as ye shall like to remain with us. . . ."[2] In conclusion, Elizabeth stated that in case of war she would join forces with Russia "against our common enemies" and "for as long as God shall spare my life." The document was countersigned by the chief officers of the crown, starting with the Chancellor, Sir Nicholas Bacon.

This missive threw Ivan into a rage. Instead of the offensive and defensive alliance he had dreamed of, he received, like a piece of charity, a confused promise of assistance against "our common enemies." Instead of reciprocal political asylum, he obtained the assurance that Elizabeth would be delighted to receive him, at his own expense, if he had trouble with his people. Instead of even a veiled allusion to a possible marriage with the Czar, silence! Moreover, Savin reported that during his conversations with the Queen's advisers, the chief subject of discussion had been commercial advantages, which the English were increasingly eager to obtain. Savin had thought he was talking to statesmen; they were only merchants. Ivan indignantly seized his pen and addressed Her Britannic Majesty in the virulent style of his epistles to Kurbsky: "The most important affair you left aside, and your boyars only talked with our ambassador about trade. We thought you were sovereign in your states, mistress of your royal will, and that you were concerned about the interests of the kingdom; it was in that belief that we wanted to treat with you of great affairs. But in fact it is your statesmen who exercise power apart from you. They are not only advisers, but also simple muzhiks of trade, who care nothing for the interests of the sovereign and the country but only for their commercial profits. And you yourself remain in the role of a common wench* and behave like one. . . . Muscovy lacked for nothing when it had no English merchandise. And the rescript that we sent you concerning trade privileges, you will please return to us. Even if you do not send it back, we shall give orders that no account is to be taken of it. Thus, all the advantages which we have hitherto granted are canceled."

Elizabeth was more amused than angered by the insulting tone of the letter, for she considered her correspondent a harebrained eccentric. But when she learned that the Czar, carrying out his threat, had confiscated the Company's merchandise and forbidden it to conduct trade, she realized the seriousness of the situation. Only one man, she thought, was capable of mollifying the tyrant. Quickly she organized a new official embassy, whose leader would be Robert Best but whose key member would be the irreplaceable Jenkinson.

In Moscow, meanwhile, the Czar was gradually getting over his great rage against Elizabeth. Surely it was the Queen's advisers who were responsible for everything. Not she. Hadn't he himself had bad advisers? Hadn't it taken much courage for him to exterminate that riffraff? Elizabeth was probably not so ener-

---

*The expression in Russian was *poshlaya devitsa.*

getic as he was. But she was intelligent, cultivated. What a couple the two of them would make! Perhaps in her heart of hearts she had not rejected the notion of becoming the Czarina.

Ivan could not stop thinking about rich, industrious, Anglican England. However, for the time being he had too many worries in Russia to take much interest in foreign policy. A new confidential adviser had his ear now: a Dutch adventurer named Elysius Bomel, or Bomelius. He had come from Germany and he claimed to be a doctor of magic sciences. During his conversations with the Czar, he urged him to be more vigilant toward those around him. According to Bomel, despite the chain of executions of the last few years Ivan still had many enemies among the boyars of the *zemshchina,* the high clergy, and even the people. Since not all the roots of the evil had been torn up, the weed was growing back and spreading. The extirpation, he said, must be pursued more vigorously. The advice of the learned doctor reawoke Ivan's suspiciousness, which had begun to drowse. Talking with this zealous servant of his cause, he agreed that Russia was sick. And nothing could equal a good purge to make the body healthy again. Trust him: He would administer the correct dose and cure the country of perfidy!

XI

Metropolitan Philip

Now that Metropolitan Athanasius had given up his post and retired to a monastery, who was to replace him? Ivan first thought of Germanus, Archbishop of Kazan. The candidate was called to Moscow, the bishops assembled, the act of election was drawn up, and the future Metropolitan was getting ready for the consecration ceremony. But during a private conversation with the Czar, Germanus dared exhort him to repent his sins and to fear the wrath of heaven. Ivan was furious; he reported the Archbishop's words to his favorites and asked them what they thought of them. "We think that Germanus wants to become another Sylvester," answered Alexei Basmanov. "He is trying to frighten your imagination in order to gain control of you. Beware of such a pastor!" This view coincided so exactly with his own that the Czar made Germanus leave the palace, canceled the festivities planned in his honor, and set about finding another Metropolitan.

His choice fell on Philip, Abbot of the Solovetsky Monastery, located on an island in the White Sea. This man was considered to be one of the most learned and devout ascetics in Russia. It was in his desolate, frozen retreat that the former Metropolitan, Sylvester, banished by Ivan, had taken refuge. Doubtless the disgraced prelate had told the Abbot about his stormy experience as the sovereign's spiritual guide. Philip understood what the Czar would require of him: If in spite of everything he consented to go to the capital, it would be because he accepted the difficult conditions of the post he was being offered. At least, this was the opinion of Ivan, who had often corresponded with Philip in the past. The monarch had a high regard for this personage of noble birth who as a young man had renounced the brilliant, easy life of the boyars, his peers, to devote himself to meditation. Ivan knew that Philip possessed a fortunate combination of qualities: While his soul aspired to heaven, his feet stood firmly on the ground. He set the monks an example of the most austere morality, but at the same time managed the worldly goods of the community admirably. He had built stone churches and dikes on the island, cleared the forests, opened roads, drained marshes, organized the raising of reindeer and cattle, established fisheries and saltworks. Ivan thoroughly approved of this sort of practical wisdom. Even the lamps that burned in front of icons had to have oil if they were not to go out.

After hesitating a long time, Philip finally set out for Moscow. On the way he met a delegation of townspeople who begged him to intercede for them with the Czar, whose wrath they feared. The closer he came to Moscow, the more humble and urgent were the pleas that reached him from His Majesty's subjects. The pomp with which he was received in the capital could not dispel his sense of foreboding. The Czar seated him at his own table and informed him that he was naming him head of the Church. At these words the pious recluse, with tears in his eyes, entreated the sovereign not to entrust "so enormous a weight to so weak a vessel." Then, as Ivan remained adamant, he said to him, "So be it. I yield to your will. But appease my conscience by abolishing the *oprichnina!* Let there be but one Russia, for according to the words of the Almighty, an empire that is divided will become a desert. It is impossible for me to bless you sincerely when I see the motherland in mourning!"

Ivan's immediate impulse was to send the madman back to his monastery, but he quickly thought better of it. How would it look if once again he dismissed a prelate whom he himself had chosen to head the Church? Would it not be better to so entangle Philip that, without realizing it, he would become an accomplice in the Czar's political machinations? In that way the Czar would have on his side the moral weight of a saint whom the whole country venerated. Instead of exploding, Ivan justified himself vehemently. "Do you not know," he said, "that my people want to devour me, that those around me are preparing to destroy me?" And when the old man asked him at least to cancel the new distribution of lands and to return to the former landowners the estates they had inherited, he explained the necessity of the vast plan of reorganization he had in mind for his people.

Disturbed by this first conversation with Ivan, Philip next confronted the bishops, who to a man implored him to accept the Czar's offer unconditionally. They believed that for the good of the Church and the nation, the metropolitan must refrain from angering the monarch by remonstrating with him and should try to use gentle persuasion. After thinking things over, Philip gave in to their arguments, not out of pride but in a spirit of sacrifice. An act was drawn up providing that the new Metropolitan promised in advance never to criticize the actions of the *oprichniki* and never to abandon his seat in protest against the Czar's conduct. Thus, the temporal domain was placed beyond his competence and the spiritual domain was singularly narrowed.

The consecration ceremony took place in the presence of the Czar, his two sons, Prince Vladimir Andreyevich, the archbishops, and the bishops. In his pastoral address Philip urged Ivan to become once again the father of his subjects, to beware of the flatterers who crowded around the throne, to make justice reign in his country, and to prefer "love without weapons" to the "triumphs of war."

For a time, the Czar seemed softened by Metropolitan Philip's words. But his new mood did not last long. Back in his lair in Alexandrovskaya Sloboda, his mind was again poisoned by doubt. Wasn't Philip a tool of the boyars? Wasn't he following their orders when he dared to ask that the *oprichnina* be dissolved? Ivan's imagination sped on at a gallop. As if to confirm his suspicions of a vast conspiracy, there came into his hands several letters that Sigismund Augustus had sent to certain boyars of the *zemshchina,* urging them to revolt against the Czar. No doubt the King of Poland thought there were enough discontented nobles to launch a civil war! It was the recipients of these secret messages themselves who, seized with fear, had spontaneously turned the letters over to their sovereign as proof of their loyalty. Among them were Princes Belsky, Mstislavsky, and Vorotynsky, as well as Grand Equerry Fedorov. Ivan personally dictated to his boyars an ironic reply to Sigismund Augustus: After expressing their indignation at this shameful call to treason, the correspondents of the King of Poland stated that they were indeed prepared to go over to his court—providing he gave their Czar "all of Lithuania, all of White Russia, Galicia, Prussia, Volhynia, and Podolia." Old Prince Fedorov even wrote, on his master's orders, "How could you have imagined that with one foot in the grave I would be willing to sacrifice my immortal soul by an infamous betrayal? And what would I do at your court? I am no longer able to lead armies, I do not like feasts, I have never learned your dances, and I do not know the art of amusing you."

Having thus settled the matter with dignity and good humor, Ivan soon regretted that he had been so magnanimous. If the King of Poland wrote to certain boyars, it was because he knew they were likely to lend a willing ear to his proposals. Without question, Sigismund's goal was to incite the *zemshchina* to insurrection against the *oprichnina* in order to dethrone the Czar and set someone else in his place. But whom? Why not *precisely* Fedorov, a man faithful to the old customs, vested for nineteen years with the dignity of Grand Equerry, and deeply respected by all who sighed for former days? Yes, yes, it was he, without a doubt, who was the leader of the conspiracy. One day, in the presence of the whole court, Ivan made Fedorov put on his own coat, placed the crown on his head, had him sit on the throne, and, bowing before him, said in a loud voice, "Greetings, great Czar of Russia! You receive from me the honor you aspired to!" Fedorov sat dumbfounded, not knowing how to respond. A few of the boyars around him, thinking it was a joke, burst out laughing. But Ivan did not laugh. Continuing his speech, he declared, "Just as I have had the power to make you czar, so I have the power to cast you down from the throne." And raising his dagger, he planted it to the hilt in Fedorov's chest. The old man collapsed. The *oprichniki* fell upon him, finished him off savagely, dragged his body out of the palace, and abandoned it to the dogs.

Fedorov's wife likewise had her throat cut. Some alleged accomplices were readily discovered and immediately executed. Princes Belsky, Mstislavsky, and Vorotynsky for some reason escaped the sovereign's vengeance. But three Rostovsky princes paid for the others. One of them, a voivode in Nizhni-Novgorod, was praying in a church when thirty *oprichniki* burst in and ordered him in the name of the Czar to follow them. They tore off his clothes and took him twenty versts from the city, completely naked, to the edge of the Volga. There he was beheaded and his body was thrown into the river. The head was carried to Ivan. He kicked it from him and said with a smile of hatred, "He used to like to bathe in the blood of enemies on the battlefield; at last he has bathed in his own."

Prince Peter Shchenyatov, who took refuge in a monastery, was pursued there and put to torture: He was slowly grilled on a roasting pan and needles were driven under his nails. Ivan Pronsky, a glorious general, was drowned. Tyutin, the state treasurer, was hacked to pieces, together with his wife, his two daughters, and his two young sons; the execution was carried out by the Circassian prince who was the Czarina's brother. Other eminent families met the same fate. The *oprichniki* looted the houses and villages of their victims. The peasant women were raped before being murdered. Corpses lay everywhere in the fields and along the roads, no one daring to give Christian burial to "enemies of the Czar." Some were disfigured, unrecognizable. Most of the bodies were naked, because they had been stripped before the massacre so that their garments—an important part of the booty—would not be stained with blood.

The inhabitants of Moscow holed up in their houses, trembling at the sound of the shouts and laughter of the executioners outside, who were hunting down their prey, stabbing them, trampling them, cutting their throats. Metropolitan Philip, witnessing these bloody disorders, powerless and in despair, could only exhort the Czar to clemency. His prayers went unheeded. Soon His Majesty even refused to receive him.

One Sunday during mass, Ivan entered the Cathedral of the Assumption wearing a monk's frock and tall bonnet. He was accompanied by a great many *oprichniki*, likewise dressed as monks. Philip, who had seen them come in, did not go to meet them but continued to celebrate the divine office. The Czar went up to him and asked for his blessing. The Metropolitan made not a move. The *oprichniki* muttered in stupefaction. One of them cried, "Holy Father, His Majesty awaits your blessing!"

Ivan at the age of six
receiving the Lithuanian ambassadors.
After a sixteenth-century miniature.
(Photo Viollet Collection)

Погомца марта . кнѣьвеликіи ранчⷮа
ѥнаⷩсⷩивеⷩарⷤⷩн . игоⷨтиповⷣеⷣлⷩиⷮкⷨ
ⷩⷩкⷩгⷩⷩⷩ елеⷩа . пелⷤⷣеⷣлⷩипреⷣⷣеⷣлⷩⷩⷩⷣⷣⷣⷣⷩⷩ
старыеⷣⷩⷩⷩⷩⷩⷩ намоⷣⷩⷩⷩⷩⷩⷩⷩⷩⷩⷩⷩⷩ тогоⷣ
ра . чⷤⷣⷣⷣⷣⷣⷣⷣⷣⷣⷣⷣⷣⷣⷣⷣⷣⷣⷣⷣⷣⷣⷣⷣⷣⷣ
крⷤⷣⷣзаⷩⷩⷩⷩⷩⷩⷩⷩⷩⷩⷩⷩⷩⷩⷩⷩⷩⷩⷩⷩⷩ

The Regent Elena Glinskaya
and her son, the future
Ivan the Terrible,
having new money coined.
After a sixteenth-
century miniature.
(Photo Viollet Collection)

Coronation ceremony of Ivan IV, the Terrible.
After a sixteenth-century miniature.
(Photo Viollet Collection)

Crown of the czars,
known as the Cap of Monomakh
*(Moscow, Museum of the Army
in the Kremlin.*

Throne and scepter of
Ivan the Terrible.
(Photo Novosty Press Agency)

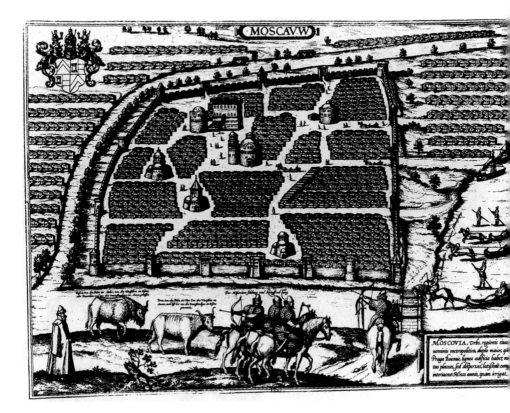

Map of Moscow in 1527.
(Paris, Bibliothèque Nationale. Photo B. N.)

Costumes of boyars
in the sixteenth century.
*(Moscow, Museum of History
and Reconstruction.
Photo Novosty Press Agency)*

Lieutenant Colonel du Corps des Strelits.

Lieutenant-Colonel of the *streltsy,*
a permanent armed force
created by Ivan the Terrible.
*(Paris, Bibliothèque Nationale.
Photo Viollet Collection)*

archevêque
en habit ordinaire
au chœur.

Russian archbishop in ordinary costume.
(Paris, Bibliothèque Nationale. Photo B. N.)

Capture of Kazan by Ivan the Terrible in 1552.
After a sixteenth-century miniature.
(Photo Viollet Collection)

Construction of the Church of
the Intercession of the Virgin
(Cathedral of Basil the Blessed).
Miniature from the
Great Collection of Chronicles.
(Moscow, National Historical Museum.
Photo Novosty Press Agency)

Banner of Ivan the Terrible at the Siege of Kazan.
(Photo Novosty Press Agency)

Moscow, Red Square, Cathedral of Basil the Blessed,
originally the Church of the Intercession of the Virgin (1554-60).
(Photo San-Viollet)

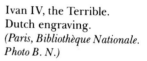

IOANNES BASILIDES
Grooten hertogh van Moſcovien

Ivan IV, the Terrible.
Dutch engraving.
*(Paris, Bibliothèque Nationale.
Photo B. N.)*

Ivan the Terrible.
Russian portrait, sixteenth century.
*(Copenhagen, National museet.
Photo by the museum)*

Ivan the Terrible.
German engraving from the sixteenth century.
(Paris, Bibliothèque Nationale. Photo B. N.)

Ivan the Terrible has one of his advisers seized and put to death.
After a sixteenth-century miniature.
(*Photo Viollet Collection*)

Massacre of the inhabitants of Novgorod in 1570.
Engraving by an unknown artist.
(Photo Viollet Collection)

Construction of the palace of the *oprichnina*.
Miniature from the *Great Collection of Chronicles*, sixteenth century.
(Moscow, National Historical Museum. Photo Novosty Press Agency)

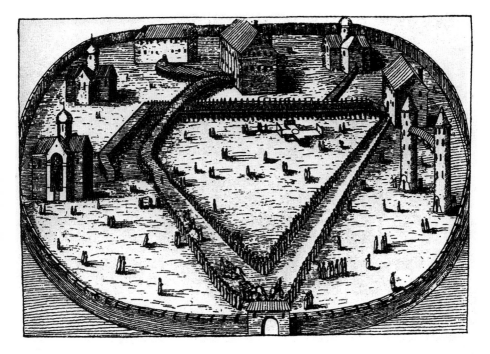

General view of Alexandrovskaya Sloboda,
the Czar's residence some hundred kilometers from Moscow
(Photo Viollet Collection)

Feast given by Ivan in his residence at Alexandrovskaya Sloboda.
(Photo Viollet Collection)

Audience given by Ivan the Terrible to various ambassadors, at Alexandrovskaya Sloboda.
(Photo Viollet Collection)

Torture in Russia at the time
of Ivan the Terrible.
(Paris, Bibliothèque Nationale
Photo Viollet Collection)

Cruelty of Ivan the Terrible.
Sixteenth-century engraving.
(Photo Viollet Collection)

Russian seal affixed to
two treaties between Russia
and Sweden in 1583-84.
(Photo Viollet Collection)

Ivan the Terrible
beside the body of his son.
Painting by V. Schwartz,
nineteenth century.
(Moscow, Tretiakov Gallery.
(Photo Novosty Press Agency)

Tomb of Ivan the Terrible in
the Cathedral of St. Michael the Archangel in Moscow.
(Photo Novosty Press Agency)

Looking down at the Czar in his monk's costume, Philip said, "In this strange garb I no longer recognize my sovereign. I do not recognize him in his acts either. . . . Oh Prince! in this place we are offering sacrifices to the Lord, and behind the altar the blood of innocent Christians is flowing in torrents. Never since the sun began to shine in the heavens has there been seen a monarch enlightened by the true faith who rent his people so cruelly. Even among the pagans there is law, justice, some compassion for men. In Russia there is none. The lives and property of our citizens are no longer protected. Everywhere there is murder and robbery, and all these crimes are committed in the name of the Czar. However high you may be on the throne, there is a supreme being, our Judge and yours! How will you appear before His tribunal, covered with the blood of the righteous, deafened by their screams of pain—for the stones of this cathedral on which you tread cry out to heaven for vengeance. Oh Prince, I speak to you as the shepherd of souls and I fear only God!"

Trembling with anger, Ivan struck the paving stones with his iron-tipped staff and cried, "Miserable monks, I have been too merciful with you until now, rebels that you are! Henceforth I shall be what you say I am!" Then he left the church, followed by his thugs.

Ivan did not yet dare to attack the Metropolitan directly, contenting himself with having a few members of the clergy arrested and tortured. Meanwhile, his *oprichniki* were quick to widen the scope of reprisals. In July 1568, at midnight, Ivan's favorites Athanasius Viazemsky, Maliuta-Skuratov, and Vasily Griaznoy, at the head of a troop of *oprichniki*, burst into the wealthy homes of certain boyars and merchants, carried off the women known for their beauty, and took them out of the city. At daybreak they were joined by the Czar, who chose for himself the loveliest of the prisoners to rape. The others were turned over to his faithful officers. The *oprichniki* carried on with their party, burning farms and killing horned cattle. Then the company returned to Moscow, the women were taken back to their homes, and "a number of them," says the chronicler, "died of shame and sorrow."[1]

A few days later, on July 28, the Czar and his henchmen were at the Monastery of the Holy Virgin while Philip was celebrating mass. Noticing an *oprichnik* wearing a skullcap, the Metropolitan reproached the Czar for allowing one of his men to remain covered in the house of God. This was too much! Ivan decided to begin Philip's trial.

The Czar sent emissaries to the Solovetsky Monastery to collect reports on the hypocrisy and impurity of his "enemy." Most of the monks were sincerely devoted to their former abbot, and cited him as a model of holiness. But the new abbot, one Paisy, moved by the hope of becoming a bishop, agreed to testify against his predecessor. He was brought to Moscow. Before a tribunal composed of the Czar, the bishops, and the boyars, he repeated his calumnies with quiet assurance. Disdaining to defend himself, Philip merely told him that "bad seed will not bring forth good fruit," and expressed the wish to resign his position. "Better to perish as an innocent martyr than to suffer in silence, in the high office of Metropolitan, the horrors and impieties of this unhappy time," he declared. "Do as you please with me. Here is the bishop's crook, here are the white miter and the mantle, the marks of honor with which you have invested me!" The Czar would not hear of it. "You cannot judge yourself!" he retorted, and ordered him to take up his vestments again and go on celebrating mass as usual, until sentence was pronounced.

On November 8, St. Michael's Day, armed *oprichniki* entered the Cathedral of the Assumption while Philip in sacerdotal robes was officiating in front of a large crowd. Alexei Basmanov, interrupting the liturgy, brandished a paper and read aloud the sentence that stripped the Metropolitan of his functions. At once the *oprichniki* tore off the pontiff's garments, put a torn frock on him, loaded him with fetters, drove him from the church with brooms, and took him on a sleigh to the Monastery of the Epiphany. Terrorized, the people ran after the vehicle weeping and shouting. They assembled in front of the monastery, expecting a miracle. But the miracle did not take place. Philip had been found guilty of sorcery and was condemned to life imprisonment.

One last time Philip entreated Ivan to have pity on Russia. His only reward was to be treated more harshly. While he was dying of cold and hunger, fettered in his cell, more and more pilgrims crowded around St. Nicholas Monastery on the banks of the Moskva, to which he had been transferred. Gazing up at the high walls, these simple folk felt a kind of spiritual radiation penetrating their souls. They stood in silent communion before the refuge of a "living saint" who was sacrificing himself for the faith. Ivan realized that instead of getting rid of a troublemaker he had created a martyr. This was intolerable, and he had Philip removed to the distant Monastery of Otroch, near Tver; after which another Metropolitan was elected: one Kirill, a weak, conciliating man.

Now that Philip was no longer dangerous, Ivan's anger toward him abated. It so happened that he was preparing a punitive expedition against Novgorod. The old man's blessing, he thought, would have the most beneficial effect on his troops. He sent Maliuta-Skuratov, his most brutal and sadistic favorite, to the Monastery of Otroch to persuade the prisoner to call down the grace of God upon His Majesty's enterprise. Philip was praying in his cell when the Czar's emissary entered. One glance at the bestial face of his visitor and Philip sensed the danger he was in. Maliuta-Skuratov repeated to him, word for word, the sovereign's demand. Undaunted, the priest haughtily refused to associate himself with fresh violence. "I give my blessing," he said, "only to good men undertaking good works. For a long time I have been waiting for death. Let the sovereign's will be accomplished." Whereupon Maliuta-Skuratov leaped on him in fury, tightened both hands around his neck, and strangled him.

Maliuta-Skuratov told the Abbot of Otroch that Philip had died in his cell "asphyxiated by the heat." The frightened monks said nothing. Ivan felt that, all things considered, this murder was in line with his politics, so there was no question of his blaming Maliuta-Skuratov. To indicate his approval, he even sent some of the dead man's relatives to execution.*

On September 1, 1569, Moscow was shocked to learn of the death of the Czarina Maria, Ivan's second wife. No doubt she had been poisoned. By whom? Everyone suspected the Czar, who had long since detached himself from his wife. Although she had played no role at court, she had nevertheless been an encumbrance to the monarch. He deceived her casually enough, but he could no longer endure to see her in his palace. Besides, she stood in the way of his plans for an English marriage. A pinch of powder or a few drops of a secret potion, and the path before him was clear. But the people around the Czar trembled as they waited to hear whom he would accuse. The boyars pretended to be deeply afflicted and put on mourning: velvet or damask pelisses without gold ornaments. After the funeral ceremony, which took place in Moscow, Ivan withdrew once again to the evil solitude of Alexandrovskaya Sloboda, without having designated the guilty party. There, among his *oprichniki,* he reviewed in his mind the great men of his empire and wondered which one he should send to death.

Of all the former conspirators, only one still remained in place, his cousin Prince Vladimir Andreyevich. Ivan had pardoned him six years earlier. Now he felt that the reprieve was undeserved. It was time to make an end of this magnificent personage who had once tried to usurp his throne. But Ivan would not accuse him of having poisoned the Czarina. No, he would claim that Vladimir Andreyevich had committed a still

---

*After the death of Ivan IV, Philip's body was laid to rest in the Solovetsky Monastery. In 1652, the fallen metropolitan was canonized and his remains were transported to the Cathedral of the Assumption in Moscow.

graver crime: He had bribed one of the palace cooks to poison the Czar himself. The Prince was summoned, with his family, to Alexandrovskaya Sloboda.

In Ivan's presence the cook repeated that he had received fifty silver rubles to sprinkle a certain powder in His Majesty's food. Vladimir Andreyevich, his wife, Eudoxia, and his two young sons fell at the sovereign's feet, protested their innocence, and asked to enter a monastery. "Traitors," cried the Czar, "you had prepared poison for me; well, you shall drink it!" And he had a cup brought that was full of a fatal brew. The Prince hesitated to take it, but his wife said courageously, "It is still better to die at the hands of the Czar than at the hands of the executioner." At these words, Vladimir Andreyevich bade farewell to his wife, blessed his sons, and put his lips to the cup. Eudoxia and the two boys did the same. All four began to pray, while the poison did its work. Ivan was present at their last convulsions. Then he called the Princess's maids-in-waiting, and as they lamented over the corpses, he gave orders that they be stripped naked and shot. For good measure, he commanded that the cook, whose testimony had been so useful, be shot as well and that Vladimir Andreyevich's mother, the ambitious Princess Euphrosyne, who had long since taken a nun's habit and withdrawn from the world, be drowned in the river.[2]

To Ivan's astonishment, the death of Vladimir Andreyevich and his family aroused general compassion. No one believed the fable of an attempt on the monarch's life. The execution of the Prince was regarded only as an abominable fratricide, inspired by hatred rather than suspicion. The Czar, however, took little notice of public opinion; for him, to listen to what others said was already to cease to reign—it was not on the people that he relied for support but on God. And he thought of God not as a judge but as a partner, maybe even an accomplice. The older he grew, the more persuaded Ivan became of the importance of rites. He was meticulous about the forms of religion. He never doubted that crossing oneself, genuflecting, and sprinkling holy water produced a magical effect on God, who thirsted for tokens of respect. To make the Almighty give in, one had only to implore Him according to the rules. Besides, the exact observance of ritual gave Ivan an almost sensual pleasure. He loved to pray in the same way that he loved to possess a woman: For him, mystical ecstasy and carnal ecstasy were complementary and sometimes merged into one. The perfume of incense and the odor of damp skin were equally pleasing to his nostrils. He had only to feel an intense pleasure of any kind to be convinced that he was acting with the Creator's approval or even carrying out His explicit will.

In the continual tête-à-tête between God and the Czar, the Church had played an entirely subordinate role. It was there only to add marginal notations to the messages going back and forth between the throne and heaven. Even so, very often Ivan bypassed the solemn intermediary to converse directly and familiarly with the Eternal. His alliance with God was never more strikingly demonstrated than on Palm Sunday. According to tradition, on that day the whole population of Moscow gathered in the Kremlin before mass. A sleigh glided through the streets bearing a tree hung with various fruits, chiefly apples. Five young boys dressed in white stood under the branches singing prayers. Others, holding aloft tapers and lanterns, walked beside the vehicle. Next, amid a forest of banners and holy images, came more than one hundred priests in sacerdotal robes glittering with gold and precious stones, then the boyars and the notables. Last, the Metropolitan appeared in a cloud of incense, mounted on an ass with white trappings. In his left hand he held a Bible bound in gold; with his right hand he blessed the people. The Czar walked beside him, deferentially holding the bridle rein. Thus, Ivan posed before them all as a faithful penitent of the Church, while in reality the new Metropolitan was trembling under his magnificent chasuble lest one day he should meet the same fate as Philip, his predecessor. Everyone in the crowd knew which of the two—prelate or Czar—held power over the other.

The people prostrated themselves before the heavenly power and the earthly power at the same time. The procession made the rounds of the major churches in the Kremlin and then returned to the Cathedral of the Assumption, where the Metropolitan himself performed the office. After the religious service, he gave a banquet for the Czar and the boyars. And the symbolic representation of Jesus' entrance into Jerusalem would end in a drunken revel.

XII

The Martyrdom of Novgorod

Driven ever further by the desire to demonstrate his omnipotence, Ivan could no longer be satisfied with punishing individuals, he had to punish whole towns. For a long time he had been irritated by the presumptuousness of Novgorod-the-Great and Pskov. The inhabitants of these two important cities, which had only recently been united to the crown,* still remembered the time when they had been independent and had traded as they pleased with the Lithuanians and the Swedes. First, the

---

*Novgorod had been conquered in 1474, then again in 1478, by Ivan's grandfather, Grand Duke Ivan III, and Pskov in 1510 by Ivan's father, Grand Duke Vasily III.

Czar's wars in the North had compromised this commerce, then English merchants had obtained exorbitant privileges, and finally, the incursions of the *oprichniki* had sown panic among a population jealous of its last remaining liberties.

Sensing that discontent was boiling in that part of the empire, Ivan began by taking hostages to ensure the good conduct of the two cities: In the spring of 1569, five hundred families from Pskov and one hundred and fifty from Novgorod were forcibly transported to Moscow. The people who were thus torn from their homes bemoaned their exile; those who were left behind trembled in expectation of even more terrible events. A few months later a habitual criminal by the name of Peter, originally from Volhynia, came out of prison in Novgorod and formed a plan to take revenge on the city's inhabitants, who had condemned him. Knowing that Ivan was strongly prejudiced against them, he wrote a letter to Sigismund Augustus, signing the names of the Archbishop of Novgorod and the notables, according to which the entire population, pushed beyond endurance by the Czar's ill treatment, was ready to submit to Poland. This letter he hid behind the icon of the Virgin in the Cathedral of St. Sophia. Then he went to Moscow and denounced the alleged conspiracy. Orders were immediately given to seek the criminal missive in the designated place. It was discovered there, of course, and the signatures of Archbishop Pimen and many magistrates were declared authentic. Ivan jumped for joy: At last he had his pretext.

In December 1569, the Czar left Moscow at the head of the army with his *oprichniki* and 1,500 *streltsy* for a punitive expedition. His heart beat with gladness—as if he were going on a picnic. He was accompanied by his eldest son, Ivan, fifteen years of age, who had been brought up in a climate of cruelty and shared his father's taste for crude pleasures and the sight of blood. For this adolescent, torture was a diversion like hunting. In his mind there was no notion of remorse connected to the violence perpetrated against a defenseless man. Some people, he thought, were destined to be victims and others executioners. It all depended on the category in which God had caused you to be born.

On the way to Novgorod the armed bands amused themselves by massacring the inhabitants of Klin—who could not in any way be accused of having sold out to the King of Poland. In Tver the Czar prayed in a monastery for five days while the *oprichniki* went from house to house, torturing whomever they pleased. The same fate awaited Torzhok, Vyshniy, Valday, and so on. All the Russian towns between Moscow and Novgorod were punished. Even peasants whom the army met on the way were killed, ostensibly because Ivan's expedition was supposed to remain secret. After the "punishers" had passed, nothing remained but charred walls, heaps of corpses, bodies hanging from the branches of trees, and cattle with their bellies ripped open.

On January 2, 1570, the advance guard of the army reached Novgorod. It was a beautiful, wealthy city, densely populated and proud of its European traditions. The soldiers began by building a high stockade around it so that no one could escape. Next, the churches were locked so that no one could seek refuge there. The monks were obliged to evacuate their monasteries, the doors of which were sealed behind them. The notables and merchants were confined to their homes. All the government officials and all the members of the lower clergy were arrested. The ecclesiastics, of whom there were a great number, were herded into an enclosure and called upon to pay a ransom of twenty rubles a head. Those who were unable to produce that sum would be given the bastinado every day. In the dead city the inhabitants did not yet know the reason for the repression, and awaited in fear the arrival of the Czar.

On January 6, Epiphany, he halted with his troops two versts from Novgorod. The next day, at his orders, all the ecclesiastics who had been unable to pay the fine were put to death; they were struck down with clubs and transported to their respective monasteries to be buried. On January 8, the Czar, with his son and his retinue, entered the deserted, silent city. Archbishop Pimen was waiting for him, with the crosses and icons, on the great bridge across the Volkhov. Instead of bowing his head, Ivan refused the prelate's blessing and cried, "Ungodly man, it is not the life-giving cross I see in your hands but a murderous weapon which you want to plunge in my heart. I know your treacherous plans and those of this vile population. I know that you are ready to deliver me up to Sigismund Augustus! From this moment forth you are no longer in my eyes the shepherd of Christians but a carnivorous wolf, a predator, the fierce enemy of the Cap of Monomakh!"

Ivan ordered the Archbishop to return to the Cathedral of St. Sophia, with the procession. He himself went there with his son and after having thus violently denounced Pimen, now listened patiently as he celebrated mass. The Czar genuflected and crossed himself, a model of piety. Could he have forgotten his fit of rage? Was he about to pardon? The priests around the venerable Pimen already saw a faint ray of hope. After the service, Ivan agreed to dine at the Archbishop's palace. At table his boyars chatted gaily with the members of the clergy. In the middle of the banquet the Czar stood up and uttered a terrible cry. At once the *oprichniki* rushed into the room, seized Pimen, tore off his vestments, tied up the other priests and the servants, and dragged them all off to prison. Then they looted the Archbishop's house and wrecked the cathedral, carrying off the treasures and the sacred vessels.

Starting the next day, Ivan briskly set about the task of bringing justice to Novgorod. Every day in the great square a thousand inhabitants were brought before him and his son— notables, merchants, or ordinary citizens. No interrogation, no hearing of witnesses, no pleading, no verdict. Simply by virtue of the fact that these people lived in Novgorod, the accursed city, they were guilty. To further perfect the punishment, husbands were tortured in front of wives, mothers in front of children. The *oprichniki* flogged their victims with knouts, broke their limbs, cut out their tongues, slit their nostrils, castrated them, roasted them over slow fires. Then, bleeding and broken, the poor wretches were tied by the head or feet to sleighs, which sped over the snow toward the Volkhov to a place where even in the depths of winter the river remained open. There they were flung into the icy water, whole families at a time, wives with their husbands, mothers with babies at their breasts. Those who rose to the surface were despatched with boat hooks, lances, and axes by *oprichniki* in boats.

The methodical slaughter lasted for five weeks. Ivan and his son never tired of the spectacle. According to the Czar, nothing was more instructive to a mind curious about the mysteries of human beings than the reactions of a defenseless victim struggling with pain and death. Even for a habitué of torture chambers, the pleasure was always new. Under the influence of suffering, faces accustomed to feign indifference, pride, courtesy, or courage became contorted. The masks fell off. The animal appeared behind the man. It was as exciting as the undressing of a virgin who struggled and screamed. The victims writhed, shrieked, grimaced, forgot all dignity. Guilty or innocent, they were all alike. One could stop their torments with a word—but one didn't. Instead, one's pleasure grew in proportion as the other was debased. Pearly white tendons, bluish viscera, green and viscous humors, and above all, the joyous spurt of blood with its warm, sweetish, intoxicating, irreplaceable smell! What better preparation for lovemaking or prayer? Having beaten, flayed, pincered, quartered, and roasted, one plunged into a woman or into God with renewed vigor. Thus, after each series of executions, Ivan and his son were to be found in church again, in a calm and pious mood. Butchery and the divine service complemented each other.

The total number of victims was to reach 15,000 according to Andrei Kurbsky, 18,000 according to the *Third Chronicle of Novgorod*, 27,000 according to Taube and Kruse, 60,000 according to the *First Chronicle of Pskov.* The Volkhov was choked with corpses and its current carried blood and human debris all the way to Lake Ladoga.

Not content with exterminating the population of Novgorod, Ivan had his men proceed to systematic pillage. It was as if, seized with uncontrollable rage, he wanted to ruin one of the greatest cities in his country so as to prevent it from rivaling Moscow. He rode through the streets encouraging his *oprichniki,* who were besieging houses and shops, breaking down doors, climbing through windows, arguing over piles of fabrics and furs, dishes and icons. All the churches were ransacked. Under the Czar's direction, the "punishment" spilled over into the surrounding countryside for a radius of two hundred and fifty versts. Farmers were murdered, houses set afire, cattle slaughtered, grain lofts burned—the magnitude of the destruction gave Ivan the measure of his genius.*

At last, at daybreak on February 12, the Monday of the second week of Lent, Ivan ordered that one survivor from each street be brought to him. They appeared—emaciated, in rags, exhausted from horror and despair, expecting death. But the Czar they saw before them wore a kindly expression. He had emerged from his bloodbath refreshed and rejuvenated. "Inhabitants of Novgorod who have remained alive," he said gently, "pray God to grant us a happy reign, pray for the Army of Christ to triumph over its visible and invisible enemies. May God judge your Archbishop Pimen and his abominable accomplices. It is they who are responsible for the blood that has flowed in this place. Now let the weeping and groaning cease. . . . Go home in peace!" Following this speech, Archbishop Pimen, mounted on a white mare, covered with rags and holding in his hands a musette and a drum, was paraded through the city like an itinerant entertainer. As he passed, the few onlookers,

---

*Novgorod was never to recover from the massacre of 1570. It remained a secondary city, poor and with a small population.

ashamed and aghast, bowed their heads and crossed themselves. After this performance, he was taken to Moscow under escort.

As for Ivan, he and his army left Novgorod and headed for the second guilty city, Pskov. They were loaded down with booty. The German adventurer Heinrich von Staden, who had enrolled in the *oprichniki*, later boasted that he had entered Novgorod with nothing but his mount and left it followed by forty-nine horses and twenty-two wagons laden with plunder.[1]

When they learned that the Czar was approaching their city, the people of Pskov flocked to the churches to pray, frozen with terror. At midnight the bells tolled mournfully. Was it a signal of welcome or a death knell? From St. Nicholas Monastery in Lubatov, where the Czar had halted, he heard the deep ringing and, it is said, his heart was touched. The next day, when he entered the town, he found a table set up in front of every house and the inhabitants kneeling to offer him the bread and salt of hospitality. Their spokesman, with tears in his eyes, said, "Do as you will with our lives and our property, for everything we possess is yours, as are our persons!"

Ivan liked that sort of talk, and he went into the Church of the Trinity to hear a Te Deum. When he came out, he decided to visit the cell of the monk Nicholas, who had mystic powers. He found himself facing an emaciated, half-naked man with a bushy beard, a chain around his neck, and a mad glint in his eye, who looked him up and down arrogantly and held out to him a piece of raw meat. "I am a Christian," the Czar told him, "I do not eat meat during Lent." The anchorite retorted fiercely, "You do worse: You feed on human flesh and blood, forgetting not only Lent but God Himself." And he prophesied that the Czar would be struck with thunderbolts from heaven if he touched so much as a hair of the head of a single child in Pskov.

Meantime, the sky had become covered with dark clouds. Thunder rolled in the distance. Was it possible that the miracle worker was right? Ivan was on the point of thrusting his spear through Nicholas when he changed his mind. He had dared to raise his hand against an archbishop and had let a metropolitan be strangled, but he stood in awe of this "holy fool." Didn't God more often choose to speak through the mouths of the simpleminded than through the mouths of prelates? These tattered, stammering intercessors were to be feared like fire. Prudently, Ivan ordered his army to evacuate the city. They would restrict themselves to a little looting in the outskirts.

A few days later, the Czar and his men set out again on the road to Moscow. Behind them, the people who had been spared by a miracle rushed to the churches. Forests of candles were lit under the icons. Incense smoked. A thousand prayers rose to God in celebration of the courage of the monk Nicholas, who had saved the city.

Ivan allowed himself the luxury of organizing a return to Moscow that was part triumph and part masquerade. To amuse the people, he had himself preceded by one of his buffoons perched on an ox. But after they had laughed at the clown's antics, the onlookers were frightened to see their all-powerful Czar riding at the head of his *oprichniki*. To make it clear that he was the leader of this band of killers, he too carried on his saddlebow the insignia of the brotherhood: a broom and a dog's head. The army following him marched as proudly as if it was returning from a victorious campaign against the Poles or Tatars. Wagons carrying the plunder collected in Russian towns closed the procession.

Ivan's first act on his return was to begin criminal proceedings against the alleged accomplices of the people of Novgorod and Pskov. The trial lasted for five months. Prisoners who had been brought back from the expedition were put to torture. Broken by pain, they confessed to whatever was wanted, and accused anyone and everyone of treason. Even some of the Czar's favorites were denounced. This was enough to persuade him that they should be put to death. Thus, Athanasius Viazemsky—a hard, cynical man whom Ivan had hitherto trusted completely, who had tasted for him the medicines prescribed by his doctors, who had accompanied him to his bedchamber every night to listen to his confidences—suddenly found himself suspected of having warned the people of Novgorod of the fate that lay in store for them. Ivan summoned him to the palace and conversed pleasantly with him about affairs of state. Meanwhile, at his orders, the Prince's house was being sacked and his servants murdered. When he went home, Viazemsky, who was himself a specialist in executions of this sort, was not unduly disturbed. He was sure that when the time came, he could prove to his master the loyalty of his intentions. But that same evening he was arrested and thrown into a dungeon. There he found two other favorites: Alexei Basmanov and his son Feodor, the Czar's companions in debauchery and violence. Ivan Viskovaty, a member of the Duma of boyars; Simeon Yakovlev; the treasurer, Nikita Funikov; and the clerks Vasiliev and Stepanov were likewise incarcerated, despite their protestations of innocence. All were tortured but not killed. Some three hundred persons, finally, were thus prepared for a mass execution in the capital.

In the great square of the Kremlin, workmen set up seventeen gallows, an enormous cauldron of water suspended over a pile of faggots, a frying pan as big as a man, ropes stretched taut to saw bodies in two by friction. On July 25, 1570, the date fixed for the great festival of blood, the Muscovites, terrified by these extraordinary instruments of torture, did not dare come to the place of execution. Although usually eager for strong sensations, they hid in their houses. The shopkeepers deserted their shops; the streets were empty. Everyone feared that the Czar might avenge himself on Moscow as he had done on Novgorod. And thus the macabre procession made its way through an abandoned city. It was a fine, hot day. A drumroll announced the arrival of the Czar. He rode forward dressed magnificently, a quiver filled with gilded arrows slung over his shoulder, his saddle glittering with pearls and emeralds. His eldest son was with him. Behind them marched the *oprichniki*, followed by the slow cohort of the condemned. Numbering more than three hundred, mutilated, broken, and bleeding, they dragged themselves along, awaiting death as a deliverance.

When Ivan reached the foot of the scaffolds, he was astonished to find the square empty. He had prepared such an exhibition that he had to have an audience before he could start, so he immediately ordered the guards to round up the people. Impatient at their slowness, he himself rode through the streets, shouting to the Muscovites to come to the spectacle. To encourage them he declared that no harm would come to them. Half reassured, the inhabitants came out of their holes. Slowly the crowd grew. A few of the more curious climbed up on the rooftops. When Ivan thought the audience was large enough, he shouted, "People of Moscow, you are going to see tortures, but those whom I am punishing are traitors! Answer me: Do you find my sentence just?" The crowd obediently roared, "Long live the Czar! Death to his enemies!" The Czar quivered with satisfaction.

The great performance began with a distribution of pardons. Some hundred prisoners from Novgorod had their lives spared. Among them was Pimen, former archbishop of the martyred city; he would be exiled to a remote monastery. Athanasius Viazemsky could not be executed because, unfortunately, he had died during the preliminary tortures. Nor was Alexei Basmanov present among the condemned: Ivan had forced young Feodor Basmanov to kill his father in prison to save his own head and Nikita Prosorovsky to stab his brother for the same reason. After which he told them: "You, you are a patricide! And you, a fratricide! So you both deserve death." He made a sign now to the executioner to seize them, while the *oprichniki*, amused by the good joke, cheered this sovereign who certainly could not be beaten at refinements of cruelty.

A secretary of the Privy Council unrolled a parchment and read aloud the names of the victims. The chief prisoner was Prince Ivan Viskovaty. Accused of having tried to deliver Novgorod up to Sigismund Augustus, of having written to the Sultan urging him to seize Astrakhan and Kazan, of having invited the Khan of Crimea to lay Russia waste, he raised his eyes to heaven and protested, "Everything that I have just heard is a tissue of atrocious calumnies! It is useless for me to try to vindicate myself, for my earthly judge is deaf to the sound of truth! But He who reigns in the heavens sees my innocence!" The *oprichniki* threw themselves upon him, gagged him, hung him by the feet, and cut his flesh into strips. Treasurer Funikov had boiling water and ice water poured over him by turns, "so that his skin came off like an eel's." The others had their throats cut, were hanged, or were hacked to pieces. Without dismounting from his horse, Ivan ran an old man through with his spear. In the space of four hours, two hundred men were put to death by the *oprichniki*. Finally, weary of killing, their clothes spattered with blood, they cheered the Czar, uttering their shout of joy: "Hoïda! Hoïda!"*

Ivan rode over the square, examining the corpses with curiosity and finding some of their postures comical. Then he went to the home of Funikov's widow, a young and lovely woman, the sister of Prince Athanasius Viazemsky, and demanded that she reveal where her husband hid his treasure. Since she swore that she did not know, he had her stripped naked in front of her daughter, a girl of fifteen and, having forced her to sit astride a stretched rope, subjected her to the slow torture by friction. According to a contemporary, Jerome Horsey, Prince Telepnev was impaled and suffered for hours before he died, while soldiers raped his mother in front of him.

After these executions, Ivan rested for three days—just long enough for the corpses to be buried and the square cleaned. Then new victims were brought out. Maliuta-Skuratov, the chief executioner, outdid himself. Eighty wives of prisoners were drowned in the Moskva. The bodies of their husbands, horribly mutilated, lay in the open air and decomposed in the July heat, giving off an unbearable stench. Ivan ordered his

---

*According to M. Karamzin, this was a cry used by the Tatars to urge on their horses.

oprichniki to cut this dead meat into small pieces so that the remains could be removed more easily. For nearly a week the dogs of Moscow fought over scraps of rotting flesh, and the dust of the square was soaked with blood. When Muscovites left their houses, they felt as if they were entering an open-air charnel house.

The slaughter en masse, before the assembled crowd, was followed by summary executions in private. The voivode Golokhvastov, learning that he was in danger, hid in a monastery on the banks of the Oka. The *oprichniki* discovered his hiding place and Ivan had him placed on a barrel of cannon powder and blown up. "Cenobites are angels who should fly up to heaven!" he said with a laugh. Another time, annoyed by some jest of Prince Gvozdev's, the Czar poured a bowl of boiling-hot soup on his head. The unfortunate prince screamed with pain and tried to flee, but Ivan planted his knife in his chest. Doctor Arnolphe Linsey, first physician to the Czar, was immediately called. "Save my good servant," Ivan said to him. "I have jested a little too roughly with him." "So roughly," replied Linsey, "that God alone can bring him back to life. He is no longer breathing." Some time later, again at table, the Czar cut off the ear of the voivode Boris Titov, as a joke. Titov never changed his expression but thanked His Majesty for this "gracious punishment" and wished him a happy reign. Another time, when Ivan rose from dinner to attend the torture of a few Livonian prisoners, one of them, a gentleman named Bykovsky, wrenched the Czar's spear away and tried to run him through with it. As swift as lightning, the Czarevich deflected the blow and stabbed the assailant with his dagger. Ivan was pleased with his son: With a bold fellow of that stamp—hard, courageous, quick—he was sure to have a worthy successor.

The two of them had long been united by love of wine, debauchery, and blood. The young man had only to appear at his father's side and the Russians were robbed of even the hope of a milder reign in the future. Sometimes, noticing peaceable citizens assembled in the square, father and son would amuse themselves by loosing raging bears among the crowd. The headlong flight of the Muscovites, their screams, their awkward and unequal struggle with the fierce beasts were a treat for the two practical jokers. Suffering that became comical meant the acme of pleasure.

Ivan's conviction that he was on the right road was strengthened by the terrorized acceptance of his people: Not only did those whom he sent to death receive his decision courageously, they did not even seem to be angry with him for punishing them unjustly. Their attitude was a mixture of religious respect for the person of the Czar, the Lord's anointed, and blind submission to the inevitable. The less a Russian understood the reason for the punishment that fell upon him, the more inclined he was to believe it was sent by God. He did not rebel against adversity, he opened his door to it. Everything that was beyond his comprehension, either good or evil, necessarily came from on high. An example cited as typical is the case of a boyar who was impaled and who during the twenty-four hours of his lingering death talked with his wife and children and kept repeating, with eyes cast up to heaven, "Great God, protect the Czar!"

Debauchery of all kinds—drinking bouts, gluttonous feasting, sexual excesses—left its mark on Ivan's appearance. At the age of forty he was wreathed in fat. His long hair and tangled beard were graying. The eyes in his coarsened face had such an expression of suspicion and cruelty that only the *oprichniki* could bear to return his gaze, and it was with them that he felt most at ease. They alone, he thought, did not hate him.

In the countryside, meanwhile, because of the ravages of the *oprichnina*, great stretches of land remained uncultivated. Farmers who had been ruined never recovered to rebuild and plant again. In addition, the summer of 1570 had been very rainy and in the fall there was already a shortage of wheat and rye. That winter, famine came. The peasants ate the bark of trees; men died of hunger and exhaustion on the roads; in certain districts there were cases of cannibalism. Ivan no longer needed to intervene with his iron hand to decimate the population: God was taking care of that.

After famine came the plague. The Czar gave orders to cut all roads leading to the capital. Suspect travelers were seized and burned, along with their horses and baggage, to avoid contagion. Among the people the idea took root that the epidemic was a punishment sent by heaven for Ivan's sack of Novgorod.

XIII

The Burning of Moscow by the Tatars

In the West nothing was settled. The war in Livonia had been dragging on for months in a series of isolated encounters, sieges, retreats, precarious truces, and feeble attempts to resume hostilities. The year before, on July 1, 1569, Poland and Lithuania had signed the Act of Union of Lublin after long negotiations. By this act the two countries came together for all questions of foreign affairs under the authority of a single king (Sigismund Augustus), a single Diet, and a single Senate. Lithuania would retain its independence only in matters of internal politics. The rich Lithuanian Ukraine, including Kiev—the Orthodox mother of all Russian cities—was ceded to Little Poland, a southern part of that nation.

All this was a serious diplomatic defeat for Ivan. He tried to compensate for it by organizing his conquests in Livonia. But before he had even acquired the entire country, he realized that if and when he did so, he would have trouble administering the remote province from Moscow. He therefore decided to make it a separate state, very strictly controlled by Russia. As king of this new country, the territory of which he had not yet wholly taken over, he chose Magnus, sovereign of the Baltic island of Oesel and brother of the King of Denmark, Frederick II. A treaty signed with the princely adventurer stipulated that once Livonia was completely "liberated," it would become the vassal of Moscow but would remain in charge of its own administration, justice, and religion. In exchange, it would give free passage to Russian troops and would help them to take Reval and Riga.

In May 1570, Magnus arrived in Moscow with a retinue of four hundred persons. The theoretical master of a country not yet entirely subdued, he was crowned with great pomp and betrothed to the Czar's own niece, Euphemia. The year before, Ivan had killed the girl's father, Prince Vladimir Andreyevich—all the more reason to give the orphan a chance. He even granted her a dowry of five barrels of gold, which he forgot to pay.

Magnus was no sooner married than he left to besiege Reval. He was defeated. Ivan realized that it would be a long and difficult war. Fearing that the Sultan of Turkey, Selim II, might take advantage of these skirmishes in the West to attack him in the South, he had his ambassadors make broad peace overtures. Selim concluded from this that the time had come for the Tatars to avenge their latest defeats. He demanded that Kazan and Astrakhan be returned to him or that Moscow pay him an annual tribute. Suddenly, early in 1571, while negotiations were bogged down, the Tatars of Crimea, numbering 100,000, invaded the southern territories of Russia. There they met some fugitive boyars whom Ivan had exiled from Moscow. These boyars urged them to march fearlessly upon the capital because, they said, the main body of the Russian army was busy in Livonia and the people were weary of the reign of terror imposed on them by the Czar and his *oprichniki*. And indeed, the regiments stationed on the Oka represented only a thin curtain of protection.

Ivan went to the scene of action and received insulting messages from Devlet-Guirey, who challenged him to single combat and threatened to cut off his ears and send them to the Sultan. The situation was undeniably grave. Bypassing the troops defending the Oka, the Khan and his horde advanced on Serpukhov, where the Czar and his eldest son were staying. Ivan was seized with panic at the idea of being either killed in the melee or taken prisoner by a pitiless enemy. Abandoning his army, he fled with the Czarevich, his treasure, and his faithful *oprichniki* to Alexandrovskaya Sloboda. But he did not feel safe there and, seeking refuge with his regiments of the northwest, continued his retreat toward Yaroslavl. In his mind, Moscow was sacrificed.

In view of the numerical inferiority of their forces, Ivan's generals fell back and occupied the approaches to the capital. Yet they already knew that they could offer only feeble resistance to the Khan's armed bands, who were approaching swiftly, destroying everything in their path. On the morning of May 24, 1571, Ascension Day, the Tatars set fire to wooden houses on the outskirts of Moscow. A high wind spread the blaze. In a few moments an ocean of flames was roaring over the city. Behind the glowing curtain of smoke, the Tatars pursued the city's inhabitants and pillaged the gutted houses. Fleeing before the conflagration, the Muscovites tried to find safety in the citadel of the Kremlin, but the gates had been barricaded on the inside by the guards. The press of new arrivals crushed and trampled those who had arrived earlier and were streaming back into the adjacent streets. It was a tidal wave of bodies thrown against each other. Unable to either advance or retreat, suffocated by the heat, crushed under falling beams, the people died amid horrible disorder—to the sound of bells ringing the death knell. Living torches ran in every direction. Some threw themselves into the Moskva and were drowned. Corpses piled up in front of the locked doors. "He who has seen that catastrophe will remember it always with terror and will pray God to spare him so appalling a spectacle," an eyewitness was to write.

In less than three hours the vast city of wood had been reduced to a mass of smoking ruins and ashes, a stinking charnel house. Only the Kremlin, protected by its high stone walls, had escaped the disaster. Metropolitan Kyrill had taken shelter there with the sacred religious objects, leaving his flock to roast in the furnace outside. The number of victims, it was said, exceeded half a million. First physician Arnolphe Linsey and twenty-five British merchants were burned to death. The river and ditches of Moscow were filled with corpses.

The Tatars, who had begun to loot the city, were soon driven out by the flames. But they captured all the Russians who had taken refuge from the fire in the northern suburbs. There, from the top of the Sparrow Hills, Devlet-Guirey surveyed with satisfaction the charred landscape covered with wildly dancing sparks. To be sure, he could await the end of the conflagration and then assault the Kremlin. But a false piece of news made him decide against it. A rumor had spread that Magnus, King of Livonia, was advancing on Moscow by forced marches, at the head of a formidable army. The Khan judged it more prudent to return with his troops to Crimea.

Couriers brought news of this to the Czar, who in the mean-time had left Yaroslavl for Rostov. He immediately ordered Mikhail Vorotynsky to pursue the retreating enemy. But the Khan had too many troops and too good a start to be worried. As the Tatars withdrew they laid the country waste, as they had done on their way in. Their booty was enormous. They took with them 100,000 captives, destined to be sold in the slave market of Theodosia (Kaffa). The most beautiful women were reserved for the Turkish Sultan himself, the others for the harems of princes. Terrorized, starving, in chains, the prisoners were urged on with whips, like cattle. Those who stumbled and fell were killed on the spot.

Ivan saw no necessity for visiting the ruins of his capital, and returned directly to Alexandrovskaya Sloboda. From there he ordered the surviving Muscovites to raise their city again. Their first task was to clear the streets of the corpses that polluted the air. As there was a shortage of manpower, only the distinguished dead were given a religious burial; the others were thrown into the Moskva, in such quantities that the course of the river was slowed. The heaps of putrid flesh poisoned its waves. The city's wells were so contaminated that no one dared drink from them anymore—people were dying of thirst. To combat the disaster, inhabitants of the neighboring towns and villages were conscripted by force and turned into gravediggers. Bodies pulled out of the Moskva were belatedly interred. Finally, the Muscovites began to rebuild their wooden houses on the now-blackened foundations.

At last, on June 15, Ivan started back to Moscow. En route he received two envoys from Devlet-Guirey. They demanded once again, in the Khan's name, that he return Kazan and Astrakhan, and symbolically presented him with a dagger in case he wished to kill himself in despair. But the envoys also delivered to him a letter from their master. "I burn, I ravage Russia," wrote Devlet-Guirey, "for no other reason than to avenge Kazan and Astrakhan, without thinking of the money, the riches, which I regard as dust. I have sought you everywhere, in Serpukhov, in Moscow itself: I wanted your crown and your head. Yet you fled those two cities and you dare boast of your greatness, prince without courage and without shame! Now I know the road to your dominions. I will soon return to them, if you do not restore to liberty my ambassador, whom you hold captive to no purpose, if you do not do what I require of you, if you refuse, lastly, to swear allegiance to me for yourself, your children, and your descendants."

Naturally, Ivan was tempted to respond to this provocative message with biblical insults. But it hardly seemed the best time for a fresh confrontation. Swallowing his pride, he therefore addressed a "humble petition" to Devlet-Guirey. He asked for a truce, promised to consider giving up Astrakhan, and agreed to free the Crimean ambassador. So far as Astrakhan was concerned, he said, one of the Khan's sons could be named governor, with a boyar designated by the Czar at his side. This patched-up solution did not satisfy Devlet-Guirey. He demanded the return of Kazan and Astrakhan without any concessions on his part, and with an advance of two thousand rubles on the annual tribute. Ivan equivocated. He was really only playing for time while he mobilized all his available reserves. Contemptuous the moment he felt himself in a position of superiority, he was capable of being patient, obsequious, and wily when he was not certain of his strength.

XIV

The Czar's Bed
and the
Throne of Poland

Ivan's troubles with the Tatars had prevented him from acting on an idea which he had had his heart set on ever since the death of his second wife, Maria: He wanted to remarry. As soon as a semblance of calm had been restored to the southern borders, he gave out the same orders as at the time of his first betrothal: that pleasing young maidens without distinction of birth should be brought to him, in Alexandrovskaya Sloboda. More than 2,000 arrived, escorted by their parents—nobles, merchants and other bourgeois. Every region of the empire was represented. Who would dare to hide his daughter from the eyes of the Czar, unless she were ill-favored?

Each girl was presented separately to Ivan, who looked her

over critically, questioned her, mentally gave her a grade, and sent her away before interviewing the next one. First, he chose twenty-four, then of those he chose twelve, whom the doctors and midwives were instructed to inspect more closely. After these examinations, of which he was given a detailed report, he compared the final contestants one last time for their beauty, plumpness, hair, sexual attractions, and manners. He gave his preference to Martha Sobakina, the daughter of a merchant from Novgorod. While he was at it, the Czar decided to have his seventeen-year-old son Ivan marry another of the chosen twelve. A competent judge of such matters, he allotted the Czarevich the next most desirable virgin after Martha, whom he had reserved for himself. She was the daughter of a bourgeois and her name was Eudoxia Saburova. The fathers of the two triumphant candidates were elevated at once from simple commoners to the rank of boyars. But Martha, the Czar's betrothed, scarcely had time to rejoice in her victory. A few days after the great choice, she fell ill. Although she was visibly wasting away and could hardly keep her feet, Ivan decided to marry her, hoping that his embraces would have a tonic effect. The Czar's wedding took place on October 28, 1571, his son's on November 3. Alas! The nuptial feasting ended in tears and anger: Martha expired on November 13.

The Czarina's coffin was taken to the convent of the Nuns of the Ascension to join those of Ivan's first two wives. The Czar promptly began talking of poison, and looked about for those who would have had a motive to do away with his young wife. The close relatives of the preceding Czarinas, Anastasia and Maria, were immediate suspects. He ordered a speedy investigation, but knew already whom he was going to annihilate. His vengeance fell on his brother-in-law, the Circassian Mikhail Temriuk (or Temriukovich), who was impaled; then on Ivan Yakovlev and the voivode Saburov,* who were knouted; and last on the boyar Leon Saltykov, the favorite Vasily Griaznoy, Prince

---

*The voivode was not related to Ivan's daughter-in-law, Eudoxia Saburova.

Gvozdev-Rostovsky, and several other noblemen, who were all poisoned with a potion prepared by the diabolical Dr. Elysius Bomel.

Widowed for the third time, Ivan wondered whether his marital career was over. According to the rule of the Orthodox church, a man could contract no more than three marriages. The *Stoglav* Council had made a strong statement to that effect: "The first marriage is the law; the second, a concession by the law; the third, a violation of the law; the fourth, an impiety, a state resembling that of the beasts." Now Ivan had no intention of remaining a bachelor. He declared, therefore, that he had had no carnal relations with his ill wife, that she had died a virgin, and that consequently his last marriage could be considered by the Church nonexistent. Secure in this conviction, on April 29, 1572, he married Anna Koltovskaya, the daughter of a courtier, without even asking the Bishop's blessing. He then convoked an ecclesiastical council.

Metropolitan Kyrill being deceased, the assembly was presided over by Leonid, Archbishop of Novgorod, a greedy, servile, venal man. When all the bishops were gathered in the Cathedral of the Assumption, Ivan addressed them as follows: "Evil men used sorcery to take the life of my first wife, Anastasia; the second, a Circassian princess, likewise poisoned, died amid painful convulsions. I hesitated long before making up my mind to marry a third time, as I was commanded to do by my temperament and by the position of my children, who have not yet reached the age of reason. Their youth prevented me from withdrawing from the world, and to live in the world without a wife is to live in constant temptation. With the blessings of Metropolitan Kyrill, I looked for a spouse for a long time and at last chose one after a careful examination. But hatred and envy caused the death of Martha, who was really Czarina in name only. She was scarcely betrothed when she lost her health, and two weeks after the wedding she died a virgin. Desperate, overcome with grief, I wanted to devote myself to the monastic life; but having once again considered the youth of my sons and the distress of my dominions, I dared to marry a fourth time. And now I beg the holy bishops to grant me absolution and their benediction."

Deeply moved by this act of contrition on the part of a powerful sovereign, the prelates confirmed his marriage. However, they forbade him to enter a church before Easter Sunday, and ordered that when he did return to worship, for one year he should take his place among the penitents and only the next year among the faithful, "except in case of war." Furthermore, so that no one among the common people should be tempted to imitate the Czar's illegal conduct, the council threatened anyone who might marry for a fourth time with a fulminating anathema. The act of absolution was signed by three archbishops, sixteen bishops, several archimandrites, and the abbots of the most respected monasteries. Having thus quieted Ivan's scruples, they turned to the election of a new Metropolitan. It was Anthony, Archbishop of Polotsk, who was honored with the title.

Ivan was so satisfied with his new wife that he decided to take her on a honeymoon trip to the city he had recently sacked: Novgorod. It never occurred to the Czar that the citizens might feel some resentment for the massacre he had perpetrated within their walls: Since he had pardoned the survivors, should they not be filled with gratitude? The Czar's two sons and his favorites accompanied the couple. When they arrived they found a dead city, three-quarters depopulated. Still ravaged by the disaster of 1570, the inhabitants dreaded this fresh visit from their sovereign. What was he going to invent now for their misery? Only the clergy welcomed him with joy. Leonid, the Archbishop of Novgorod, was his creature. Ivan liked to debate with him on obscure points of theology and to direct the cathedral choirs with his spear.

The real reason for Ivan's presence in Novgorod was that he intended to conclude an armistice with Sweden, whose territory Magnus, King of Livonia, had been attacking for some time.

Once again the Czar needed all his armed forces to confront a new threat of invasion by the Tatars. According to information provided by his spies, Devlet-Guirey had not even "unsaddled his horses," and was making ready to descend on Moscow again. Honor demanded that Ivan remain in the capital, which had barely risen from its ashes, so that his presence might bolster the morale of the population; but as usual, he thought first of his own safety. He believed that even if the Khan reached Moscow, he would never push as far north as Novgorod. Therefore, Ivan had 450 wagons laden with treasure brought to his retreat and ordered his generals to prepare to contain the Tatars on the banks of the Oka.

In the meantime, he was overjoyed by an event of the greatest importance: Sigismund Augustus died on July 18, 1572, without leaving a male heir. This circumstance offered Russia the possibility of acquiring Poland and Lithuania by installing a puppet sovereign. No doubt if Ivan maneuvered skillfully he could even be a successful pretender to the double crown himself. Without delay he wrote a hypocritical letter expressing the grief he felt at the death of his brother Sigismund Augustus, the last of Poland's Jagiello dynasty. Unfortunately, he did not have time to advance his pawns in that direction.

As Ivan feared, Devlet-Guirey and his Tatar hordes started to move along the usual route, found a ford on the Oka, and, escaping detection by the Russians, crossed the river and once again threatened Moscow. The news reached Ivan on July 31, but instead of sending reinforcements toward the capital, he took no action, merely cursed his incompetent generals. Prince Vorotynsky, however, evacuating his now-useless positions on the left bank of the Oka, raced after the enemy, managed to catch up with them fifty versts from Moscow, and on August 1 engaged them in bloody battle. The Khan's army numbered 120,000. Vorotynsky had fewer men, but they were driven by fear of seeing the old city, symbol of the Orthodox faith and national tradition, once again profaned. They fought with the energy of despair, at first from a distance, with arrows, then hand to hand in a furious melee of screaming men and neighing horses. The issue of the battle was still in doubt when Vorotynsky executed a flanking maneuver and fell upon the enemy's rear. His artillery captured the positions of the adversary, one after another. At nightfall, of the 120,000 Tatar warriors only some 20,000 remained. Devlet-Guirey beat a retreat, abandoning to the Russians his tents, his baggage, and even his flag. When Vorotynsky's messengers announced this success to the Czar, they brought him as trophies two bows and two sabers that had belonged to the Khan. Ivan, relieved of his anxiety, had the Novgorod bells rung and Te Deums sung day and night for a week.

The unlooked-for victory strengthened his personal prestige and rid the Khan of Crimea of any desire to invade Russia again. The Sultan himself accepted the military decision. Astrakhan and Kazan, it was now confirmed, were destined to be Russian cities. And Ivan could take a scornful tone with Johan III, King of Sweden, who was blustering again: "Inquire," he wrote him, "how the Khan of Crimea was treated by our voivodes!"

Moscow being now quite out of danger, Ivan returned there in great pomp. Never before had he had such a feeling of power and of popular support. Although he had had nothing to do with the defeat of the Tatars, and had even fled at their approach, his subjects gave him all the credit for the Russian victory. The strength of his army now gave him confidence, too, in his own future. Accordingly, he decided to rely on it henceforth and to dissolve the *oprichnina,* which was detested throughout the country. Another factor in this decision was the sinister reputation Ivan's "legion of death" had acquired beyond Russia's borders: Too many Polish noblemen, whose agreement he needed if he was to be crowned King of Poland, feared the introduction into their country of a band of mercenaries with authority to do anything they pleased. The Poles were less concerned about the

Czar's personal violence than about that of his henchmen; the former, they felt, was simply a manifestation of his dominating character, the latter the reign of murderous madness. Thus, to gratify his own people and to disarm the hostility of the Poles and Livonians, Ivan separated himself from his dear *oprichniki*, who for seven years had been covering Russia with blood and ruin. He published the following order: "Henceforth anyone who pronounces the name *oprichnik* will be beaten with the knout in the public square."

When Ivan's decision was announced, the people blessed the wisdom of their sovereign. They no longer had to fear the terrible horsemen with their dogs' heads and brooms. The marauders became courtiers once again, soldiers, high officials without special rights. Surprisingly, not one of them rebelled against the ukase that stripped them of their privileges. Fierce adventurers, hired assassins, bloody debauchees, all accepted their fall from grace without a murmur. What the Czar had given he could take back at any moment. Once again Ivan relished the pleasure of casting down those whom he had raised up on a sudden impulse. If he needed a fresh proof of his omnipotence, the *oprichniki* had just given it to him: The wolves had submitted like lambs. Having formerly tipped the scales in their direction, he now inclined them to the other side. The members of the *zemshchina* regained possession of their property. The Abbot of Solovetsky Monastery, Paisy, who had borne false witness against Metropolitan Philip, was exiled to the island of Valamo, and certain bad advisers were dismissed from the palace. Nevertheless, the ferocious Maliuta-Skuratov retained his dominant place at court.

Maliuta-Skuratov's son-in-law, Boris Godunov, a distant relative of the Czar's first wife, began gradually to grow closer to the throne. Day by day, Ivan came to have increasing regard for this handsome young man with the majestic stature and wily brain. Godunov was opposed to violence and in all circumstances he counseled temporizing and guile. But he understood his sovereign's character perfectly and never took it into his head to talk to him about virtue—he invoked only reason and expediency to persuade his master to moderate his rages. No doubt it was at Godunov's urging that Ivan had dissolved the *oprichnina,* whose excesses were a blot on his image abroad. It was also Godunov who suggested that the Czar cajole the Poles and Lithuanians with honeyed words so as to win their confidence and obtain, without striking a blow, the crown he so eagerly desired.

The army, meanwhile, was sent to the Northwest against Sweden. Magnus, fighting to enlarge his domain under Ivan's protection, naively imagined that as a reward for his efforts he would receive Livonia, as promised. But Ivan and Boris Godunov had no intention of yielding a territory long coveted by Russia to a Dane. They would leave him his illusions so long as he could serve their interests. At present, Ivan was aiming his blows at the Estonian front. Towns fell, one after another, before his troops and those of Magnus. They looted, burned, killed, raped. During one of these clashes the bloodthirsty Maliuta-Skuratov was killed.

Ivan was furious at the disappearance of his best companion in debauchery and slaughter. As a reprisal he rounded up his German and Swedish prisoners, in chains, threw them into a heap, covered them with faggots, and burned them alive. The screams of the victims and the smell of burning flesh consoled him in part for the loss of his friend. Ivan had no doubt that Maliuta-Skuratov, despite all his crimes, was already in paradise. How could the man fail to be pleasing to God, since in his cruelest deeds he had obeyed the orders of the Czar? Seen from that point of view, the combustion of a few captives was not a pointless execution but a quasi-religious holocaust.

"We are punishing you," wrote Ivan to the King of Sweden, "you and your country. The righteous always triumph. . . . Tell me, whose son was your father? What was the name of your grandfather? Send me your genealogy to convince me of my mistake, for until now I have been persuaded that you were bred of common stock. . . . The seal of the Roman Empire is not foreign to me, since I descend from Caesar Augustus. I do not say this in order to boast and to disparage you, but to make you realize what you are. Do you want peace? Order your ambassadors to appear in my presence."

Instead of sending his ambassadors, King Johan III of Sweden replied in the same tone: "You write in a discourteous manner, as if you had been raised among peasants or vagabonds who knew nothing of honor. . . . You lie impudently and loudly whenever you open your mouth. . . . You look down on us disdainfully from the heights of your intelligence, the intelligence of a pig. . . ." And then the Swedish troops, for all that they were outnumbered, inflicted a severe defeat on the Russians at Lode. This circumstance, together with the news that the Cheremiss tribes had revolted in the Kazan region, persuaded Ivan to slacken the war against Sweden and send an army to the Volga.

The pacification was carried out with dispatch. Taking advantage of the lull that came with the suspension of hostilities in the west, Ivan decided to put an end to Magnus's territorial claims—his services were no longer needed. Magnus's first wife (the Czar's niece) had died some time earlier, so Ivan began his charade by offering the widower as second wife the deceased woman's sister, a girl of thirteen. Magnus, who was thirty-five, accepted gladly, and the marriage was celebrated with much gaiety in Novgorod on April 12, 1573. Many German guests joined in the festivities. During the religious ceremony, the Czar directed the choirs, beating time with his staff. Afterward, he entertained himself by ordering the dances and encouraging the couples to be freer in their movements. Seeing so much benevolence, Magnus already looked upon himself as king and imagined that in addition to the rich dowry he was promised, he would receive all the Russian-occupied towns in Livonia. But instead of the five barrels of gold he was counting on, he was sent only chests of clothes for his young bride. And far from ceding him Russia's share of Livonia, the Czar only granted him a small domain. Magnus, disillusioned, left for his estates and lived there in poverty—"having only three courses at dinner," according to his brother Frederick II, King of Denmark, "amusing his thirteen-year-old wife with toys, feeding her delicacies, and to the great dissatisfaction of the Russians, causing her to dress in the German fashion."

In Warsaw, meanwhile, the Polish Diet was trying to elect a king. There were several candidates for the vacant throne: young Ernst, the son of Emperor Maximilian II; Johan III of Sweden and his son Sigismund; Henri de Valois, the Duc d'Anjou, brother of King Charles IX of France; and the Czar of Russia, Ivan IV. Each of the aspirants was going hard at it with presents and promises. Certain Polish noblemen were considering offering the crown to Ivan's second son, Feodor. When the Polish envoy in Moscow, Feodor Voropai, hinted at this possibility, the Czar responded with indignation: "My two sons are like my two eyes. Do you want to make me half blind?" Then, pleading his own cause, he explained: "Many people in your country say that I am inhuman; it is true that I am cruel and irascible, but only for those who behave badly toward me. The good ones? Ah, I would not hesitate to give them my gold chain and the coat off my back! . . . My subjects would have gladly delivered me up to the Tatars of Crimea. . . . It was not the enemy I feared but betrayal by my own people. They let Moscow burn when it could have been defended with a thousand men. But when great men don't want to fight, how can the humble do it? . . . If anyone was punished afterward, it was for his crime. . . ." Suspecting that the renegade Andrei Kurbsky, who had gone over to the service of Poland, was conducting a campaign of defamation against him, Ivan added: "Who can be blackening me in the eyes of your compatriots? My enemies! Traitors! Kurbsky deprived my son of his mother; he took from me a beloved wife, and I call God to witness, I did not mean to punish him with death, but only

to deprive him for a time of the rank of boyar and the property
he had acquired through my liberality. In a word, do you want
to know if I am good or evil? Send me your children to serve me
faithfully: Loaded with favors, they will be able to judge the
truth! . . . If, by the will of the Almighty, I am called upon to
reign over you, I promise to observe your laws scrupulously, to
respect your freedoms and privileges, and even to extend them
if need be."

Having thus justified himself before Feodor Voropai and
his retinue, Ivan awaited the arrival of a new ambassador bearing a favorable response from Poland. It was Mikolaj Haraburda
who presented himself. He was ready to support the Czar's
candidacy but posed certain conditions: In exchange for his
election, Ivan should rectify the border to Poland's advantage
and abandon Polotsk, Smolensk, and other Russian cities.

Ivan dug his heels in. Did they take him for a beggar? "It
is they," he cried, "who need me!" On February 23, he summoned Haraburda, reproached him for the presumptuousness
of his compatriots, curtly refused to accept the conditions
posed, and demanded that Kiev be yielded to him, that Livonia
become his undivided property, that all his titles, starting with
that of Czar, be inscribed in full in diplomatic documents, and
that in future the Polish monarchy be no longer elective but
hereditary, united to Russia "until the end of time." As for his
rivals for the throne of Poland, he had only contempt for their
maneuvers. "I know that Austria and France show more conde-
scension in their relations with you," he said, "but they cannot
set an example for Russia, for we know for a fact that except for
us and the Sultan there is no sovereign in Europe whose dynasty
is two centuries old. Some of them are descendants of simple
princes, others come from a line of foreigners, and it is quite
natural that they should be fascinated by royalty. But for us, *czar*
by birth, we are descended from Caesar Augustus, as the whole
world knows."

Timidly, Haraburda pointed out that Moscow was too far

away from Warsaw, where the presence of a king was indispensable, and that it might be better if he reconsidered his decision and consented to stand aside in favor of his son, so far as ruling Poland was concerned. Ivan remained adamant. "After mature reflection, I believe that I could govern three states at the same time [Russia, Poland, Lithuania] by traveling from one to another," he said. "But I ask to be crowned by a Russian metropolitan and not by a Latin archbishop."

Haraburda left for Warsaw again with this reply. Ivan thought he had the advantage. His most serious rival, he felt, was Henri de Valois, whose envoy, the Comte de Montluc, had dangled countless preposterous promises in front of the Poles: the creation of a Polish fleet, the training of Polish squadrons in Paris, development of the Academy of Cracow by French scholars . . . But, Ivan thought, half of the Polish nobility were Protestants. How could they vote for a Catholic who was deeply compromised in the St. Bartholomew's Day massacre that had been ordered the year before by Charles IX? Actually, that massacre gave Ivan a clear conscience. He was not the only monarch who hacked up his subjects. Of course, he could have pressed harder to obtain the crown of Poland, but while he desired it, he also feared it. In Poland the king had to take into account the Senate, composed of magnates, and the Szlachta, a Diet elected every two years by the lesser nobility. How could a czar, the symbol of absolute power, be content with this limited power over citizens who claimed the right to have their say? Would not the Polish aristocracy, proud of these privileges, set a dangerous example for Russia, which for centuries had been subject to the will of the sovereign? It is never good to associate an enslaved people with a free people. The perverse taste for discussion and representation is quickly transmitted even to the most submissive minds. Perhaps it was better for the Russians to keep to themselves, in a country with a firm hierarchical structure, rather than to seek a false rapprochement with the Poles, who had too many ideas in their heads.

It was with a mixture of irritation and relief that Ivan learned of the Poles' final choice. After endless discussions, the electing Diet had decided in favor of the Frenchman, Henri de Valois, the Duc d'Anjou. Thus, because the Czar had been too arrogant in his demands and too stingy of gifts that might have bought the electors' consciences, he lost the chance to rule Poland and Lithuania. Nevertheless, he was firmly convinced that another opportunity would soon present itself in that region.

XV

Stephen Bathory

The abolition of the *oprichnina* led to incessant disputes among the Czar's high dignitaries, each eager to assert his right of precedence over the others. In the army an officer whose father or grandfather had been a voivode in command of the center didn't want to take orders from a voivode whose father or grandfather had only commanded the advance guard or the rear guard, the right wing or the left wing. By the same token, at court everyone cited his birth and refused to give way before a newcomer. The Czar grew weary of arbitrating these petty quarrels. Generally he consulted registers and based his decisions on seniority, but sometimes—as for Boris Godunov—he imposed his will without giving the least explanation to those around him. When a minister of the Duke of Kurland asked Ambassador Sukorsky how the Russians could put up with a tyrant like Ivan IV, the diplomat replied, "We are always devoted to our czars, whether they are kind or cruel."

This devotion to the sovereign struck all foreigners who were received in public. The Russians made a rule of impressing visitors with the richness of their costumes and the strictness of their etiquette. When the Czar went to church, he walked slowly, leaning on a long cane of gilded silver, his body buried under a robe of cloth of gold cut like a dalmatic and studded with precious stones, his head crowned with a glittering tiara surrounded with sable. There was something pontifical about his splendor. He was escorted by four sons of boyars wearing white boots and robes of cloth of silver lined with ermine, each carrying a silver ax on his shoulder. Behind them came a lengthy procession of boyars in magnificent costumes. After mass and before sitting down at table, the Czar's retinue would change their clothes, taking advantage of the opportunity to let the travelers admire the luxury of the garments underneath. Actually, the costumes and undergarments came from the Czar's wardrobe and would be returned there after the banquet. This was to remind the nobles that everything in this world belonged to the monarch.

The ceremonial during a feast also contributed to this impression of omnipotence. When the guests had taken their places around the Czar, they would remain frozen in mystical respect, awaiting his first gesture. He would begin by distributing the bread and salt. The boyars then divided these among the guests, and when each had received his portion, he rose and bowed. Next, the Czar had a great cup of wine brought to every foreigner, on his behalf, and again everyone rose to his feet. When the meats arrived, the drill was the same. After having served himself, the Czar offered pieces dripping with sauce to a few high personages. The officers would say to each one, "The

Czar sends you this," and each would again stand up to thank him. When the Czar drank to someone's health, which often happened, he first made the sign of the cross three times over the cup held out to him by the cupbearer; a nobleman seated next to Ivan would inform the guest of the honor that fell to him; and the whole company would leap to their feet and bow their heads. There was no end to the thanks offered the master for the wine and food. Everything came from him! His table companions were obligated to him for life.

Because of the tirelessly repeated rituals, meals sometimes lasted five hours. On the table would appear a succession of cocks in ginger, roasted swans, spiced cranes, boned chickens, grouse in cream, ducks with cucumbers, hares with turnips, elks' brains, stuffed fish, and pâtés of all sorts. Over this avalanche of victuals floated a strong odor of garlic, saffron, onion, and sour milk. The guests ate with their fingers, placing the bones in gold plates. Juice flowed into beards, faces flushed, voices grew louder. The obligation to do honor to all the cups sent by the Czar induced in some a stupor bordering on coma. In their stomachs mead was mixed with Rhine wines, French wines, Malmsey, *kvas,* and vodka. And when they rose from table to go home, it was not unusual for Ivan to send to their residences, as a token of friendship, more alcohol and food to be downed on the spot, in front of the officers who had brought it.

In private homes as at court, immoderate eating and drinking constituted the chief diversion. Every Christian holiday was the occasion for feasting. As for the indispositions that followed these blowouts, the Czar, like his subjects, treated them with contempt. To cure an illness of any kind, the best thing was still to empty a glass of brandy seasoned with garlic or pepper, eat a slice of onion, and go sweat in the steam baths. While he listened to his English physicians, the Czar did not disdain Russian medicines. A heavy eater and a heavy drinker, he believed that a man's strength depended on the amount of nourishment he consumed.

Other profane pleasures, although proscribed by the Church, were tolerated in the palace. The Czar's courtiers played cards in his presence and he himself played chess. He also liked to be amused by the jests of his clowns. With their blunt speech that spared no one, they would sometimes provoke a burst of laughter that dissipated the heavy atmosphere in which the Muscovite court crouched. But if one of them went beyond the bounds, beware the iron-tipped staff! One scowl and the clown fell silent. Every living creature in the Kremlin dove back into its hole.

For some time those who were close to Ivan had hoped that as he grew older, his passions would moderate. But at forty-five, though he had grown fat, become short of breath, and taken to sleeping later, he had lost none of his gluttony, ferocity, or sexual appetite. After two years of marriage he tired of his wife, the Czarina Anna, blamed her for her sterility, repudiated her, and sent her to a convent, where she became Sister Daria.* Then, without asking for the least ecclesiastical absolution, he took into his bed another daughter of the people, Anna Vassil-chikova. Doubtless there had been no solemn marriage for her, only a simple blessing. In any case, she soon disappeared, struck down apparently by violent death. In her place appeared the very beautiful Vasilissa Melentieva. With this new companion Ivan enjoyed his sixth honeymoon. But in his matrimonial experiments he was to be persistently dogged by ill luck. A few months later Vasilissa, caught in adultery with Prince Ivan Dev-telev, was obliged to witness the slow execution of her lover, who was impaled under her windows, and then found herself in a cloister with her head shorn. Another wife, Maria Dol-gorukaya, chosen immediately afterward, was even more disappointing than the preceding: On his wedding night the Czar found that she was not a virgin. This discovery of fraud left him beside himself with rage. In his eyes it was more than an insult

---

*She lived another fifty-one years, until 1626.

to the Czar's virility, it was a sacrilege that besmirched God himself. The very next day the young woman was bound in a carriage and drawn by galloping horses to the river, where she was drowned. The terrified Church dared neither condemn the murder nor refuse to bless the successive unions of the aging goat.

At this time, Ivan freely declared that he was weary of life, honors, and politics. He said that he yearned to wear the black cowl of a monk. And as if he were preparing to renounce the world, he unexpectedly announced that he was relinquishing his functions in favor of one of the Tatar princes in his retinue, who had been baptized under the name Simeon Bekbulatovich and married to the daughter of Prince Mstislavsky. "From this day forth, you will be the czar and I will be your subject," Ivan said to the dull-witted, good-natured youth, who thought at first it was a sinister joke. No one could forget that some seven years earlier the Czar had mockingly given his robe and crown to old Prince Fedorov and then killed him with his own hand. Was not the same fate in store for Simeon, now that he was asked to ascend the throne? He shuddered with fear, smiled humbly, and prepared himself for death. But this time Ivan proved benign. He sincerely desired that Simeon take charge of the affairs of the country in his place.

The astounded Tatar soon found himself receiving petitions, signing ukases, giving audiences to prelates, noblemen, and foreign ambassadors. Lost among the crowd of courtiers, Ivan was amused at the serious air affected by his monkey. He even lavished upon him public marks of the deepest respect, addressed petitions to him, stepped down from his carriage at the approaches to the palace where his double was installed. Observing this newcomer to glory, he told himself that the real power lay elsewhere. Simeon was the appearance without the reality; *he* was the reality without the appearance. It was not the crown that conferred power but birth, the heart, the glance. So far as Ivan was concerned, since he could still do precisely as he pleased, he remained Czar even though he was Czar no longer. In any case, no one was deceived. While they bowed before the other, it was before Ivan that they trembled. Chosen by God, he had no need of the scepter to reign. When he felt like it, he would take the empire into his own hands again.

This strange "vacation" lasted an entire year—after which, Czar Simeon made his exit through a trapdoor, and Czar Ivan returned to center stage, delighted to have put on this act for his people.* For he loved to laugh at others' expense. One day, he ordered the Moscow authorities to deliver to him a hat filled to the brim with live fleas, in order, he said, that he might prepare a medicine. When the city proved unable to do as bidden, he imposed a fine of seven thousand rubles on its inhabitants, and boasted of the exploit, holding his sides with laughter while his entourage noisily echoed his merriment.

The reason Ivan wanted to remove the doltish Simeon from the throne and resume his old place was that he was again preoccupied with Polish affairs. Immediately after being elected, the Duc d'Anjou had taken an oath, in the Cathedral of Notre Dame in Paris, to respect Poland's liberty. But he had waited six months before going to Warsaw for the coronation. As a fervent Catholic, he found it repugnant to swear that he would never interfere with the practice of any religion within his realm, yet the Poles insisted that he must pronounce those words before he received the scepter. He resigned himself, resentfully. A French fop, pomaded and powdered, he felt ill at ease among the rough, proud magnates. In private they said that they didn't know whether they should call him a woman-king or a man-queen. Visibly, they were as dissatisfied with him as he was with them, and it was with a sense of relief that the Duc d'Anjou learned of the demise of his brother Charles IX. The timely

---

*Peter the Great was to show the same inclination for this kind of masquerade, living in a little wooden house while his favorite, Menshikov, strutted in a palace, posing as a simple courtier during his "Great Embassy" abroad, and paying homage to Romoda-novsky seated in a throne and dressed up as Caesar.

death restored him, as it were, to France. He escaped secretly at night, galloping his horse and returning to Paris to ascend the throne under the name Henri III. Naturally, despite the entreaties of his former subjects, he refused to go back to Poland. The Diet solemnly deposed him in May 1575.

Once more, the Poles were feverishly casting about for a king. It started all over again: the intriguing, the bribery, one contender outbidding the other. Taking advantage of the disorders in the country, the Tatars ravaged the Ukraine, and the Polish nobles realized they must make a decision without delay. Again Ivan was passed over because of his intransigence. Finally, on December 12, 1575, the Diet, unable to choose among the candidates, elected two kings: the Emperor Maximilian and Prince Stephen Bathory of Hungary. But Maximilian was ill and could not come to be crowned. Stephen, on the other hand, was full of vigor and determination. He hurried to Cracow, impressed the electors with his energetic speeches, and further strengthened his position by marrying Anna, sister of the late king, Sigismund Augustus. The couple were crowned on May 1, 1576. And, very opportunely, Maximilian breathed his last the following 12th of October.

So now there was only one king in Poland, Stephen Bathory. At forty-three he had character, piety, courage, a solid knowledge of military affairs, an inclination for justice, and a taste for power. First, he bought peace with Islam by paying a tribute to the Sultan. Then, in November 1576, he sent ambassadors to Ivan, who, seated on his throne with the Czarevich at his side, received them haughtily. Both the Czar and his son were dressed in cloth of gold; the boyars were sitting on benches in the audience chamber. Courtiers crowded the antechamber, the galleries, and the staircases. Outside, the square was black with people, and armed *streltsy* had to hold them back. This display of magnificence and strength was obviously designed to impress the envoys of Stephen Bathory, who was a mere soldier of fortune.

Bathory's ambassadors held their heads high, nonetheless.

The letter from their king, which they delivered to Ivan, aroused his ire, for his correspondent did not deign to call him "Czar," left out the titles of Grand Duke of Smolensk and Polotsk, and referred to himself as sovereign of Livonia. To be sure, Stephen Bathory said he was ready to observe the three-year armistice concluded between Russia and Poland "until the time agreed." But he gave no promise for the future. Icily, Ivan replied that he would consider the King of Poland as his "brother" only when the latter, "a simple voivode from Transylvania," should have given up his claims to Livonia and consented to name him in his communications "Czar of Russia and Grand Duke of Smolensk and Polotsk." Having spoken, he dismissed the ambassadors without inviting them to dinner but gave them letters of safe-conduct so that they might return to their country in peace.

As Ivan saw it, when the armistice expired, war with Poland would be inevitable. He decided, therefore, to take advantage of the interim to seize Swedish and Polish possessions in Livonia and on the Baltic coast. Early in 1577, 50,000 Russians laid siege to Reval. Stephen Bathory was himself busy besieging Danzig, (Gdansk) and did not interfere. The Swedish garrison in Reval defended itself so well that on March 13, after several costly assaults, the Russians withdrew—promising, however, to return in force. The fierce determination to resist displayed by the populations under attack was a direct consequence of the fearful reputation of the Czar. He inspired such terror that the Livonians, Estonians, and Latvians deliberately risked their lives to avoid falling under his yoke. Armed peasants commanded by one Yves Schenkenberg, nicknamed "Hannibal" because of his daring, made surprise attacks on the enemy and looted their encampments and towns. They occupied Wittenstein, burned Pernau (Parnu), and repaid Ivan in kind by torturing and massacring their prisoners. Ivan retaliated with even greater savagery. In Lenewarden he had old Marshal Gaspard von Münster's eyes torn out, then ordered him whipped to death; other commanders of fortified towns were quartered, impaled, hacked to pieces;

in Ascheraden, people all the way across the Dvina could hear the screams of forty virgins whom soldiers were raping in a garden.

The major part of the Russian army was now operating in the country, sweeping all before it and occupying town after town. Magnus reappeared and with the Czar's consent resumed the conquest of the kingdom he had so long coveted. In reality, he was acting on his own account, under cover of submission to the policies of Moscow. When Ivan allowed him to attack Wenden (Tsesis), he won entrance to the city without drawing his sword, by promising immunity against Russian tyranny—the Livonians felt that in welcoming him they were choosing the lesser evil. He continued his progress, acclaimed everywhere as the savior and as King of Livonia. Intoxicated by his success, Magnus even sent the Czar a list of towns that had recognized his sovereignty, including Dorpat.

Ivan was furious. He had the emissaries of the impudent princeling beaten; rushed to Kokenhausen, which was one of the towns on the list; organized a massacre there; and, having decimated the population, sent a letter to his "vassal" Magnus ordering him to appear before his eyes: "It is easy for me to bring you to your senses. I have soldiers and bread. That is all I need. Obey at once! And if you are not satisfied with the cities I have given you, cross the sea and return to your own country." While awaiting the arrival of the disloyal king, the Czar walked about the smoking ruins of Kokenhausen and discussed theology with a German pastor. But since the latter praised the virtues of Luther and dared to compare him to the Apostle Paul, Ivan struck him dead with his spear and cried, "Go to the devil with your Luther!"

Notwithstanding the Czar's summons, Magnus was slow to make up his mind. It was only when Ivan had recaptured most of "the King's towns" that finally, seized with fear, he went to the Russian encampment under the walls of Wenden. Twenty-five Germans accompanied him. Dismounting from his horse with an ashen face, he prostrated himself at the feet of his master. Ivan considered him with a mixture of anger and contempt. "You fool!" he shouted, "How could you have thought that you would be King of Livonia, you, a vagabond, a beggar, whom I took into my family, whom I married to a beloved niece, whom I have clothed and shod, to whom I have given riches and cities? And you have betrayed me, me, your sovereign, your father, your benefactor? Answer if you dare! How many times have I not heard talk of your hateful plans? But I did not wish to believe them and I kept silent. Now all is revealed! You wanted to invade Livonia by intrigue and cunning to become the servant of Poland. But the Good Lord has saved me and delivered you into my hands. Now, therefore, be the victim of your own disloyalty. Return what belongs to me and go back to crawl in obscurity!" Guards raised Magnus up and took him roughly, along with his followers, to a hut. There the captives were thrown on a litter of straw to await the Czar's decision.

Since the traitor's flag was still flying over Wenden, Ivan had the city shelled by cannon. Instead of surrendering, men, women, and children took refuge in the old castle that dominated the city. Desperate but resolute, they fired harquebuses at the approaching Russians, wounding a great many. Then Ivan had a Livonian prisoner, George Wilke, the famous defender of Volmar, impaled before their eyes. Next, he gave orders for the cannon to be aimed at the castle and to open fire at close range. For three long days the artillery battered the town walls, which gradually crumbled. Just before the final assault, the besieged decided to blow themselves up amid the ruins. They filled their cellars with powder, took communion, and knelt in rows, by families. At the moment when the Russians burst through the breach, one of Magnus's officers, named Boismann, waved a flaming torch. A formidable explosion pulverized everything, flesh and stone. Somehow Boismann survived, burned and mutilated, only to be planted on a stake while the Russian troops, thirsty for vengeance, beat and tortured the remaining inhabitants.

Rape and murder kept the soldiers busy for several days. Ivan, who was present, urged his men on to excesses. The "Punishment of Wenden" sowed terror throughout Livonia. Everyone knew from hearsay that the Czar was more cruel than all his generals put together. For the surrounding populations, his mere name constituted a threat of death. Cities were terrified at his approach and opened their gates at the first summons. Thus, he appropriated the major part of Livonia without fighting, though he gave up the idea of besieging Riga and Reval, whose defenses worried him.

Satisfied with his territorial gains, the Czar gave a great banquet in Volmar for his officers, distributed furs and gold cups to them, and freed a few distinguished Polish prisoners. "Go back to King Stephen," he told them; "persuade him to conclude peace with me on the conditions I am pleased to impose, for my arm is powerful, you have had proof of that." And remembering the deserter Kurbsky, who was still hiding in Poland, he dreamed of the day when Stephen Bathory, at a loss how to respond, would deliver Kurbsky to him bound hand and foot. Already in his head he imagined exquisite tortures for the traitor.

As if savoring his victory in anticipation, he wrote Kurbsky a triumphant letter: "We, Ivan, son of Vasily, by the grace of Almighty God sovereign, Czar, and Grand Duke of all Russia . . . to our former boyar. . . . Even if my crimes are more numerous than the sands of the sea, I continue to trust in divine clemency, for the Lord can drown my transgressions in the waves of His mercy. Already He has shed His grace on me—me, a sinner, an adulterer and torturer—by casting down Amalek and Maxentius* by virtue of the life-giving Cross. . . . For my part, I do not wish to enumerate all these victories, for it is not I who achieved them but God. You have written me that my understanding was more corrupt than that of a pagan, and be-

---

*Amalek: King of the Amalekites, and enemy of Jehovah (Exodus 17:8); Maxentius: Roman emperor, relentless opponent of the first Christian emperor, Constantine.

hold, I place you as judge between us: Which of us—all of you, or I—has the more corrupt mind? Is it I who, wanting to show that I was your master, incited your rebellion and rage, or rather you who refused me submission and obedience, who sought to rule me, to rob me of my power so as to govern as you pleased, removing me from the throne? . . . You, along with Alexei Adashev . . . imagined that the whole land of Russia was under your feet, but divine mercy changed your wisdom into vanity. It is precisely for this reason that I have trimmed my pen to write to you. Did you not use to say, 'There are no men of worth in Russia, no one is there to defend her'? Now that you are no longer here, who is it then who takes the fortified towns of the Germans? . . . Henceforth, Lithuania will no longer dare to say that the hooves of our horses have not passed over it from one end to the other."

The traitor Kurbsky might be out of reach for the moment, but Ivan had another traitor in his hand: Magnus. What should he do with him? The prisoner was expecting slow death by torture. But to general surprise, Ivan pardoned him. Perhaps victory had made him generous; or perhaps he wanted to imitate God, who dispensed storm and rainbow arbitrarily. He freed Magnus, granted him a few unimportant towns by way of a kingdom, and imposed on him a tribute of 40,000 gold florins, which the Dane did not have and would never pay. To proclaim his sovereignty over Livonia, the Czar ordered that the following inscription be engraved in stone on all the churches of that province: "I am Ivan, sovereign of a great number of countries, which are designated in my titles. I confess the faith of my fathers, the truly Christian faith according to the doctrine of the Apostle Saint Paul, as do the good Muscovites. I am their czar by birth, a title which I neither sought nor purchased, and my own czar is Jesus Christ."

At the end of autumn 1577, Ivan returned to his beloved residence in Alexandrovskaya Sloboda, where he planned to rest after the strains of his military expedition. But despite the successes achieved in Livonia, he was unable to recover his peace of mind. The last letter he had written to Kurbsky had reawakened his old grievances. Tirelessly he went over in his mind the alleged crimes of those around him. Twenty-four years later, he still could not forgive the clique of boyars who, when he had been ill and they had thought him dying, had wanted to keep the Czarina Anastasia and her son from the throne and to set Prince Vladimir Andreyevich upon it instead. To be sure, all the guilty persons, including Prince Vladimir, had paid for their presumption with their lives. Even the families of the conspirators had been destroyed and their property confiscated. One was left, however, a former friend of Adashev—Prince Mikhail Vorotynsky, hero of the capture of Kazan.

Banished in 1560 with all his family to Belozersk, Vorotynsky had been restored to favor five years later but had never been granted an absolute pardon. During seventeen years of loyal service, he had constantly felt hanging over him the threat of delayed punishment. Even after his recent victory over the Tatars of Devlet-Guirey, fifty versts from Moscow, he did not feel safe from the Czar's anger. Indeed, it seemed to him rather that that high deed, which had received unanimous praise, had done him a disservice in the eyes of his sovereign, for it was true that Ivan could not bear to have one of his subjects supplant him in the people's admiration. By becoming a national hero at the age of sixty, Mikhail Vorotynsky had definitively lost his chance of being pardoned. Henceforth, the Czar thought of him as a rival. Vorotynsky was aware that his fame placed him in danger, but he made no attempt to escape his fate. "If my sovereign wishes to put me to death," he said calmly, "he has a right to do so, for I am on earth to execute his will."

He had not long to wait. On Ivan's orders, a runaway serf from Vorotynsky's estate accused his master of practicing magic and holding secret interviews with witches for the purpose of making an attempt on the monarch's life. Arrested and loaded with fetters, the illustrious old man was brought before the Czar and confronted with the informer. "I have not learned, O tsar," cried Vorotynsky, "nor have I received the custom from my ancestors, to practise magic and to believe in devilry; but I have learned to praise one God, who is glorified in the Trinity, and to serve you, my tsar and sovereign, truly. This man accusing me is a servant of mine who ran away from me after robbing me. You should not believe him, nor should you accept evidence from such a man, for he is an evil-doer and has betrayed me, bearing false evidence against me."[1]

Unmoved by these protestations of innocence and devotion, Ivan ordered the execution of the voivode who had taken Kazan and saved Moscow. He was tied to a stake and placed between two blazing fires. During the torture the Czar, blinking his eyes in the smoke, used his long iron-tipped staff to move burning brands up to the sizzling body. In satisfying this old hatred, he felt as if he were setting his house in order—as if he were settling an affair that had dragged on for too long. The Prince was horribly burned but still alive when he was taken down and placed on a litter to be transported to the Monastery of Belozersk. He died on the way. "O must excellent and most steadfast of men," wrote Prince Kurbsky, "filled with much understanding, great and glorious is your blessed memory! . . . [Y]ou have been counted worthy to receive the very great reward by suffering in your innocence at the hands of that drinker of blood, and you have been counted worthy together with all the great martyrs to receive crowns from Christ our God in His Kingdom, in that from your youth up to a little before your sixtieth year you many a time bravely defended His sheep against the Mussulman wolf."[2]

To Ivan, the hideous death of Mikhail Vorotynsky was like the overture to a bloody opera. His appetite whetted by the torture of his voivode, he also had Nikita Odoyevsky and Mikhail Morozov executed, the latter along with his wife and two sons. Cornelius, Abbot of Pskov, and his disciple Vassian Muromtzev were slowly crushed by a millstone; Archimandrite Theodoret,

Kurbsky's former confessor, was drowned in a river; Leonid, Archbishop of Novgorod, was sewn into a bearskin and thrown to ravenous hounds, which tore him to shreds. Other, less illustrious victims also appeared on the list. In settling his scores, Ivan deliberately included both old boyars hostile to his policies and newcomers he didn't like the looks of. The virtuous and the wicked were equally exposed to his wrath. It was his way of being impartial.

Indeed, the morality Ivan IV had gradually forged for himself throughout his life would not let him be content to pursue only the truly guilty. When he tortured a man who was truly guilty, his chief feeling was one of satisfied vengeance and, beyond that, of agreement with the tribunal of God. No doubt this was agreeable. But when he tortured an innocent man, the enjoyment was at the same time more subtle and more intense. What he felt at such a time was the gratuitous pleasure of doing evil for evil's sake . . . the intoxication of destroying his fellow creature for no reason . . . the pride of affirming that he was above human laws. Yes, the scent of a body burning or bleeding was a hundred times more exciting when one knew that the suffering was not deserved. Unjust justice was a feast for a gourmet. When he punished for a reason, the Czar was conforming to the will of God; when he punished for no reason, he became the equal of God. One more step was thus ascended in the exaltation of absolute power.

While the energetic purge was going on inside the country, Ivan still kept a close watch on events abroad. Fearing that, despite the assurances of Stephen Bathory, Poland might be preparing to march against Russia, the Czar sought an alliance with Rudolf II, Maximilian's successor on the throne of the German Holy Roman Empire. In case of victory, he promised Rudolf Hungary; he would keep Poland for himself. But the new emperor, notwithstanding his hatred for Stephen Bathory, was afraid of the Sultan's reactions if he and Ivan should touch Hungary. He was therefore evasive with the Czar. King Frederick of Denmark, meantime, proposed to Ivan that they march together against Sweden. What Frederick had in mind was that the booty—Livonia and Estonia—should be shared between them. This time it was Ivan who found the bargain unacceptable. They settled for a fifteen-year armistice between Russia and Denmark. To be on the safe side, the Czar also sent gold to Mahomet-Guirey, son of Devlet-Guirey, who had died that year, to buy the neutrality of the Tatars. And through his emissaries he now carried on an amiable conversation with Stephen Bathory, who was obviously playing for time.

Suddenly, at the beginning of 1578, Ivan learned that Bathory had signed a treaty of offensive and defensive alliance with Sweden for the recapture of Livonia, the Narva River being the intended future line of demarcation between the two states. Operations began immediately. The Livonians sent barrels of brandy to the officers at Duneburg as a token of friendship, and when the entire garrison was drunk, forced the gates of the fortress and massacred the Russians inside. Russian-held Wenden also fell into the hands of the assailants, who attacked in the middle of the night and surprised the sleeping sentries. Last, the Polish army, commanded by Andrzej Sapieha, together with the Swedish army, under the orders of Boë, crushed the forces of Prince Golitzin. Six thousand Russians lay on the field. The artillerymen had committed suicide on their guns rather than surrender.

Fighting broke out everywhere, but it was only in June of 1579 that the courier Wenceslas Lopacinski brought to Moscow Stephen Bathory's declaration of war. This document, printed in several languages on presses that followed the army, included a historical account bristling with dates, several ironic allusions to Ivan's claim to be descended from Caesar Augustus, and the promise to respect the persons and property of nonbelligerents.

Indeed, the Polish army, some 20,000 strong, was subject to very strict discipline. Composed for the most part of foreign mercenaries (Russians, Hungarians, Frenchmen, Englishmen,

Italians, Belgians, Scots), it was nevertheless highly unified and very efficient. The Russians had nearly five times as many men, but, being badly armed and badly trained, they were inferior in combat to those commanded by Bathory. On the one side stood a shapeless Asiatic army split by rivalries among its generals; on the other side, a modern European army composed of soldiers of every country, under the rigid discipline of their officers—and accompanied by scribes and printers. Although they belonged to the same family, the two peoples represented two different and historically rival worlds. In their confrontation, two civilizations clashed. Under the Polish banners the Latin West was setting out to conquer the Slavic East.

At the beginning of August 1579, Stephen Bathory laid siege to Polotsk. Caught under artillery fire that smashed the wooden fortifications and set fire to the houses, the city fell after three weeks of resistance. A Russian army sent to its relief refused to fight in open country, shut itself up in the fortress of Sokol, and tried to cut the enemy's supply lines. But Sokol was taken by force of arms. Karsnoy and Starodub likewise capitulated. Faced with these repeated disasters, Ivan, who had set up his headquarters in Novgorod, retreated in haste to Pskov. One small consolation in the avalanche of bad news: The redoubtable "Hannibal," leader of the partisans, was captured, taken to Pskov, and executed.

Bathory was still advancing, and his reputation for generosity preceded him, winning the hearts of the people. It was said that he was justice itself. Simple, sober, courageous, he slept on the straw along with his soldiers, ate at their mess, wore no gloves, and disdained the use of stockings. He knew how to choose his officers, his men worshiped him, his manner of speaking was as grave and inspired as if he were praying. Ivan decided that so virtuous a prince could not be insensible to the language of the heart. Changing from arrogance to humility, Ivan invited him to send ambassadors to discuss a reasonable peace. Bathory refused, and demanded before anything else the release of Wenceslas Lopacinski, his emissary, whom the Czar had thrown into prison. Ivan obediently let the Pole out of his cell and invited him to his table. Then, swallowing the remainder of his pride, he sent his victorious enemy a delegation of five hundred superbly dressed dignitaries in an effort at conciliation. On the way they learned that Bathory, far from being prepared to parley, had gone on campaign again with an army of 18,000 men. The negotiators retraced their steps in consternation and informed the Czar of the failure of their mission. Ivan felt the chill breath of defeat pass across the back of his neck.

In September 1580, Bathory opened a path through thick forests, threw makeshift bridges across marshes, and laid siege to the great city of Veliki Luki, which the Muscovites used as a war depot and base of operations against Lithuania. The wooden ramparts, made of a double row of timbers and earth, seemed proof against shot. But a fire broke out and the garrison surrendered. After the city was captured, Bathory defeated the troops of Prince Khilkov, which had been sent as reinforcements, and went on to conquer the entire province inside of a month. "Even a hen defends her brood better when a falcon attacks," he wrote in a letter circulated in several languages. "But the Czar, the two-headed eagle of Muscovy, goes into hiding."

While the Poles were sweeping up Russian towns one after another, the Swedes, commanded by General Klas Horn and a Frenchman, Pontus de La Gardie, invaded Karelia and Estonia. They occupied Narva, Ivangorod, Yam, and Koporie. Beaten, bewildered, demoralized, the Russians gave ground in every sector. Most of Ivan's former conquests were wiped out. In view of the deficiency of his troops, he placed all his hope in God. Holed up in Alexandrovskaya Sloboda, he spent hours in prayer, waiting for celestial inspiration. Andrei Kurbsky, who was still fighting under the banners of Stephen Bathory, wrote to his former master: "Well, where are your victories now? In the graves of the heroes, the true defenders of Russia, the voivodes whom you have exterminated! . . . Instead of the love of the people and their blessings, which were once so dear to your heart, you reap only hatred and universal curses! Instead of military glory, you drink deep of shame! . . . Do we not see the judgment of God carried out on the tyrant? . . . I am silent and I weep!"

Ivan did not reply to this epistle, but to shake off the gloomy thoughts that tormented him he suddenly decided to marry for the eighth time. Violating all the laws of the Orthodox Church yet again, he married Maria Feodorovna Nagaya, the daughter of a court dignitary. At the same time his second son, Feodor, took to wife Boris Godunov's sister Irina. Only a few intimate friends were present at the double ceremony. Having a fresh young beauty in his bed was not enough, however, to cure Ivan of his hypochondria. On the contrary, it simply made him more cruelly aware of the deficiency of his own body and the disorder of his mind. He was obsessed with foreign affairs. He must have peace at any price.

The new negotiators whom Ivan sent to Stephen Bathory had orders to be conciliatory and affable, to accept the worst affronts, "including insults and blows," and to offer the insatiable Hungarian all of Livonia with the exception of four cities. He could have saved himself the trouble: Bathory demanded not only all of Livonia but also Novgorod, Pskov, Smolensk, all of "Sieverie,"* and an indemnity of four hundred thousand gold ducats.

Ivan choked with rage, and answered his adversary with a twenty-three-page letter that was a tissue of biblical quotations, protestations of innocence, and stinging insults. According to him, Poland had no right to Livonia, which was Russian territory. As for the war indemnity that was demanded, that was "a Moslem custom." "Such demands," he wrote, "are made by the Tatars, but in Christian states a sovereign does not pay tribute

---

*A former principality of Russia, in the Ukraine.

to another sovereign. . . . You who claim to be a Christian, why do you demand a tribute of Christians, as the infidels do? And why should we give you money? It is you who have made war on us, you who have taken a great number of prisoners, and is it we who owe you tribute? It would rather be appropriate for you to pay us indemnification, you who have attacked us without cause and conquered our territories. . . . We place our trust in the Almighty, we rely on the strength of the life-giving Cross, and you will do well to remember Maxentius, who perished in Rome through the effects of the holy, saving Cross."

When Bathory finished reading the interminable message, he burst out laughing, and said, "Never before has His Majesty sent us such a long-winded epistle! Perhaps he can trace his ancestry back to Adam?" And he instructed his chancellor, Jan Zamojsky, to draft a reply twice as long. He himself determined what the main points should be. To return good measure for Ivan's abuse, he declared that the Czar was a crowned madman, that his soldiers conducted themselves on campaign like bandits, that he made himself ridiculous by invoking his Roman origins when, "as everyone knows," his mother was the simple Princess Glinskaya, the daughter of a Lithuanian deserter, that he had no right to reproach the King for seeking the support of the Turks when he himself had once married a converted Moslem (Maria Temriukovna), and that he was only a coward fleeing the battlefields where his regiments died for nothing. In conclusion, Bathory challenged Ivan to single combat: "Take up your weapons, mount your horse, Ivan! Let us agree upon a time and place for the meeting, show your courage and your confidence in the justice of your cause, let us cross swords, we two alone! Thus, much Christian blood will be saved. . . . If you refuse us this satisfaction, you will have ratified your condemnation and proved that there is in your soul no strain of truth and no sense of the dignity of a sovereign, as you claim, nor the dignity of a man or even of a woman."

During this exchange of insults the military operations continued. Bathory, having obtained further funds from the Diet and pawned the crown jewels to pay his mercenaries, arrived under the walls of Pskov with 20,000 men and twenty cannon. The city, surrounded by a stone rampart and flanked with towers, contained a garrison of 40,000 soldiers, warehouses crammed with food and ammunition, and many churches. From a distance it looked so imposing to the Poles that Abbot Piotrowski exclaimed, "Heavens! Pskov is another Paris!" To galvanize the city's defenders, their commander, Prince Ivan Shuisky, had soldiers and civilians swear before the image of Our Lady of Vladimir that they would die rather than surrender. Venerable icons and relics of saints were borne in procession around the ramparts.

On September 8, 1581, after a few light attacks designed to feel out the enemy's resistance, Bathory's men launched a general assault, to the sound of trumpets. When the Polish artillery had opened breaches in the walls, they rushed into the city trampling corpses underfoot, seized two towers, and planted their flag on them. From there they riddled the Russians with bullets as these fell back in disorder. Prince Shuisky, covered with blood and powder, dismounted from his horse, stopped the fleeing men, and, pointing to the picture of Our Lady that the priests were waving above the melee, ordered them to return to combat. At the same moment, by a miraculous coincidence, one of the towers occupied by the assailants, which the defenders had mined beforehand, blew up in a deafening explosion with the soldiers and standards of the Polish King. German, Polish, and Hungarian corpses piled up in the ditches while the Russians counterattacked with renewed courage. In a supreme effort, the enemy was driven outside the encircling walls. Stephen Bathory, who had left 5,000 dead on the field of battle, did not give up the idea of taking the city. But early in October the cold and a lack of supplies began to decimate his army.

Ivan, for his part, had not abandoned the notion of an honorable peace with Poland. Especially since the Swedes were completing the conquest of the Gulf of Finland and threatening Pernau, Dorpat, and Fellin, the Danes appeared to be on the point of breaking the truce concluded two years earlier, and in all probability the Tatars, seeing Moscow in difficulties, were waiting for a propitious moment to recapture Kazan and Astrakhan. With his back against the wall, the Czar had a dazzling inspiration: Why not propose to the Pope and to Emperor Rudolf that they organize a crusade against the infidels in which all the Christian states would participate—including Russia and Poland, which would have been reconciled beforehand. Of course, in Ivan's mind the crusade was only a pretext to get the Pope and the Emperor to put pressure on Stephen Bathory and bring him to repentance.

Istoma Shevrigin, the son of a boyar, was entrusted with the mission. Furnished with detailed instructions, he went first to Prague to see Rudolf II, who answered neither yes nor no. From there he left for Venice, where the Doge also equivocated. Finally he arrived in Rome, with two interpreters. Received by Pope Gregory XIII in a private audience, Shevrigin knelt, kissed the sovereign pontiff's slipper, presented him with a gift of sables, and gave him a long letter from the Czar. In this message Ivan asked the Holy Father to order Stephen Bathory to "cease allying himself with the Moslems and making war on Christians"; but he was careful not to promise the slightest rapprochement between the Orthodox and Roman Catholic churches in exchange for the potential crusade. The Holy See, which in the fifteenth century had vainly attempted to bring about such a rapprochement, still cherished the hope that it could be accomplished. Notwithstanding the Czar's deliberate silence on the question, Gregory XIII decided to send a representative to Moscow to propose religious union first and a political agreement afterward.

This complex task fell to Antonio Possevino, a highly cultivated Jesuit who knew the north well. In Venice he enthusiastically explained how desirable it would be for Christendom to create a league around Russia and Poland, aimed against the Turks. The Venetians, however, valued their commercial relations with the Ottoman Empire too highly to enter into so disadvantageous a scheme; as earlier, they gave an evasive reply. Traveling by way of Vienna and Prague, Possevino went to Vilna to see Stephen Bathory. There, a fresh disappointment. Despite his respect for the papal authority, the King of Poland stuck to his guns: He wanted all of Livonia, the destruction or surrender of certain Russian fortresses, and the payment of a large sum in tribute. Nevertheless, he agreed to give the traveler a passport for Russia.

The indefatigable Possevino set out again. In Smolensk he was received with great ceremony, but his ignorance of the Russian language played a trick on him. Thinking he was going to a dinner to which he had been invited (*obied*), he found himself at the door of an Orthodox church, where the bishop was celebrating mass (*obiednia*). In a panic he retreated, refusing to kiss the bishop's hand. At last, on August 18, 1581 (while Bathory's army was nearing Pskov), Possevino arrived in Staritsa, a small fortified town where the Czar had chosen to reside temporarily. Two days later the Italian was allowed to "present himself before the serene eyes of the Czar." At first, Possevino was amazed by the barbaric magnificence of the setting and costumes, the entourage of bearded boyars in long brocade tunics. Ivan, seated on his throne, wrapped in a robe of cloth of gold spangled with precious stones, his scepter in his hand and the Cap of Monomakh on his head, was studying him with a cold and predatory eye. Under this imperious stare, the Pope's representative, in his poor black cassock, bowed humbly. After having inquired after the health of the Holy Father and received a document in which Gregory XIII graciously called him his "beloved son," the Czar examined the presents sent by the pontiff: a crucifix of rock crystal decorated with gold and containing a fragment of the True Cross, a superbly bound copy in Greek of the Acts of the Council of Florence, a rosary mounted in gold with precious stones, and a gold cup. At the last moment, Possevino had decided not to include a picture of the Holy Family, in which St. John the Baptist appeared completely nude; it would surely have offended the Russians, who were accustomed to a more modest iconography. There were also gifts for the Czar's eldest son and the Czarina Anastasia Romanovna ("our beloved daughter"), who had been dead for twenty-one years and replaced seven times since—a circumstance unknown to the Vatican. Ivan thanked the Pope's envoy without batting an eye, and ordered that the negotiations should begin at once.

Six boyars, assisted by interpreters, conducted the debate with the papal legate, running to consult the Czar as soon as the slightest difficulty arose; then, when the meeting resumed, they would take turns reading scrolls containing the sovereign's exceedingly subtle and complicated replies. Each reader would begin by invoking the Holy Trinity and enumerating Ivan's many titles. Possevino heard them repeated fifty times over, hiding his impatience behind a courteous manner. Then he had to put up with quarrels among the interpreters, who split hairs over the meaning of the text and accused each other of betraying His Majesty's thought.

The negotiators argued solidly for a month without understanding each other, exchanged notes, thrashed about in a fog. Sometimes the Czar would summon Possevino for a private conversation. As soon as the legate had kissed his fingertips, as a sign of respect, Ivan would wash his hands in a gold basin so as to remove the stain left by contact with the mouth of a heretic. Then, craftily and tenaciously he would defend his positions, extol the merits of the Pope, and describe in detail the advantages Christendom would derive from a cessation of hostilities between Russia and Poland—but say not a word about the crusade against Turkey or a rapprochement between the two churches. The Czar was encouraged in his stubbornness by long-awaited news of the failure of Bathory's siege of Pskov. He knew that the attackers were short of food, munitions, and money. This was no time to be making concessions.

In mid-September, the Jesuit realized that he was wasting his time with the Russians, and decided to try what could be done with the Poles. "You will go to see King Stephen," the Czar said as Possevino took his leave, "you will greet him on our behalf, and, after negotiating peace according to the Pope's orders, you will come back to us, for your presence will always be pleasing to us because of him who sends you and because of your faithfulness in our affairs."

When Possevino reached the Polish camp before Pskov, on October 5, Bathory, despite the poor condition of his troops, maintained all his territorial claims. He agreed, nevertheless, to drop the demand for an indemnity. On October 9 the Jesuit, feeling that he had exhausted all the resources of diplomacy, wrote to Ivan advising him to start negotiations as soon as possible. Ivan, weary of war, agreed to send plenipotentiaries. They met the Polish representatives in the ruined village of Kiverova-Gorka, fifteen versts from Yam Zapolsky. The meetings were held in Possevino's wretched hut; the negotiators sat on benches between an improvised altar and a brazier whose smoke had no outlet but a hole in the roof. At the end of each meeting the delegates on both sides looked like chimney sweeps. The Jesuit acted as moderator, with the Poles seated on his right and the Russians on his left. The interpreter remained standing. The discussions were so violent that on several occasions the Poles stormed out, shouting that they would never again set foot in this trap. One day Possevino, at the end of his patience, seized a member of the Russian delegation by the button of his pelisse, gave him a good shaking, and threw him out.

Despite the repeated quarrels, however, the two sides eventually reached agreement. A ten-year armistice was signed on January 15, 1582. The Russians abandoned all of Livonia, as well as Polotsk; the Poles evacuated the Russian towns they had conquered. For the Czar it was a compromise of last resort. In reality he was giving up only what he had already sacrificed three months earlier. His adversaries' threats had gotten nothing more out of him. But he was nonetheless bitterly disappointed.

After twenty years of struggle, having thought he had already achieved his ends, Ivan found his Muscovy as before, cut off from the Baltic and from western Europe.

And Europe constantly occupied his thoughts. While he was afraid of letting himself be caught up in enthusiasm for foreign innovations, Ivan secretly envied them. He felt proud to be Russian and at the same time ashamed of the backwardness of his nation compared to others. When he considered France, Italy, England, Germany, Spain, and Poland, where art and literature, humanism and religious debate thrived, he realized that his country was frozen in the contemplation of a dusty past. At a time when, elsewhere, people were reading Chaucer and Villon, Petrarch and Boccaccio, Dante and Ariosto, Rabelais and Ronsard, not one writer raised his voice in Muscovy. A horror of profane pleasures, taught by the Orthodox Church, stifled any impulse toward original creation in Russia. Only architecture was free of the iron restraint. Painting, sculpture, music, and literature were interdicted by the clergy. The painter's imagination was liberated—within very strict rules—only in icons. Makers of myths had to content themselves with folk tales and songs as their only vehicles for poetic thought. So far as the life of the mind was concerned, the great Russian land lay shrouded in darkness. A heavy torpor prevented it from thinking and expressing itself.

Years before, when a first letterpress, operated by Danish craftsmen, was destroyed by the people of Moscow—incensed at "Satan's workmen"—Ivan had another installed in Alexandrov-skaya Sloboda. Very few books were printed there, and all were of a religious nature. Even works imported from abroad were rare in Russia. According to an inventory made in 1578, the incalculably wealthy Stroganov family possessed in all 208 volumes, of which only 86 were printed. Metropolitan Macarius, a tireless writer in his own right, had gathered together in twelve huge tomes the works of the Fathers of the Church, some lives of saints, accounts of travels. Ivan himself had worked on some of these chronicles. Steeped in Church Slavonic, he wrote easily and with a fertile imagination. The core of his personal library consisted of the Bible, books of hours, psalters, the famous *Domostroy*, and the *Chety-Meneye*, a series of edifying texts for each day of the month, connected with the life of the saint indicated by the calendar. But he had also read profane books: the *Iliad*, the *Odyssey*, everything that fell under his hand. Gifted with an exceptional memory, Ivan loaded his epistles with allusions and quotations. He wanted to be the most erudite man in Russia, and he may indeed have been. But he still had to face the problem, on both the cultural level and the political level: How could he remain fundamentally Russian and yet take advantage of the intellectual movements of the sixteenth-century world? How could he launch into the future and yet keep a hold on the traditions of the past? Faced with this dilemma, the Czar had one cardinal rule: Distrust Europe but at the same time steal some sparks from it here and there. A day would come, he thought, when, having assimilated all the knowledge of her neighbors, Russia would dominate them by the genius of her artists and scholars, without surrendering any part of her national heritage.

XVI

The Czarevich

The Czar had had three sons by his first wife, Anastasia: Dimitri, who had died when only a few months old, Ivan, and Feodor. Feodor, who was sickly and a dreamer, did not count for much at court. On the other hand Ivan, the elder and heir to the throne, was in 1581 a tall, vigorous man of twenty-seven with a lively intelligence and violent tastes. Literate like his father, he spent his leisure moments writing a life of St. Anthony. Also like his father, he was attracted to the spectacle of human suffering. The Czar, who loved and admired him, liked to have him present at meetings of the Council of Boyars and at audiences with ambassadors, as well as at nocturnal orgies, massacres, and torture sessions.

Through experiences of debauchery and cruelty, Ivan hoped to make his namesake a mirror image of himself. Together they presided over the torture of Dr. Elysius Bomel, the Czar's physician and supplier of poisons, who was accused by his enemies of carrying on a secret correspondence with Poland. Stretched on a rack with his arms and legs disjointed and his body lacerated with a wire whip, the learned man screamed out the most preposterous confessions. Then the Czar gave the order to have him roasted. Bound and bleeding on a wooden spit, Elysius Bomel was presented to the flames, which licked his back. His smoking flesh quickly shriveled, but he was still alive when they untied him. Brought back to his cell, he died almost immediately, cursed by the Czar whose trust he had enjoyed only a short time before. Another day, Ivan and his son, side by side, treated themselves to the spectacle of the execution of some recalcitrant monks. These frocked scoundrels had refused to deliver to His Majesty an exact inventory of their treasure, for fear it would be confiscated. Ivan had them gathered together in a courtyard surrounded by high walls. As a favor, he permitted each of them to arm himself with a rosary and a spear. Then he gave the order to loose upon them the wild bears he kept in cages for his sport. The furious animals rushed on the monks, clawed them, ripped open their bellies, tore out their entrails— "as a cat does with a mouse," as one witness put it. Only one of the rebellious brothers was able to use his spear to kill the beast that attacked him, but he too succumbed to his wounds. He would later be canonized for his valor. The Czar and his son withdrew, satisfied. They were so happy together, they understood each other so well!

The chronicler Oderborn states that the two exchanged mistresses. In any case, the Czarevich, following his father's example, had sent his first two wives, Eudoxia Saburova and Prascovia Solova, to a convent. The third, Elena Sheremeteva, received all his affection, although he deceived her left and right. In the fall of 1581 she was pregnant, which made her all the dearer to her husband, who, as it happened, was hoping for a male offspring. In this season of mist and cold, the Czar's complete family was gathered in Alexandrovskaya Sloboda.

The Czarevich, closely following the progress of the peace negotiations with Poland, reproached his father for proceeding so timidly and asked to be entrusted with troops to liberate Pskov. When he heard this criticism, Ivan boiled with anger, but he contained himself. On the morning of November 9, a delegation of boyars presented themselves before him with bowed heads. Their leader, Prince Sergei Kubensky, addressed His Majesty. "Great Czar," he said, "the armies of King Stephen Bathory have invaded our country. We are all ready to shed our blood to save Russia, but it is time to oppose the enemy if we do not wish to perish. We entreat you, therefore, to place yourself at the head of your troops, or at least to send your son, the Czarevich Ivan, in your stead."

Coming on top of his son's words, this speech confirmed in the Czar's mind the mad idea that a conspiracy was afoot to dispossess him of his power in favor of the Czarevich. Furious, with his eyes starting from his head and his beard trembling, he shouted, "How dare you speak to me like this? All you have ever wanted was to have another master than the one whom God has given you, and now you would like to see my son on the throne in my place!" And despite the tears and protests of the boyars, he had them thrown out. Shortly afterward he calmed down.

A few days later, on November 15, meeting his daughter-in-law Elena in a room of his residence, Ivan noted that in spite of her advanced pregnancy, she was wearing only a single light dress instead of three, one on top of the other, according to custom. Considering this costume indecent for a princess, he raised his hand to her and struck her so brutally that she fell. That night she miscarried. When the Czarevich returned to the palace, he rushed to his father and reproached him angrily. It was the second time in a short space that he had allowed himself to raise his voice before the sovereign. Ivan could not tolerate this. Forgetting his minor grievances against his daughter-in-law, he returned to the main cause of his resentment. "You poor fool!" he screamed. "How dare you foment a rebellion against me?" The Czarevich declared that he had never had any such intention, that he had not even known about the visit from the delegation of boyars, but that he did indeed think it necessary to assemble an army to raise the siege of Pskov.

At these words the Czar, filled with demented rage, leaped up from his seat, brandished his long spear, and struck his son with it at random, on the shoulders, on the head. Boris Godunov, who was present at the scene, tried to stop the hail of blows, and received a few himself. The Czarevich crumpled to the floor with a hole in his temple.

For an instant, Ivan remained standing in a daze, his bloody staff in his hand, as if it had been someone else who had acted in his place. Then he threw himself on the body, covered with kisses the pale, bearded face in which the whites of the eyes were showing, and tried in vain to stop the blood that was flowing from a deep wound in the skull. Terror-stricken, he shrieked in despair, "Wretch that I am, I have killed my son! I have killed my son!" Boris Godunov ran for help. Servants hurried in with basins of water and cloths. A doctor leaned over the wounded man, examined his injuries, and shook his head with an air of authority: There was scarcely any hope. Having regained consciousness, the Czarevich kissed his father's hands and murmured, "I die as your devoted son and the most submissive of your subjects."

For four days and four nights the Czar waited in anguish for a miracle that would give him back the life that was so dear to him. Torn by remorse, he roamed the palace, groaning and pulling the hairs from his beard. His features were sunken, his hair had turned white. It was an old man, bent by years and sorrow, who from time to time dragged himself to the bedchamber of the dying Czarevich to watch for his respiration. Young Ivan was barely breathing. But all was not lost. Ivan would stagger back to his own room and lie down, staring at the flicker-ing flames of the lamps. When he fell asleep from exhaustion he was visited by nightmares. He would wake with a start and rush to the icons. Kneeling before them, he promised God not to inflict any more tortures, to free the prisoners, build churches, distribute the rest of his fortune to the poor. But heaven re-mained deaf to his voice. Already the Metropolitan had adminis-tered the last rites.

On November 19, the Czarevich expired. All the bells in the town tolled the knell. Ivan, overwhelmed, sobbing, his chest shaken with spasms, sat for several days by his victim's corpse. He refused to sleep or eat. As the Czarevich's assassin, he felt doubly guilty: because he had slain his son and because that son was the heir to the throne. By destroying him in a fit of anger, he had offended both God and Russia.*

On November 22, the funeral procession left Alexandrov-skaya Sloboda for Moscow. Ivan, dressed like the humblest of his subjects, followed the hearse on foot. All along the way he lamented and gesticulated, imploring his son to forgive him. During the service at the Cathedral of St. Michael the Archangel, he uttered cries like an animal and struck his head alternately against the stone floor and against the coffin. In the days follow-ing, Ivan's disorder bordered on madness. In the middle of the night he would get up and roam the palace with his arms held out like a sleepwalker, looking for the son he had lost. In the morning he would be found collapsed on the floor somewhere. With great difficulty, attendants would stretch him out on his bed; he seemed to grow calm; but immediately afterward, as if beset by a specter, he would fall from his bed and roll bellowing on the floor.

Soon after his son's burial, Ivan summoned the boyars and said to them gravely, "The hand of God has fallen heavily upon

---

*Officially, the Czarevich had succumbed to a high fever. His wife, Elena, retired to a convent, where she died not long afterward.

me, and nothing remains for me but to end my days in the solitude of a monastery. My second son, Feodor, is incapable of governing Russia and could not reign long. You yourselves, therefore, must choose a worthy monarch. I will immediately turn over to him my scepter and my dominions." But the boyars remembered what had happened in 1553, at the time of Ivan's illness. Those who had dared to choose a successor for him while he lived had died a cruel death. Suspecting a trap, the courtiers begged the Czar not to abdicate. He gave in with an expression of great weariness.

Every day he attended funeral services and imposed penances on himself. Had he not been wrong, only the year before, to forbid the monasteries to acquire land? He had written to Gurius, Bishop of Kazan: "It is hearts and not land that monks should cultivate. It is not wheat they should sow but the divine word. Their inheritance should be the Kingdom of Heaven, not villages and lands. Some of our bishops think more about their secular goods than about the Church." Offensive words to the clergy, and ones the Czar now repented of. This was no time for him to anger the men of God. Dreading the wrath of heaven, Ivan reversed himself and loaded with gold the religious communities which he had formerly blamed for their wealth. Going further and higher, he sent ten thousand rubles to the Patriarchs of Constantinople, Antioch, Alexandria, and Jerusalem so that they would pray for the repose of the Czarevich's soul. He wondered if God, who had clearly forgiven him all his past crimes, would also forgive him the latest and most monstrous. Then, little by little, he was reassured. Overhead all was quiet. The Almighty had swallowed this too. But Ivan was no less sad on that account. He wept for his son; but he was no longer afraid of divine retribution. His only punishment was regret.

To shake off his dark thoughts, Ivan had a few military men executed on suspicion of not having fought the Poles energetically enough. Then he took it into his head to torture his father-in-law, Athanasius Nagoï, who was guilty of having spoken ill of

Boris Godunov. At his orders, painful setons were placed on the slanderer's chest and sides. But Ivan's pleasures were no longer the same. He regretted the blessed time when he had had his son at his side to enjoy the executioner's work. Without that closest of companions, and surfeited as he was with such diversions, the spectacle of agonizing death hardly had an effect on him any more. He was distressed at his inability to take pleasure in bloodshed. He felt that this was a sort of sexual impotence. Had he lost forever the gift of battening on raw meat? No, no, he had to hope it was only a temporary loss of appetite due to an excess of violence and debauchery.

When Possevino returned to Moscow, on February 14, 1582, together with the plenipotentiaries bearing the text of the treaty of armistice with Poland, the Jesuit was struck by the lugubrious look of the once-magnificent court, now dressed in mourning. He thought he was, as he himself put it, in the midst of "a humble retreat of monks." When the Czar gave him an audience, he presented his condolences and once again pleaded for a crusade against the infidels and a rapprochement between the two churches. "The Greek Church of the Athanasiuses, the Chrysostoms, and the Basils," he said, "is bound to the Roman Church by indissoluble ties of unity. Consequently, there would be no question of breaking with ancient, venerable Byzantium. On the contrary, the Pope himself desires that people remain faithful to the earliest traditions of the East, to the councils of the first centuries. It would only be necessary to renounce the innovations, the later abuses introduced by men like Photius and Michael Caerularius."

So far as the crusade against the infidels was concerned, Ivan shrewdly replied that before making up his mind he would like to know if the Pope had been able to convince the other Christian countries of the urgency of the holy war. He was equally evasive on the subject of the rapprochement between the two churches. Instead of speaking of the possibility of an understanding between religions that were so close in spirit, he sighed, "I am already fifty-one years old and I do not have long to live. Raised in the principles of our Christian Church, which has been separated for centuries from the Latin Church, how could I become unfaithful to it at the end of my existence? The day of God's judgment is approaching; He will show us which of the two religions is the truer, the more holy." Possevino would not admit defeat, and insisted on the primacy of Rome, the true capital of Christianity.

At these words, Ivan lost patience and flew into a temper, tapping his foot. "You boast of your piety and you shave your beards!" he cried. "Your Pope has himself carried on a throne and gives people his slipper to kiss, with a crucifix sewn on it! What a profanation of holy things!" "There is no profanation," replied Possevino; "it is justice done to one who is worthy of it. The Holy Father . . ." The Czar interrupted him: "Christians have only one Father, Who is in heaven. Your pontiff, who has himself carried on a seat as on a cloud supported by angels, is not a shepherd but a wolf!" Standing imperturbable in his worn, tight cassock, the Jesuit retorted, "If he is a wolf, why did Your Majesty choose him for a mediator?"

Ivan's eyes flashed fire. "No doubt it is in the public square," he said, "that peasants taught you to speak to me as if I were a peasant myself!" And he raised the spear with which he had slain his son. Then, suddenly calm again, he softened his glance and concluded: "That is why I did not wish to talk with you about religion. Without meaning to, we might lose our tempers. Besides, it is not Gregory XIII whom I am calling a wolf, it is the Pope who would stray from the doctrine of Christ. Let us leave it at that!"

Having embraced the legate, the Czar dismissed him kindly and ordered his officers to bring him the choicest dishes from his own table. Shortly afterward, he asked him to attend a service in the Cathedral of the Assumption. "There," he said, "we worship what is in heaven and not the things of this world. We honor our Metropolitan, but we do not carry him in our arms. Never was St. Peter carried by the faithful. He walked barefoot. And your Pope dares to call himself his vicar!"

The courtiers dragged Possevino toward the church. Were they going to push him forcibly into that den of schism? He shuddered with horror at the idea. Without doubt Ivan wanted to show his subjects the triumph of their religion. What a wonderful sight for them: Rome's envoy bowing before the Orthodox Metropolitan! But at the last minute Possevino, risking all, escaped from those around him and lost himself in the crowd. When the Czar was informed of the incident, he reflected, rubbed his forehead, and finally said, "He is free to act as he wishes." However, Ivan categorically refused Possevino the right to open a Catholic church in Moscow, though in the past he had given permission for the building of both a Lutheran church and a Calvinist church.

Possevino was no more successful when he suggested that the Czar send to Rome young Russians "versed in letters," so that there they might teach Russian and learn Latin, Italian, and the modern sciences. Ivan was dumbfounded by the ridiculous proposal. To be sure, he was willing to welcome to Russia a few learned foreigners, on the condition that they didn't meddle in politics. But his whole being revolted at the idea of sending Russians to study abroad. He knew only too well that, once there, they would let themselves be won over to European customs and opinions. When they returned they would bring back to Russia the plagues of disorder, freethinking, and the debased fashions of the western world. A true Russian should stay at home; for him to cross a border was already to betray his country.

Possevino did not insist, and until the end of his stay he was treated with great respect. When he was taken to see the Czar, he always passed between ranks of guards lined up to do him honor. He left Moscow on March 11, bearing gifts for the Holy Father and accompanied by Yakov Molvaninov, whom Ivan was sending to Vienna and Rome. This new ambassador brought with him a letter for the Pope. It said that Russia was ready for a general crusade against the Ottomans, but made no mention of a union of the two churches.

A short time later, the Polish ambassadors came to Moscow for the exchange of final signatures. Now that he was rid of that business, Ivan, who was weary, decided to wind things up with Sweden as well. A truce was concluded the following year, the Czar ceding to Sweden Estonia and all the Russian possessions from Narva to Lake Ladoga.

As fate would have it, this double failure in the west was balanced by a glorious conquest in the east. And that conquest was achieved, as it were, unbeknownst to Ivan.

Ever since the annexation of Nizhni-Novgorod in the fifteenth century, the Grand Princes of Muscovy had been organizing military expeditions to Siberia, a vast, frozen region little known and sparsely populated but rich in metals, precious stones, and furs. In 1558, Ivan had conceded to the Stroganov family, which operated salt mines beyond the Urals, the possession in perpetuity of a vast territory on the banks of the Kama and granted the Stroganovs the exceptional privileges of administering justice, hiring soldiers, procuring cannon and munitions, and building fortresses against the Tatars and other natives. In return, the Stroganovs promised not to exploit the silver, copper, or tin mines they might discover but to draw them to the attention of the Treasury. Exempted from taxes, dependent solely on the authority of the Czar, these fabulously wealthy colonialists founded a number of fortified towns and organized an army composed of Cossacks, Cheremiss, Bashkirs, and Nogays. They employed 10,000 workers and 5,000 serfs in their various establishments. Alarmed by the ever-expanding activity of these neighbors, Prince Kuchum of Siberia instructed his nephew Makhmetkul to ravage the Russian domains. Semën Stroganov immediately called upon two Cossack chieftains— Ermak Timofeyev, the daring leader of a band of outlaws, and Ivan Koltzo, a raider of caravans who had been sentenced to death in absentia—and placed them at the head of a troop of 1,000 men who were more bandits than soldiers.

On September 1, 1581, Ermak left to cross the Urals. In a few days Makhmetkul's hordes, armed with only bows and arrows, were decimated by harquebus and artillery fire. As early as October, Sibir, Prince Kuchum's capital, fell into the hands of the Russians. Meanwhile, the Tatar prince of Pelim quickly began raiding the province of Perm. When the voivode of the province, finding himself hard pressed, asked Stroganov for reinforcements, the latter said that he was sorry but his troops were on campaign beyond the Urals, with Ermak. The voivode complained to Moscow. Ivan, furious, sent Stroganov a threatening letter: "You have taken it upon yourself to call back banished Cossacks, real bandits, whom you have sent to make war in Siberia," he wrote. "This enterprise, calculated to anger the Prince of Pelim and Sultan Kuchum, is treachery deserving of the extreme penalty. . . . If Perm ever again suffers the attacks of the Prince of Pelim and the Sultan of Siberia, I will crush you with the weight of my disgrace and have all these Cossack traitors hanged." And he ordered Stroganov to bring back at once the expeditionary corps he had rashly sent to Siberia. But Ermak was already too far away to receive instructions.

In his blindness, Ivan never suspected that the men he called "bandits" were in the process of conquering an empire for him. In three bloody battles the intrepid adventurers had seized a large part of Siberia—from the Urals to the banks of the Ob and the Tobol. Many Siberian princes, including Makhmetkul, submitted to Ermak and paid him tribute. In the towns and villages he had swept up furs and gold. Master of an immense country, recognized by all as the leader of an invincible army, he informed the Czar and the Stroganovs of his victories. In his letter to Ivan, he rejoiced that his poor banished Cossacks had been able, by braving death, "to unite a vast domain to Russia until the end of time, for so long as it shall please the Lord to prolong the existence of the universe." And he added humbly,

"We await the orders of the Russian voivodes, to whom we are ready to deliver the kingdom of Siberia, without any kind of condition, prepared to die for glory or on a scaffold, according as it shall please God and our master."

It was Koltzo, Ermak's second in command, who, although under sentence of death, courageously offered to take this letter to Moscow. He threw himself at the Czar's feet, kissed his hand, and on behalf of Ermak offered him "the kingdom of Siberia," together with precious furs of sable, black fox, and beaver.

For the first time in a long time, Ivan found that fortune smiled upon him again. After the Polish and Swedish reverses, after the terrible death of the Czarevich, a ray of sunshine at last entered the palace. God was no longer frowning. A faint smile of triumph passed over the Czar's face. He pardoned Ermak's envoy for his past crimes, made him the gift of a considerable sum of money, and in addition rewarded the Stroganovs. All the bells of Moscow pealed joyously. Acts of thanksgiving were celebrated in the churches. At court as in the street, people were beaming with pride and repeating, "God has sent Russia a new empire!"

Koltzo left for Siberia again with five hundred *streltsy*. He took with him two cuirasses decorated with gold, a silver cup, and a pelisse which had been worn by Ivan himself—all intended for Ermak, along with a letter from the sovereign granting a pardon to all the Cossacks and assuring them of Russia's eternal gratitude. Two voivodes had instructions to take possession, in the Czar's name, of the territories won from Kuchum. Thus, once again, Ivan was given credit in the eyes of posterity for a victory that he had had nothing to do with and which he had even at first disavowed. But Ermak was not forgotten by the people. He became a legendary personage and was raised to the level of the greatest heroes. Celebrated by the singers of *byliny*, popular epics in verse, the former bandit achieved the fame accorded to all discoverers of virgin territories. But scurvy and famine would soon decimate the Russian troops in Siberia; Koltzo was to die in an ambush; and Ermak, defeated in a surprise attack, was to drown in the waters of the Irtysh, dragged down by the weight of the cuirass that Ivan had given him. In spite of these failures, Siberia would remain an integral part of the realm. Ivan had an almost divine premonition of that.

Now he was back in the saddle again. He felt rejuvenated, and although he was married to Maria Nagaya, he intermittently dreamed again of a legitimate British union. Decidedly, he was tempted by English flesh. Since the haughty Queen Elizabeth refused him, could she not offer him one of her more outstanding subjects? He set forth this plan to an English doctor, Robert Jacob, who had recently replaced the deceased poisoner Elysius Bomel. Better yet, he ordered his own father-in-law, Athanasius —now recovered from the after-effects of his tortures—to question Dr. Jacob on his behalf. Without batting an eye, Athanasius Nagoï listened to an enumeration of all the women of noble birth, unmarried or widows, who might replace his daughter in the monarch's bed. Finally, the doctor named the person he thought the best candidate: Mary Hastings, daughter of the Earl of Huntingdon and grand-niece of Her Majesty the Queen of England.

Ivan forthwith sent to London a gentleman of the Duma, Feodor Pissemsky, who was charged with a double mission: to conclude a treaty of alliance with England and to gather information about Mary Hastings. According to the written instructions Pissemsky had been given, he was secretly to confide the Czar's matrimonial intentions to the Queen, have an interview with the young lady, ask for her portrait "painted on wood or on paper," examine "if she is tall, buxom, and of a fair complexion," warn her that she would be baptized Orthodox, assure her that she would receive appanages, and, if she were to object that the Czar was already married, reply that the sovereign's present spouse, merely the daughter of an ordinary boyar, could easily be repudiated. In exchange for his flattering union with the Queen's grand-niece, Ivan demanded that England help him to resume war against Stephen Bathory's Poland.

Pissemsky, accompanied by Dr. Robert Jacob, reached London on September 16, 1582, but had to wait until November 4 before the Queen received him at Windsor, in the presence of the peers and other dignitaries of the court and the merchants of the Russia Company of England. Very graciously she accepted the Czar's letter and his presents, inquired after his health, deplored the death of the Czarevich, expressed the desire to see her "good brother" one day with her own eyes, and was concerned to find out whether peace reigned at last in Russia. The ambassador shamelessly assured her that all rebellions had ceased in his country and that "the repentance of the criminals had moved the Czar to clemency and he had pardoned them."

On December 18, the negotiations began, Pissemsky proposing a close military alliance against Poland and Elizabeth's ministers objecting that the war between the two countries was over and that the Pope took credit for having reconciled the belligerents. Pissemsky, caught unprepared, exclaimed, "The Pope can say what he pleases; our monarch knows better than anyone else who are his friends and who are his enemies!"

A few days later, Elizabeth received him in the presence of Dr. Jacob, who served as interpreter, to discuss the "secret business." While she declared that she was happy to consider a connection with the Czar, she warned that Lady Mary Hastings, who was remarkable for her moral qualities, might displease a prince "known as a lover of beauty." "Besides," she added, "she has just had the smallpox; I could never allow you to see her in that state, or that the painter should draw her portrait when her face is flushed and covered with the marks of that disease." Since the ambassador insisted, saying that in judging her he would take into account the temporary deterioration of the charms of the chosen one, Elizabeth ultimately promised to content him as soon as the lady was presentable again. The truth was that the daughter of Henry VIII, who had had six wives, could not hold it against the Czar that he sought a ninth spouse while still married; but first, she wanted Russia to sign a treaty granting England a monopoly on all its foreign trade.

Pissemsky, in a hurry to see the marriage business successfully concluded, nevertheless quibbled over the form of the document, demanding that the Czar be designated not as the Queen's "cousin" but as her "brother"; but finally he gave in on the substance. Whereupon a high dignitary informed him that Elizabeth would immediately grant him his farewell audience. Thunderstruck, the unfortunate ambassador exclaimed, "And the marriage business?" The dignitary replied by showing him gazettes announcing a great piece of news for Russia: On October 19, Maria Nagaya had presented the Czar with a healthy son named Dimitri.*

Just as he had denied the existence of peace with Poland, Pissemsky denied this unfortunate revelation. "Treacherous persons have invented this fable," he said, "to interrupt the course of the negotiations for a marriage as advantageous to England as it is to Russia. The Queen should rely solely on the Czar's letter and on my assertions!" Of course, in his heart of hearts he had no doubt that the information was correct. But knowing the Czar, he knew that this birth would not prevent him from repudiating his wife in order to marry Elizabeth's grandniece. Accordingly, he returned to the charge, and the Queen, eager to serve the interests of British trade, at last consented to arrange an interview for him with Mary Hastings.

On May 18, 1583, Pissemsky, accompanied by Dr. Jacob, was received at the country house of Lord Chancellor Thomas Bromley. Refreshments were laid in the garden. Shortly afterward, a group of women appeared in the path. Between Lady Bromley and Lady Huntingdon walked she whom the ambassador already called "the Czar's betrothed." "Here she is," whispered Lord Bromley, "you may look at her at leisure. The

---

*Little Dimitri was to die by an assassin's hand in 1591, at Uglich. It was rumored that Boris Godunov had ordered the murder.

Queen wanted Lady Mary to be shown to you in broad daylight and not under the dark ceiling of an apartment." Filled with anxiety at having to make so momentous a decision, the Russian stared with all his might. Lord Bromley invited him to take a turn in the park and arranged to cross paths with the three ladies several times. Each time, Pissemsky bowed to Mary, who replied with a curtsy. When she had disappeared for good, Lord Bromley asked, "Did you have a good look at her?" "I obeyed my instructions," replied Pissemsky with military stiffness. And in his report to the Czar he wrote: "The Princess Hountinks [sic], Mary Hantis [sic], is tall, slim, and white of skin; she has blue eyes, fair hair, a straight nose, long tapered fingers."

Having summoned the ambassador, Elizabeth again expressed the fear that her grand-niece was not beautiful enough to captivate the Czar. "I think you did not like her yourself," she said. The Russian replied imperturbably, "I think she is beautiful. The rest is God's affair!" In mid-June the portrait of Lady Mary that was to go to the Czar was finished at last, and after having attended an impressive review of the English fleet (twenty-four ships of seventy or eighty guns, each carrying more than 1,000 men), Pissemsky embarked with Sir Jerome Bowes, the new English ambassador chosen by the Queen. All things considered, Pissemsky was not dissatisfied with the results of his mission—little did he suspect that Ivan's reputation as the murderer of his own son was a serious obstacle to the proposed marriage. In fact, neither the Queen nor her grand-niece, despite the interview in the Lord Chancellor's garden, thought of the Czar as a possible match. The entire court had been playacting in front of the ambassador to support the prerogatives of the English merchants.

In October 1583, when Jerome Bowes arrived in Russia, Ivan welcomed him as a friend. Misinformed by the reports of the naive Pissemsky, the Czar was under the impression that both the political alliance and the marriage were practically settled and that only details remained to be worked out. But from the beginning the discussions between the Russian negotiators and the British ambassador proved difficult. Unlike the flexible, wily Anthony Jenkinson, Jerome Bowes was a hard man with a peremptory manner, haughty and quick to take offense. Not only did he maintain the demand for a monopoly on trade, but he declared that England would help Russia against its enemies only after having exhausted all attempts at conciliation with them. This last condition made it impossible to resume hostilities against Stephen Bathory immediately.

After twenty sessions of fruitless talks, Ivan summoned Bowes on December 13, and said to him through the interpreter, "How do you expect me to become the Queen's ally if my greatest enemies [Sweden, Denmark, Poland] are her friends? Elizabeth must either force Bathory to return Livonia and Polotsk to me or declare war on him with me!" "The Queen would think me mad if I consented to such a treaty," said Bowes. "You have assumed airs of superiority over my plenipotentiaries which cannot be endured," cried the Czar, "for among sovereigns, my equals, I know some who take precedence of your mistress!" "The Queen my mistress is as great a prince as any in Christendom," retorted the ambassador of England, "equal to him that thinks himself the greatest." At these words Ivan, beside himself with rage, threatened to throw Jerome Bowes out. Standing rigid, Bowes replied that he had a mistress who would no doubt be revenged for any injury done to him.

Abruptly calm again, Ivan returned to his plan of marriage. The diplomat assured him that the portrait of Lady Mary was very flattering, that she was more than thirty years old, that she was ill-favored, in poor health, and in any case hostile to the idea of conversion. However, he said, the Queen had other kinswomen who were very beautiful. The Czar's eyes lit up with lust. When he had dismissed his interlocutor, he sighed, "Would to God that I myself had so faithful a servant!"

At another meeting, on December 18, Ivan returned to the charge: "You have spoken to us of ten or twenty young maidens in your country among whom we could choose a wife, but you refuse to name them. We could never go to any sort of trouble on the basis of such a vague indication. Apparently there are more than a thousand marriageable girls in England, including more than one cook: Do you want us to seek out all of them?" And he added, "You are an ignorant man and you have no idea of the way an envoy should behave!"

For two months the Czar had one interview after another with the English ambassador, all of them stormy and fruitless. On February 14, 1584, Jerome Bowes announced to Ivan that the Queen had ordered him to return by land to France. Since the loss of Livonia, the land route had been Polish. "You will take advantage of this to betray me to my enemies!" shouted Ivan, his eyes small and hard. "Since you did not come to negotiate seriously, you can go away, taking with you only what you brought! We dismiss you at this moment!"

Accustomed to these angry outbursts, Bowes waited philosophically for the Czar's mood to change. And indeed, three days later Ivan gave him a draft treaty demanding, in exchange for the commercial monopoly, an offensive alliance to recapture Livonia. Bowes prudently replied that his very pious mistress rejected the idea of conquests. "But it is not a question of conquests," replied the Czar. "Livonia is our ancient inheritance." "Is that quite certain?" asked the ambassador ironically. Ivan leaped up at the insult. "We are not asking the Queen to be the judge between us and the King of Poland!" he roared, and set the farewell audience for February 20. That day, when Jerome Bowes presented himself at the palace, he was informed that the Czar was ill and could not receive him. Bowes was not given permission to leave Russia until four months later, bearing a letter from Feodor, Ivan's son, in which there was no further mention either of an alliance or of exceptional favors for the English merchants.

XVII

The Final Days

For a year now the Czar had been busy putting in order his bloody record of repression. Although he had no regrets about his many victims, he was intent on ensuring the repose of their souls in the hereafter. Thus, to straighten out his accounts and his conscience he tirelessly drew up lists of the persons he had slain. Pen in hand, he searched the corners of his memory, hunted out forgotten ghosts, wrote down the various executions. This grim, painstaking labor enabled him to pass in review the stages of his life. His secretary and his confessor helped him to remember. Names crudely written in capital letters lined up on the parchment. The death rolls were sent to the monasteries, with large sums of money, so that prayers would be recited for the deceased.

In these documents could be read: ". . . Remember, Lord, the souls of Thy servants of Novgorod, numbering one thousand five hundred and seven persons . . . Prince Kazarin Dubrovsky, plus ten men who had come in his retinue . . . Twenty men from the village of Kolomeskoye, eighty from Matveïché . . . Remember the faithful Christians who died, numbering eighty-four, and also three who succumbed after having had their hands cut off . . ." After certain names appeared a terse notation, "with his wife," or "with his wife and children," "with his sons," "with his daughters." But Ivan was nagged by the thought that in view of the quantity of corpses he had accumulated, he must certainly have left some out, so he relied on God—whose records were complete—to fill in the blanks. He told Him straight out: "Thou wilt no doubt remember their names. . . ." Or: "Thou, alone, Lord, knowest their names!" The list of the dead destined for the Monastery of Sviazhsk mentioned, among others, ". . . the nun Princess Eudoxia [a distant aunt of Ivan's], the nun Alexandra [his sister-in-law, Yuri's widow], the nun Maria [sister of his cousin germane Vladimir]" —all three drowned at Belozersk. One such list gives a total of 3,148 persons exterminated; another comes to 3,750.

Even after Ivan had sent off these macabre reckonings, names came back to him. An entire people of bloody martyrs crowded behind his back. While he felt no guilt over their death, he had the sense that he was never alone in his room any more. An unbearable weight was crushing him. Debauchery and the excesses of the table had ruined his health. Since the murder of his son he could sleep only a few hours a night. He had gone back to his palace in the Kremlin, fleeing Alexandrovskaya Sloboda, whose sinister walls reminded him of the last days of the Czarevich. One evening, he was informed that a comet with a tail in the shape of a cross had appeared in the sky over Moscow. Muffled up in furs, he had himself carried out to the steps to see. The cold was sharp, the air transparent. The immense city was shrouded in snow. His head thrown back, the Czar gazed for a long time at the premonitory star with its glowing tail. Then he murmured, "That is the sign of my death!"

Since the beginning of 1584, Ivan's health had been failing more rapidly. The doctors spoke of a "decomposition of the blood" and "corruption of the bowels." Ivan's body began to swell; his skin peeled in shreds, giving off a terrible stench. The unguents he coated himself with could not eliminate the odor. It sometimes seemed to him that he carried in his clothes the smell of the charnel houses where he had once loved to walk. But no, it was his own flesh that stank. Or perhaps his soul? What if God did not love him any longer? What if, instead of welcoming him with open arms into His Paradise, He made him cool his heels at the door?

Yet he had done a great deal for the motherland. To be sure, his wars in the west had been disastrous, but in the east he had conquered Kazan, Astrakhan, Siberia. He had unified his country despite the opposition of the boyars. How could he have achieved this glorious result without ridding himself by torture of his worst enemies? What did a few thousand mangled corpses weigh in the scales against all the populations, all the lands acquired for Russia by force? But one never knew, with God! After having always supported him, the Almighty might still blame him at the final moment for the hecatomb of Novgorod, or for his many marriages, or for the murder of the Czarevich. This last act of violence might be the last drop of blood that would make the vessel overflow. No, no, for God too was accountable for the blood of His child, the Christ. He had let Jesus perish on the cross. Both of them had murdered their sons. God and the Czar were two of a kind. And to tell the truth, while God might act with stern and absolute justice on the day of the Last Judgment, here on earth He indulged in the purest caprice. In this world He caused crime to go unpunished and innocence to be trampled underfoot. He distributed His blows without rhyme or reason, caring about the deserts of neither those whom He raised up nor those whom He struck down. He set before all monarchs, who were the representatives of His power on earth, an example of cruelty and inconsistency. How could He be angry with them for being like Him? The more arbitrary Ivan was in his punishments, the more pleasing he must be to the Master of nature.

The Czar repeated this to himself all day long, for reassurance. Between conversations with his advisers, he would wander about the palace, talking out loud to himself. He dreaded the coming of nightfall, because it brought apocalyptic visions. Every night in the semidarkness he was visited by the image of his son, sometimes superbly dressed and smiling, sometimes livid and with a gaping wound in his temple. The specter would speak to him. Ivan would answer. Then suddenly he would utter a cry and leap up from bed. His servants would come running; they would put him to bed again. But sometimes he refused to go back to sleep, summoned priests, had the bells rung, ordered them to celebrate mass. Dawn would find him exhausted, haggard, incapable of making any decision. He discovered that there were instruments of torture more effective than those he had used on others. Yes, remorse and fear were worse than burning faggots, the rope, or the pincers. The Czar changed from executioner to victim.

Now Ivan increased his gifts to churches; he tried to atone by humbling himself. He wrote to all the monasteries in Russia: "To the very celebrated and holy monasteries. To all the virtuous and deserving monks! Grand Prince Ivan Vasilyevich bows very low before you and places himself at your feet, begging you to obtain pardon for his sins and to pray all together, or separately in your cells, for the Lord and the Very Holy Virgin to forgive his wickedness, grant him cure, and deliver him from the malady that afflicts him." In his delirium he hoped that the monks whom he had spared would speak louder in God's ear than those whom he had put to death by the hundreds, in Novgorod and elsewhere, louder than Metropolitan Philip, louder than Archbishop Leonid.

Soon, as neither the potions of the doctors nor the prayers of the monks halted the course of his illness, Ivan turned to magicians. From every side astrologers, soothsayers, and sorcerors flocked to Moscow. They were shut up, some sixty of them, in a house near the palace. Never had there been such a concentration of learned men versed in the occult sciences. Their meals were brought to them. Every day Prince Bogdan Belsky, one of the Czar's close advisers, questioned them. They were pessimistic. All the signs of heaven were in agreement: The death of the sovereign would occur soon. Not wishing to frighten his master, Belsky concealed from him the conclusions of the fortune-tellers.

Despite the soothing words of his entourage, Ivan felt himself lost beyond recall. The putrid smell of his body increased; his testicles swelled painfully. He was worried about the succession. In 1572, he had made a will in favor of his eldest son, the Czarevich Ivan. The latter being dead, he now dictated, in the presence of the boyars, new provisions making Feodor heir to the throne. He advised him to reign piously and to spare his country useless wars with Christian states. To guide the young Prince, who was feeble in body and mind, he appointed a Council of Regents, composed of five boyars: Ivan Shuisky, hero of the siege of Pskov; Ivan Mstislavsky, son of Grand Duke Vasily's niece; Nikita Yuriev, brother of the Czarina Anastasia; Bogdan Belsky; and especially Boris Godunov, the most intelligent of all, whose sister Irina was Feodor's wife. Turning affectionate and pusillanimous at the approach of death, he called them his "friends," his "comrades in arms." He urged them to free the Polish and German prisoners and to reduce taxes.

Once again Ivan complained that all his life long the wicked boyars with their subversive schemes had forced him to assume a severity that was not in his character. His persecution mania now turned to madness. Everyone was guilty, except himself. A paranoiac pursued by imaginary enemies, he sobbed, "They returned me evil for good, hate for love!" Whom did he hope to deceive by this final address to the jury: the men around him or God, future generations or the guardian of the hereafter? Yet even in the midst of his angelic mildness he had fits of violence. Thus, having learned through an indiscretion that the astrologers had been able to calculate the exact date of his death—March 18, 1584—he swore to have them burned alive if their prediction proved wrong. When his daughter-in-law, Feodor's wife, visited him in his room, she "recoiled in horror," it was said, before his obscene words and gestures. The dying man had a burst of incestuous desire. The devil had suddenly reawakened in his flesh. Immediately afterward, he was overcome by such prostration that the new ambassador from Poland was asked to postpone his arrival in Moscow.

Ivan's favorite distraction now was to have himself carried on a chair to his treasure chamber. There, for hours at a time, he would gaze in fascination at the precious stones in the chests. On March 15 he invited the English ambassador, Sir Jerome Horsey, to come with him. As the diplomat watched, he trickled through his trembling fingers a stream of diamonds, emeralds, sapphires, rubies, pearls, zircons. His greedy eyes shone with the reflection of the fortune. Lovingly, he indicated the origin and price of each jewel. It was as if he could not get over being so rich, as if it pained him to have to leave all this.

Taking some turquoises in the palm of his hand, he whispered to his guest, "See how they change color. They turn pale, they announce my death, I am poisoned." Then he pointed to his scepter of "unicorn horn"—ivory, which had the magic power to combat poison—set with precious stones ("They cost seventy thousand rubles," he said) and asked his doctor to draw a circle on the table with this symbol of his power. The doctor did so. Then Ivan had spiders brought and placed them near the circle. Those which entered it died at once; those which crawled away remained alive. "That is a sure sign," said the Czar. "The unicorn horn can no longer save me." And turning back to the gems, he confided to Horsey, "This diamond is the richest and most famous in the Orient. I never used it. It moderates rage and lust, and makes men abstinent and chaste. The smallest part of it ground to powder would poison a horse, let alone a man." He pointed to a ruby: "Oh! This one does the greatest good to the heart, the brain; it strengthens the memory, clarifies impure blood. . . . See this emerald: It has all the colors of the rainbow. This precious stone is the enemy of uncleanness. Try it. I love to look at this sapphire. It maintains and increases courage and the joys of the heart; it is pleasing to all the vital senses; it is sovereign for the eye, for sight; it cures apoplectic fits, gives strength to the muscles and their fibers. . . . All of them are gifts of God, secret by nature, but He reveals them for man's use and contemplation as friends of grace and virtue and enemies of vice . . ." Ivan's tongue grew thick. He spoke with increasing difficulty. Suddenly he fainted. He was carried away.

When the Czar regained consciousness, he did not ask for the holy sacraments. Doubtless he still believed he would recover, thanks to the combined efforts of the priests, doctors, and sorcerors. He merely told the Metropolitan that in the event of his death, he wanted to be buried not as a czar but as a monk. His father, Vasily III, had expressed the same wish. Around him in the Kremlin there reigned an anxious silence. In the churches the faithful were praying.

On March 17, Ivan took a hot bath and afterward felt more alert. The next morning he was definitely improved. Remembering that the astrologers had predicted his death for March 18, he told Bogdan Belsky, "According to the soothsayers, today is the day I should draw my last breath; but I feel my strength reviving. So let the impostors prepare for death themselves!" Belsky went to bring this sentence to the magicians gathered in their lodging. They replied imperturbably, "Wait, the day is not yet over!" A second hot bath was prepared and Ivan sank into it with delight. He stayed there for three hours, after which he lay down and had a nap. When he awoke he was in high good humor. He arose, slipped a dressing gown over his shirt, called the palace singers, joined his voice with theirs, then dismissed them, and sat down in front of his chessboard and asked Belsky to play a game with him. But he was so weak that he could not set the pieces on their squares. The king and queen fell from his hand and rolled on the floor. In a moment Ivan himself collapsed, blasted by an attack, his arms hanging, his head on the chessboard. People shouted and rushed to him, the doctors consulted with one another and rubbed his body with vodka and vegetable essences to bring him back to life. Wasted effort.

Carrying out the will of the deceased, the Metropolitan read over the corpse the prayers with which a living man would have been received into a community of monks. Washed, tonsured, dressed in the garb of renunciation, Ivan was given for eternity the name Brother Jonas. A wooden cross and an icon depicting the Resurrection rested on his chest. In the antechamber there were some who whispered that the Czar had not died a natural death but had been poisoned by Bogdan Belsky and Boris Godunov, who were in a hurry to seize power.* There was no doubt that the feeble Feodor would be a plaything in their hands.

Massed in front of the body clad in the coarse woolen habit, the boyars trembled in retrospect. But behind their expressions of consternation they could scarcely conceal their feeling of deliverance. But was it possible that the nightmare was over? Would not Ivan suddenly rise up from his bed full of energy again, with glittering eyes, and send them all to the scaffold?

Outside the Kremlin, meanwhile, a vast and quiet crowd was awaiting news of the master. Fearing an insurrection or a

---

*This was the opinion of the British ambassador, Sir Jerome Horsey, among others. It is more probable that Ivan succumbed to some disease of the intestines and the genito-urinary tract.

palace revolt, Godunov delayed the announcement of the death for a day. Only after all the details of the dynastic succession had been worked out by the Council of Regents did he have the death knell tolled. When a herald cried from the top of the Red Steps, "The Czar is no more!" he was answered with groans, and the multitude fell to their knees.

To the Russian people, whom he had terrorized for nearly forty years, Ivan IV, despite his crimes and mistakes, had been the representative on earth of the Almighty. He could not be judged any more than God could be judged. He was the father of the nation and had all rights over it. Besides, it was chiefly the detested boyars who had endured his blows. Pitiless toward traitors, be they aristocrats or refractory monks, he had only very rarely struck the common folk. Who could tell whether in losing this fearsome Czar the humble people had not lost their best defender? Forgetting the murder of the Czarevich, the public tortures, the disastrous war in Livonia, the abysmal poverty of the Russian nation, they remembered only the conquests of Kazan, Astrakhan, and Siberia. The Czar's very excesses guaranteed his survival in the popular imagination: In Russia the favor of the oppressed masses has always gone to the strongest personalities. The fear of the whip does not exclude love, and sometimes contributes to it; by the very terror he inspires, the tyrant keeps his hold on his people's hearts.

A vast assemblage of people attended the Czar's funeral in the Cathedral of St. Michael the Archangel. Ivan was buried beside the son whom he had killed in a fit of lunatic rage. On his tomb was carved the following inscription: "In the year 7092–1584,* on the eighteenth day of March, there appeared [before God] the very faithful sovereign, Czar and Grand Prince of all Russia, Ivan Vasilyevich, in monasticism Jonas."

---

*In Russia at that time years were counted not from the birth of Jesus Christ but from the creation of the world, which according to tradition had taken place 5,508 years before. Thus, the year 1584 was considered to be 7092.

245

Feodor ascended the throne reluctantly. Possessed of a weak constitution and a dim mind, he was overwhelmed by the responsibility that suddenly fell to him. His father had often said of Feodor that he was more of a sacristan than an heir apparent, and had nicknamed him "the bell ringer." From the moment the new Czar took his first steps, he leaned on his strong and ambitious brother-in-law; soon Boris Godunov would be governing Russia in his stead. As for Ivan, the singers of *byliny* were already taking possession of his shade and turning it into that of an avenger, a conqueror, the pride of Russia, the terror of the mighty. While the archives preserved the record of his true crimes, the storytellers exalted his alleged virtues. Considered by some a bloodthirsty monster, by others a ruler who dispensed retribution and gathered lands together, he would stride toward the tribunal of posterity through a fog pierced by gleams of light.

Notes

II. CHILDHOOD

1. *Prince A. M. Kurbsky's History of Ivan IV,* ed. with trans. and notes by J. L. I. Fennell (Cambridge: Cambridge University Press, 1965), pp. 73–77. (Trans.)

2. Nikolai Karamzin, *Histoire de l'Empire de Russie,* 11 vol., trans. from the Russian. Paris-Berlin, 1819–26.

III. CZAR IVAN IV

1. Baron Sigismund von Herberstein, *Notes upon Russia,* trans. (from the Latin) and ed. R. H. Major (London: Hakluyt Society, No. 10, 1851–52), vol. I, p. 93. (Trans.)

IV. REFORMS

1. Heinrich von Staden, *The Land and Government of Muscovy*, trans. (from the German) and ed. Thomas Esper (Stanford: Stanford University Press, 1967), pp. 14, 16, 17. (Trans.)

VI. ILLNESS AND ITS CONSEQUENCES

1. Fennell, *Kurbsky's History of Ivan IV*, p. 83. (Trans.)
2. Richard Hakluyt, *The Principal Navigations, Voyages, Traffiques and Discoveries of the English Nation* (Glasgow: James Maclehose and Sons, 1903), vol. II, pp. 209–11. (Trans.)

VIII. SORROW AND VIOLENCE

1. *Early Voyages and Travels to Russia and Persia,* ed. E. Delmar Morgan and C. H. Coote (London: Hakluyt Society, First Series, No. 73, 1886; reprinted New York: Burt Franklin, n. d.), vol. II, pp. 367–68. (Trans.) Also in Hakluyt, *Principle Navigations,* pp. 438–39.

X. THE *OPRICHNIKI*

1. *Memoirs,* Taube and Kruse, German nobles from Livonia.
2. Letter of May 18, 1570 (spelling modernized). Morgan and Coote, *Early Voyages,* pp. 290–92. (Trans.)

XI. METROPOLITAN PHILIP

1. See Karamzin, *Histoire de l'Empire de Russie,* quoting the *Memoirs* of Taube and Kruse.
2. *Memoirs,* Taube and Kruse. Confirmed by the Danish ambassador Ulfeld, who arrived in Russia in 1578.

XII. THE MARTYRDOM OF NOVGOROD

1. *Memoirs,* Heinrich von Staden.

XV. STEPHEN BATHORY

1. Fennell, *Kurbsky's History of Ivan IV*, pp. 197, 199. (Trans.)
2. Ibid., pp. 199, 201. (Trans.)

Chronology

EVENTS IN RUSSIA AND IN THE LIFE OF IVAN	PRINCIPAL EVENTS IN OTHER COUNTRIES
1530 *August 15:* Birth in Moscow of Ivan, eldest son of Vasily III and Elena Glinskaya.	Charles V of Spain crowned Holy Roman Emperor. Diet of Augsburg opened. Confession of Augsburg.
1531	The League of Schmalkalden formed to protect Lutheranism in Germany. Swiss Protestant cantons crushed at Keppel; Zwingli killed.

1532   Embassy sent by Sultan Baber of Delhi arrives in Moscow. Construction of the Church of the Assumption at Kolomenskoye.

Administrative union between Brittany and France. Peace of Nuremburg. Henry VIII challenges the papacy. Ottomans invade Hungary. Calvin starts his Reformation movement in France.

1533   *October 30:* Birth of Yuri, Ivan's younger brother. *December 4:* Death of the Grand Duke of Moscow, Vasily III. Regency of Elena. Boyar conspiracies. Assassination of the late Grand Duke's two brothers. War against Lithuania resumed.

Henry VIII marries Anne Boleyn and is excommunicated. Andrea Doria campaigns in Greece. Ottomans conquer Azerbaijan. Birth of Elizabeth I of England.

1534

"Affaire des Placards" in France and worsening persecution of Protestants. Treaty of Augsburg between France and the League of Schmalkalden. Religious peace treaty of Cadan. Anabaptists take control of Münster. Act of Supremacy breaks the union of the English Church with Rome; Henry VIII becomes Head of the Church of England. Pope Paul III succeeds Pope Clement VII. Ottomans capture Tabriz and Baghdad. Cartier's first voyage to the New World.

1535

War between Francis I of France and Charles V

renewed. Alliance between Francis I and the Ottomans. Anabaptists massacred in Münster. Battle of Svendborg; Lübeck sacked. Sir Thomas More tried and beheaded by Henry VIII. Rabelais publishes *Gargantua.* Charles V captures Tunis for the Spanish. Antonio Mendoza brings first printing press to New World.

1536   Ivan receives the Lithuanian ambassadors.

Francis I occupies Turin; Charles V invades Provence; Treaty of Lyons. Execution of Anne Boleyn; Henry VIII marries Jane Seymour. England and Wales united administratively. Confession of faith in Geneva. Michelangelo begins *Last Judgment.* Buenos Aires founded by Pedro Mendoza. Spanish rule in Peru. Canada annexed to French Crown.

1537   New truce with Lithuania. Gomel falls. Signature in Novgorod of a sixty-year treaty with Gustav I of Sweden.

Treaty signed between France and the Ottomans. Henry VIII confiscates Church property. Alessandro de' Medici assassinated by Lorenzino. Death of Jane Seymour; birth of Edward VI of England.

1538   *April 3:* Elena dies, probably poisoned by boyars. Boyars

Truce of Nice: Charles V and Francis I meet at Aigues-

fight over the regency, held first by Prince Vasily Shuisky, then by Ivan Belsky, and then by the Shuiskys.

Mortes. Rebellion in Florence against Cosimo de' Medici. Calvin exiled from Geneva. Holy League against the Ottomans. Catholic princes in Germany form the League of Nuremberg. Earthquake in Sicily.

1539

Congress of the League of Schmalkalden: a truce between Charles V and German Protestants. Rebellion in Gent. Hernando de Soto lands in Florida. Turks ravage Mediterranean.

1540

Charles V subdues rebellion in Gent. Henry VIII marries Anne of Cleves, then annuls the marriage and marries Catherine Howard. Thomas Cromwell executed. Venice signs peace treaty with Ottoman Empire. Spanish explorers discover the Grand Canyon.

1541

Diet of Ratisbon. Calvin returns to Geneva. Ottomans capture Buda. Earthquake destroys Guatemala City.

1542 Macarius, new Metropolitan of Moscow, undertakes education of Ivan. Metropolitan Joseph, supporter of Ivan

Francis I again at war with Charles V. Catherine Howard beheaded; sixth marriage of Henry VIII, to Catherine

Belsky, exiled to a monastery.

Parr. James V of Scotland defeated and killed; accession of Mary Stuart. Cabrillo explores California coast.

1543 Andrei Shuisky imprisons Feodor Verontzov and Ivan orders Shuisky killed. The Glinskys seize power.

Franco-Turkish fleet takes Nice. Charles V takes Gelderland and joins it to the Netherlands. Alliance between Charles V and Henry VIII. Portuguese arrive in Japan. Copernicus publishes his theory. Spanish Inquisition, Protestants burned at the stake.

1544

War in northern France. The English invade Scotland.

1545

Council of Trent convenes.

1546 Tatars defeated at the Oka, then at the Volga.

Treaty of Ardres: completes end of war between England, France, and Charles V. Maurice of Saxony allies with Charles V to wage war on the League of Schmalkalden. John Knox leads Scottish Protestant revolt.

1547 *January 16:* Coronation of Ivan, who takes the title Czar and begins his autocratic reign. *February 3:* Marries Anastasia Romanovna. *June 3:* Ivan abuses delegation of prominent men from

Battle of Mühlberg: Charles V defeats the League of Schmalkalden and breaks with Paul III. Diet of Augsburg opens. Edward VI succeeds Henry VIII in England. John Knox and his

city of Pskov. *June 20:* Third fire that year in Moscow; Glinskys blamed and disgraced.

supporters defeated. Henry II succeeds Francis I in France. Ferdinand of Bohemia quells Hussite revolt in Prague. Ottomans invade Persia.

1548 Birth of Anne, first daughter of Ivan and Anastasia. New council created, the Izbrannaya Rada (Chosen Council) headed by Ivan's favorites: Metropolitan Macarius, the priest Sylvester, Alexei Adashev, and Andrei Kurbsky.

Interim vote of the Diet of Augsburg restores Catholicism to England. Mary Stuart betrothed to the Dauphin (later Francis II). England at war with France. Sigismund II succeeds Sigismund I in Poland. Paul III suspends Council of Trent. La Paz, Bolivia, founded. Pizarro executed in Peru.

1549

First *Book of Common Prayer* published. Catholic risings in Cornwall and Norfolk. Netherlands separates from the Empire. Death of Pope Paul III.

1550 Death of Ivan's daughter, Anne. Assembly of representatives from all provinces of Russia (Zemsky Sobor). Promulgation of Sylvester's *Domostroy,* a household guide, and of the Czar's Code of 1550, a new code of justice. Reorganization of the army. Campaign against Kazan and foundation of Sviazhsk.

Anglo-French treaty. France recovers Boulogne. Election of Pope Julius III. Discovery of great temple mounds in southeastern North America.

1551 Birth of Marie, second daughter of Ivan and Anastasia. *February 23:* Convocation of the third ecclesiastical council. Proposals for ecclesiastical reforms (the *Stoglav*). Reorganization of the nobility.

Italian wars between Henry II and the Pope resumed. Council of Trent reopened. Maurice of Saxony forms League of Dresden among German princes. Ottomans take Tripoli (Libya) and Algeria.

1552 Birth of Czarevich Dimitri, first son of Ivan and Anastasia. *June 16:* Ivan departs on campaign against the Tatars. *August 23:* Siege of Kazan begins. *October 2:* Yadigar-Mohammed, the governor of Kazan, surrenders. *October 29:* Ivan's triumphal return to Moscow.

Treaty of Chambord: Henry II occupies German Protestant territory. Hostilities renewed between Charles V and France. Second Act of Uniformity and second *Book of Common Prayer* issued in England. War in Transylvania. Council of Trent suspended again.

1553 Baptism of Czarevich Dimitri. *February 26:* Baptism of Yadigar-Mohammed. *March:* Ivan falls ill and prepares his will. Ivan and family undertake pilgrimage to Kirillov. Czarevich Dimitri dies at Kirillov. *June:* Dimitri buried. The priest Sylvester and Alexei Adashev in disgrace. Epidemic of ulcerous plague in the city of Pskov. Death of Archbishop Serapion. Mongolian tribes revolt against Russian tax collectors and kill Boris Saltykov. Boyar conspiracies abound during Ivan's illness. *August 24:* En-

Charles V defeated at Metz: retreat is calamitous. Catholic Mary Tudor succeeds Edward VI of England.

glish ship commanded by Richard Chancellor arrives at the mouth of the Dvina. *December:* Chancellor arrives in Moscow with letter from Edward VI.

1554 *February:* Richard Chancellor leaves for England with a letter for Mary Tudor. *March 28:* Birth of Ivan, second son of Ivan and Anastasia. Conquest of Astrakhan. Short war against Sweden for possession of Finland.

Mary Tudor marries Philip of Spain. Princess Elizabeth imprisoned. Catholicism reinstituted in England. Tobacco brought to Spain from America.

1555 Richard Chancellor returns to Russia. Charter authorizes English subjects to trade freely throughout Russia.

Peace of Augsburg allows for Catholicism or Lutheranism, but not Calvinism, in German states. Calvin suppresses revolt in Geneva with reign of terror.

1556 *July 21:* Osip Napeia sent as an ambassador to England. Richard Chancellor perishes in a shipwreck. Astrakhan annexed to Russian territory.

Charles V abdicates and is succeeded as Emperor by his brother Ferdinand I and as King of Spain and the Netherlands by his son, Philip II.

1557 *May 31:* Birth of Feodor, third son of Ivan and Anastasia.

First Protestant "Covenant" signed in Scotland. Portuguese establish trading post in Macao, China.

1558 *January 22:* Russian army invades Livonia. *May 12:* Narva captured. *July 18:* Dorpat

French capture Calais from the English. Elizabeth I succeeds Mary Tudor in En-

surrenders. Large territory on the banks of the Kama ceded to the Stroganov family. The Englishman Anthony Jenkinson leaves for Khiva and Bukhava via the Caspian Sea.

gland. Marriage of the Dauphin (later Francis II) to Mary Stuart. Death of Charles V.

1559 Sigismund Augustus of Poland undertakes defense of Livonia. Livonian Order of the Knights of the Sword defeated at Ermes. Series of signal victories over the Tatars in the Crimea.

Francis II, a minor, succeeds Henry II in France. First national Calvinist synod held in Paris. English Commons restore Act of Supremacy and Bill of Uniformity. Election of Pope Pius IV.

1560 *August 7:* Death of Anastasia. The priest Sylvester exiled and Alexei Adashev dies. New favorites: Alexei and Feodor Basmanov, Maliuta Skuratov, Vasily Griaznoy. Ivan demands to take Sigismund Augustus's sister Catherine, as his wife. Reprisals against the boyars. Cathedral of Basil the Blessed completed.

Conspiracy of Amboise. Edict of Romorantin. Upon death of Francis II, Charles IX, also a minor, becomes king of France. Regency of Catherine de' Medici. Uprising in Ireland. John Knox initiates Presbyterian church in Scotland. Nobunaga seizes power in Japan.

1561 *August 21:* Ivan marries Maria, daughter of Circassian Prince Temriak. *November 21:* Kettler cedes Livonia to the King of Poland. Jenkinson's second commercial voyage to Persia. Patriarch of Constantinople recognizes Ivan's title as Czar.

Estates-General meets at Orléans. Mary Stuart returns to Scotland. Eric XIV of Sweden attempts conquest of Estonia.

1562   Andrei Kurbsky, defeated by the Poles at Nevel, falls into disfavor.

Massacre of Vassy marks beginning of religious wars. Treaty of Hampton Court: Le Havre ceded to England. Council of Trent recalled. Treaty of Prague between Ferdinand I and the Ottomans. Abortive Huguenot settlements in Florida and South Carolina. Sir John Hawkins's first voyage to the West Indies.

1563   *March:* Birth of Vasily, Ivan's fourth son. *May:* Death of Vasily. Death of Yuri, Ivan's younger brother. Ivan becomes known as "the Terrible." Russian army dispatched to Lithuania. *February 15:* Capture of Polotsk. Six-month truce with Poland. Death of Macarius; Athanasius elected Metropolitan.

Duke of Guise, leader of French Catholics, murdered. Peace of Amboise grants Huguenots limited freedom. Eric of Sweden captures his brother John of Finland. Council of Trent disbanded.

1564   Andrei Kurbsky flees to Poland; long and extravagant correspondence between him and Ivan begins. *December 3:* Ivan leaves Moscow. *December 25:* Ivan in residence at Alexandrovskaya Sloboda. Defeat of the Khan of Crimea, Devlet-Guirey. Poles defeated at Polotsk. First Russian printing press installed in Moscow.

Agitation against the Spanish in the Netherlands. Maximilian II succeeds Ferdinand I as Holy Roman Emperor. French-Spanish meeting in Bayonne. The Ottomans besiege Malta.

1565 Ivan transfers his residence from Moscow to Alexandrovskaya Sloboda. *January-February:* Ivan renounces throne of Russia, is begged by Delegation to return, and returns. *February 4: Oprichnina* and *oprichniki* formed. Executions of boyars. Lutherans authorized to open a church in Moscow. Extension of the English trade monopoly.

Another unsuccessful rebellion in Ireland. Mary Stuart marries Henry, Lord Darnley. Increasing Protestant repression in the Netherlands. Spanish destroy French colony of Fort Caroline in Florida and found St. Augustine. Spanish conquer the Philippines.

1566 First meeting of the Zemsky Sobor (General Assembly) votes to pursue the war against Lithuania.

Calvinist riots in the Netherlands. Ottomans capture Sziget in Hungary. Election of Pope Pius V. Death of Sulayman the Magnificent, Ottoman sultan.

1567 Ivan demands the hand of Elizabeth I in marriage.

Darnley murdered and Mary Stuart, imprisoned, abdicates in favor of her son James. Conspiracy of Meaux sparks off second religious war in France. Reign of terror against Protestants in the Spanish Netherlands.

1568 Trial and life imprisonment of Metropolitan Philip. Election of Metropolitan Kirill.

Brief Peace of Longjumeau followed by third religious war in France. Mary Stuart flees to England and is imprisoned there. Eric XIV of Sweden deposed by John III, Duke of Finland. Rio de Janeiro founded.

1569   *September 1:* Death of Czarina Maria. Imprisonment of Vladimir Andreyevich and his family. Five hundred families from Pskov and one hundred and fifty from Novgorod deported to Moscow. *August:* Savin leaves for England to negotiate a treaty of political alliance. *December:* Punitive expedition massacres inhabitants of all Russian towns between Moscow and Novgorod.

French Huguenots defeated at Jarnac and Moncontour. Catholic rebellion in north of England. Diet of Lublin centralizes government of Poland and Lithuania. Cervantes publishes his first work.

1570   Euphemis, Ivan's niece, marries Magnus, brother of the King of Denmark. Disgrace and execution of Basmanov and Viazemsky, former favorites. *January 8:* Ivan invades Novgorod and massacres the inhabitants. Famine and plague spread throughout Russia. Administration of Livonia conferred on Magnus, who is defeated in the siege of Reval.

Peace of St. Germain ends third religious war. The Pope, Spain, and Venice ally against the Ottomans occupying Cyprus. Peace of Stettin between Denmark and Sweden. Elizabeth I excommunicated by the Pope.

1571   Ivan flees to Alexandrovskaya Sloboda; he returns to Moscow in June and marries Martha Sobakina in October. *November:* Czarevich Ivan marries Eudoxia Saburova. *November 13:* Death of Czarina Martha. Tatars of Crimea invade southern ter-

Ottoman fleet defeated in naval battle of Lepanto. Moor rebellion in Spain suppressed. Stephen Bathory succeeds King Sigismund of Transylvania. Royal Exchange opens in London. Spanish city of Manila founded.

ritories and set fire to Moscow. Renewed retaliations against the boyars.

1572 Ivan's fourth marriage, to Anna Koltovskaya, is at first condemned then later approved by Leonid, Archbishop of Novgorod. Death of Metropolitan Athanasius; appointment of Metropolitan Anthony. Boris Godunov in favor. Death of Maliuta-Skuratov. New Tatar invasion arrested by Prince Vorotynsky. Conquest of Estonia. Swedish troops defeat Russians at Lode. Dissolution of the *oprichnina*. Cheremiss tribes in Kazan region revolt.

St. Bartholomew's Day Massacre in Paris sparks fourth religious war. Henry of Navarre abdicates. Francis Drake captures Spanish fleet off Panama. Pope Gregory XIII succeeds Pius V. Death of Sigismund Augustus of Poland.

1573 Ivan solicits the throne of Poland.

The Pacification of Boulogne ends fourth religious war. Separate peace made between Venice and the Ottomans. Duc d'Anjou elected King of Poland.

1574 Ivan repudiates Czarina Anna and marries Anna Vassilchikova; then, after her death, marries Vasilissa Melentieva; dismisses her and briefly marries Maria Dolgorukaya. Tatars pillage the Ukraine. Between reigns in Poland, Russians occupy

Duc d'Anjou relinquishes Polish crown to succeed Charles IX as Henry III of France. Treaty of Bristol between Spain and England. Ottomans capture Bizerta and Tunis. Fifth religious war in France.

Livonia and part of Lith-
uania.

1575	Ivan installs a Tatar prince, Simeon, on the throne.	Spanish bankruptcy. Stephen Bathory elected King of Poland.

1576   Ivan returns to the Kremlin and exiles Simeon to Tver.

Peace of Monsieur and Edict of Beaulieu ends fifth religious war: Huguenots allowed religious freedom except in Paris. League for the Defense of the Catholic Faith formed in France. Spanish mutiny in the Netherlands. Frobisher voyages to the Arctic. Rudolf II is Holy Roman Emperor.

1577   Ivan returns to Alexandrovskaya Sloboda. Defeat at the siege of Reval. Estonia, Livonia, and Lithuania in fierce resistance; siege and "punishment" of Wenden; executions. Armistice between Russia and Denmark. Death of Devlet-Guirey.

Revocation of Edict of Beaulieu leads to sixth religious war, ended by Peace of Bergerac and Edict of Poitiers. Union of Brussels unites Catholic provinces in southern Netherlands. Disruption in Persia. Sir Francis Drake circumnavigates the world in the *Golden Hind.*

1578   Poles recapture Wenden and defeat the Russians.

Portuguese defeated by the Moroccans. Spain victorious in the Netherlands.

1579   *August:* Stephen Bathory of Poland invades Lithuania and liberates Polotsk, Sokol, and Karsnoy.

Peace of Arras and Union of Utrecht: United Provinces (modern Holland) formed. Seventh religious war in France. Irish revolt.

1580 Ivan's eighth marriage, to Maria Feodorovna Nagaya. Feodor, Ivan's second son, marries Irina, Boris Godunov's sister. Stephen Bathory captures Veliki Luki. Swedes invade Karelia and Estonia.

Treaty of Fleix concludes seventh religious war. Philip II of Spain gains dominion over Portugal. Buenos Aires re-founded. Montaigne's *Essays* published.

1581 *September 1:* Ermak and his cossacks, in the service of Stroganov, set off to cross the Urals. *October:* Sibir captured. *November 19:* Ivan murders his eldest son Ivan. Stephen Bathory defeated near Pskov. Swedes occupy Narva and conquer the Gulf of Finland. Ivan proposes crusade against Moslems.

United Provinces (Holland) renounce allegiance to Philip II of Spain.

1582 Ivan proposes to marry Mary Hastings. Ermak's cossacks and Koltzo conquer all of Siberia. Negotiations with Sweden and Poland through Possevino. Ten-year armistice with Poland: Russia loses Livonia.

New war in Germany between Catholic princes and the Calvinist Archbishop of Cologne. Nobunaga assassinated in Kyoto.

1583 *October 19:* Birth of Dimitri, son of Ivan and Maria Nagaya. Truce signed ceding Estonia to Sweden.

Bavarian Catholic victory over the army of the Archbishop of Cologne.

1584 Death of Ivan the Terrible. The "Time of Troubles" begins, a period of dynastic disruptions.

Treaty of Joinville. Assassination of William of Orange.

Bibliography

Ivan the Terrible is a complex figure, and among historians he has both moderate supporters and fanatical opponents. While Karamzin, Kovalevsky, and Idanov condemn him for the fury of his passions, others—such as Soloviev, Bielov, and Zabielin—forgetting all the evil he did, praise him for his political genius. The revolutionary democrats Bielinsky, Herzen, and Dobroliubov considered him a precursor. Marx admired his talents as a diplomat and organizer. Lenin and Stalin saw him as the founder of the centralized Russian state. The *Great Soviet Encyclopedia* even goes so far as to call him "one of the greatest civilizers of his time." After the death of Stalin there appears to have been a change in this attitude, and in Moscow there is now a tendency to criticize those who "idealize" Ivan the Terrible.

There are not many contemporary documents giving direct testimony about the first czar in Russian history, but a great deal has been written about him in more recent times. I list below only the main works I consulted.

ALEXANDROV, VICTOR. *Les Mystères du Kremlin.* Paris, 1960.

BEUCLER, A. *La Vie d'Ivan le Terrible.* Paris, 1931.

BRIAN-CHANINOV, N. *Histoire de la Russie.* Paris, 1929.

DUCHESNE, E. *Le Domostroï.* Paris, 1910.

—— *Le Stoglav.* Paris, 1920.

DURAND-CHEYNET, CATHERINE. *Ivan le Terrible.* Paris, 1981.

ECK, ALEXANDRE. *Le Moyen Age russe.* Paris, 1933.

FLETSCHER, GILLES. *La Russie au XVIe siècle.* Leipzig-Paris, 1864. [For original English, see Giles Fletcher in *Russia at the Close of the Sixteenth Century*, ed. Edward A. Bond. London: Hakluyt Society, First Series, No. 20, 1856. Trans.]

GRAHAM, STEPHEN. *Ivan le Terrible, le premier tsar.* Paris, 1933. [For original English, see Graham's *Ivan the Terrible.* Hamden, Conn.: Archon Books, 1968 (reprint from 1933); first published London: E. Benn Ltd., 1932; New Haven: Yale University Press, 1933. Trans.]

Great Soviet Encyclopedia, in Russian, vol. XVIII. Article on Ivan the Terrible.

HERBERSTEIN, BARON SIGISMUND VON. *La Moscovie du XVIe siècle.* Introduction by Robert Delort. Paris, 1965. [For an English translation (from the Latin), see Herberstein's *Notes upon Russia*, trans. and ed. R. H. Major. London: Hakluyt Society, No. 10, 1851–52. Trans.]

Ivan the Terrible. *Correspondence*, trans. from the Russian and with an introduction by Daria Olivier. Paris, 1959.

—— *Epistles*, in Russian. Moscow-Leningrad, 1951. [For an English translation of the epistles to Kurbsky, see *The Correspondence Between Prince A. M. Kurbsky and Tsar Ivan IV of Russia 1565–1579*, ed. with trans. and notes by J. L. I. Fennell. Cambridge: Cambridge University Press, 1955. Trans.]

JENKINSON, ANTHONY. In *Early Voyages and Travels to Russia and Persia*, ed. E. Delmar Morgan and C. H. Coote. London: Hakluyt Society, First Series, No. 73, 1886.

KARAMZIN, N. *Histoire de l'Empire de Russie*, 11 vols., trans. from the Russian. Paris-Berlin, 1819–26.

KOURBSKI, PRINCE ANDRÉ. *Histoire du règne d'Ivan IV*, trans. from the Russian. Geneva, 1965. [For an English translation, see *Prince A. M. Kurbsky's History of Ivan IV*, ed. with trans. and notes by J. L. I. Fennell. Cambridge: Cambridge University Press, 1965. Trans.]

LÉGER, LOUIS. *La Femme et la société russe au XVIe siècle*. Paris, 1887.

LEROY-BEAULIEU, ANATOLE. *L'Empire des tsars et les Russes*, 3 vols. Paris, 1883.

MERILYS, JEAN. *Ivan le Terrible*. Paris, 1948.

MILIOUKOV, SEIGNOBOS, and EISENMANN. *Histoire de Russie*, 3 vols. Paris, 1932.

NAZAREVSKI, V. V. *Histoire de Moscou*. Paris, 1932.

PERCHERON, M. *Moscou*. Paris, 1937.

PIERLING, LE PÈRE. *Bathory et Possevino. Les rapports du Saint-Siège avec les Slaves*. Paris, 1887.

——*Papes et tsars*. Paris, 1890.

——*La Russie et l'Orient*. Paris, 1891.

PLATONOV, S. *Histoire de Russie*. Paris, 1929.

——*Ivan the Terrible*, in Russian. Berlin, 1924. [For an English translation, see Platonov's *Ivan the Terrible*, ed. and trans. Joseph L. Wieczynski. Gulf Breeze, Fla.: Academic International Press, 1974. Trans.]

RAMBAUD, ALFRED. *Histoire de Russie*. Paris, 1879.

Russian Biographical Dictionary, in Russian. St. Petersburg, 1897. Article by S. Seredonin on Ivan the Terrible.

SCHAKOVSKOY, ZINAÏDA. *La Vie quotidienne à Moscou au XVIIe siècle*. Paris: Hachette, 1963.

SEMENOFF, M. *Ivan le Terrible*. Paris, 1928.

STAHLIN, G. *La Russie, des origines à la naissance de Pierre le Grand*. Paris, 1946.

VALLOTTON, HENRY. *Ivan le Terrible*. Paris, 1959.

WALISZEWSKI, K. *Ivan le Terrible*. Paris, 1904. [For an English translation, see Waliszewski's *Ivan the Terrible*, trans. Lady Mary Loyd. Philadelphia: J. B. Lippincott Company; London: William Heinemann, 1904. Trans.]

ZIEGLER, CHARLES. *Ivan IV, dit le Terrible*. Paris, 1957.

ZIMIN, A. A. *The Oprichnina of Ivan the Terrible*, in Russian. Moscow, 1964.

Index

PHOENIX
PRESS

GENERAL EDITORS:
SIMON SCHAMA AND ANTONIA FRASER

Phoenix Press publishes and re-publishes hundreds of the very best new and out of print books about the past. For a free colour catalogue listing more than 400 titles please

telephone: +44 (0) 1903 828 503
fax: +44 (0) 1903 828 802
e-mail: mailorder@lbsltd.co.uk
or visit our website at www.phoenixpress.co.uk

The following books might be of particular interest to you:

The Fall of the Russian Monarchy

BERNARD PARES

The foremost expert on Russian history of his generation, Pares tells the story of the Russian Revolution from the point of view of the Romanovs, beginning with Nicholas II's accession in 1894 and ending with his and his family's murder at Ekaterinburg in 1918.

Paperback
UK £12.99   528pp + Maps   1 84212 114 6
USA $19.95
CAN $29.95

The Life of Lenin

LOUIS FISCHER

Lenin was revolution: his absolute determination can truly be said to have changed the course of world history. No-one else of his time could have overcome the chaos in Russia, the foreign intervention, and the economic ruin without losing control of the revolution. Fischer knew Lenin personally and was given privileged access to his archives to create this landmark biography.

Paperback £16.99   720pp + 8pp b/w   1 84212 230 4

Roots of Revolution
INTRODUCED BY ISAIAH BERLIN

FRANCO VENTURI

Venturi offers nothing less than a history of the populist and socialist movements in 19th-century Russia that spawned the events of 1917 that shook the world. Isaiah Berlin, who was himself uprooted by that Revolution, contributes an introduction, and a later essay by the author on Russian Populism is also included.

Paperback

UK £16.99   96opp   1 84212 253 3
USA $24.95
CAN $36.95

On Sledge and Horseback to Outcast Siberian Lepers
KATE MARSDEN

Kate Marsden recounts her extraordinary journey, sponsored by Queen Victoria, from Constantinople to Yakutsk in north-east Siberia in the 1890s. A fervent Christian, Marsden was driven to research leprosy and its then widely differing treatments from the Middle East to Siberia. Illustrated with some of the author's own photographs and drawings.

Paperback

UK £12.99   272pp + 24pp b/w   1 84212 397 1
USA $19.95
CAN $29.95

The History of Pugachev
ALEXANDER PUSHKIN

A history of Russia's greatest peasant rebellion by its greatest national poet. With a new introduction by Orlando Figes.

Paperback

UK £9.99   16opp   1 84212 418 8
USA $16.95
CAN $24.95

Catherine the Great

HENRI TROYAT

The Prix Goncourt-winning French historian reveals the true nature of the ambitious and ruthless despot. 'Theoretically straightforward biography, it illuminates far more than the life of that amazing woman; a brilliant court, Russian itself, sparkle before our eyes' Antonia Fraser, *The Good Book Guide*.

Paperback £14.99   400pp + 16pp b/w   1 84212 029 8

Journey for our Time

The Journals of the Marquis de Custine

The 'de Tocqueville of Russia' provides a timeless insight into the divisions and distempers of one of the world's most enigmatic nations. With a new introduction by Simon Sebag Montefiore.

Paperback
UK £9.99   240pp   1 84212 436 6
USA $16.95
CAN $24.95

Peasant Russia, Civil War

The Volga Countryside in Revolution 1917–1921

ORLANDO FIGES

Britain's most celebrated historian of Russia investigates why and how the October Revolution occurred.

Paperback
UK £12.99   432pp + 8pp b/w + Maps   1 84212 419 6
USA $19.95
CAN $29.95

Cursed Days

IVAN BUNIN

This great anti-Bolshevik diary won Russia's first Nobel Prize for literature. Originally published in 1936 but banned by the Soviets, it relives the experience of civil war in 1918 Moscow and Odessa.

Paperback
UK £12.99   304pp   1 84212 063 8
CAN $24.95

A Lifelong Passion

Nicholas and Alexandra – Their Own Story

ANDREI MAYLUNAS AND SERGEI MIRONENKO

The love affair of Nicholas, the last Tsar of Russia, and his wife
Alix, a granddaughter of Queen Victoria, was a lifelong passion
with a tragic end. 'Reads like a thriller, filled as it is with stories of
plots, betrayals and sexual intrigues'. *Sunday Telegraph*

Paperback £10.99   736pp + 16pp col   0 75380 044 6

Michael & Natasha

ROSEMARY AND DONALD CRAWFORD

The life and love of Michael, the brother of the executed Nicholas
II. 'It is a long time since I have read so moving a story, and it is
one that I defy any reader to put down once begun' Count Nikolai
Tolstoy, *Sunday Times.*

Paperback £9.99   464pp + 24pp b/w   0 75380 516 2

01 - 01

B
Ivan
Troyat
Ivan, the terrible

GAYLORD S